The grandson of Irish immigrants, Rodolfo Walsh was born in a small Patagonian town in 1927. He wrote crime fiction and worked as a translator before publishing *Operación Masacre* in 1957. He traveled to Cuba in the midst of the revolution and launched a newspaper with Gabriel García Márquez, among others. Upon his return to Argentina in 1961 he was shunned by the journalistic community for his connections to the Cuban Revolution. In 1972, Walsh updated *Operación Masacre* for the fourth and final time before joining the radical Peronist group, the Montoneros, the following year. A day after submitting his now famous 1977 "Open Letter from a Writer to the Military Junta," Walsh was gunned down in the street by agents of the State.

OPERATION
MASSACRE

OPERATION MASSACRE

Rodolfo Walsh

TRANSLATED FROM THE SPANISH BY
Daniella Gitlin

FOREWORD BY
Michael Greenberg

AFTERWORD BY
Ricardo Piglia

∼

To Enriqueta Muñiz

∼

The declarant adds that the task with which he had been charged was horribly unpleasant, and went far beyond the stipulated duties of the police.

—Police Commissioner Rodolfo Rodríguez Moreno

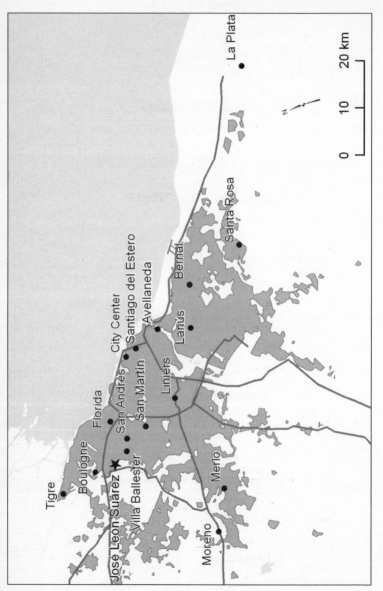

Greater Buenos Aires

CONTENTS

Foreword
xiii

Translator's Introduction
xxiii

Prologue
1

PART ONE: THE PEOPLE
9

1. Carranza
11

2. Garibotti
14

3. Mr. Horacio
17

4. Giunta
20

5. Díaz: Two Snapshots
21

6. Lizaso
22

7. Warnings and Premonitions
24

8. Gavino
25

9. Explanations in an Embassy
26

10. Mario
28

11. "The Executed Man Who Lives"
30

12."I'm Going to Work . . ."
32

13. The Unknowns
34

PART TWO: THE EVENTS
37

14. Where is Tanco?
39

15. Valle's Rebellion
43

16. "Watch Out, They Could Execute You . . ."
47

17. "Cheer Up"
50

18. Calm and Confident
53

19. Make No Mistake . . .
55

20. Execute Them!
59

21. He Felt He was Committing a Sin . . .
60

22. The End of the Journey
65

23. The Slaughter
67

24. Time Stands Still
70

25. The End of a Long Night
73

26. The Ministry of Fear
77

27. An Image in the Night
79

28. "They're Taking You Away"
82

29. A Dead Man Seeks Asylum
86

30. The Telegram Guerrilla
92

31. The Rest is Silence . . .
96

PART THREE: THE EVIDENCE
101

32. The Ghosts
103

33. Fernández Suárez Confesses
106

34. The Livraga File
110

35. Blind Justice
141

36. Epilogue
146

37. Aramburu and the Historical Trial
148

APPENDICES
153

Prologue to the Book Edition
(from the first edition, July 1957)
155

Introduction
(*to the first edition, March 1957*)
157

Obligatory Appendix
(*from the first edition, July 1957*)
165

Provisional Epilogue
(*from the first edition, July 1957*)
183

Epilogue
(*to the second edition, 1964*)
187

Portrait of the Dominant Oligarchy
(*end of the epilogue to the third edition, 1969*)
191

Operation in the Movies
193

Open Letter from a Writer to the Military Junta
197

Notes
211

Glossary
217

Afterword
221

About the Translator
233

FOREWORD

I was nineteen when I arrived in Argentina in the fall of 1972. I had been drawn to South America by the literary explosion that began in the 1950s and was still going on—a historical burst of creativity exemplified by Julio Cortázar, García Márquez, Borges, Ernesto Sábato and other equally potent, unclassifiable writers who were, collectively, in the process of changing the tenor of world literature.

Upon arriving, however, what immediately captured my attention wasn't literature but the political upheavals of the continent with their alarming urgency of living, present time. In those vintage Cold War years, the political fate of South America—the "mood" in the Latino forests and highlands and streets—was as pressing to US foreign policy as that of the Muslim world is today. Fidel Castro was ten years into his reign over Cuba and at the height of his influence. Salvador Allende, a cultivated, European-style Socialist, was the democratically elected president of Chile. And set to return to Argentina was Juan Domingo Perón, an aging populist with a bewildering, fascist-inflected philosophy who was beloved by Argentina's working class.

Perón had been deposed by a violent military coup in 1955. He had been in exile—first in Panama, then in Spain—for eighteen years. During that time, his Peronist party was outlawed, despite or perhaps because of the fact that it would have won any open election by a landslide. After the 1955 coup, the mere utterance of Perón's name was prohibited and punishable by law.

But in 1972, after a seemingly unending succession of inept military and civilian governments, Perón had struck a deal to return, assume the presidency, and save the country from a leftist guerrilla movement that had been operating in his name.

I hadn't been in Buenos Aires long before I became familiar with the name Rodolfo Walsh. A writer and intellectual hero of the left, Walsh was known to anyone with even a glancing interest in the political scene. In a country of adventurers, avant gardists, gangs, demagogues, and sloganeers from every point on the political spectrum, he was a rare voice of integrity—a staunch, clear-eyed realist, more swayed by concrete events than abstract political strategies and ideas. With his strong moral compass, his horse sense, and independent investigative rigor, Walsh was, in the benighted land of Argentina of the 1970s, a cross between Orwell and Woodward and Bernstein.

Operation Massacre is Walsh's most famous work—a precise, meticulously researched account of the execution, on June 9, 1956, of five men suspected of participating in a failed coup against the military government designed to return Perón to power. No major Argentine news outlet would touch the story, and Walsh's exposé was published in a small journal between May 27 and July 29, 1957, and then as a book later that year.

Walsh was thirty when he wrote *Operation Massacre*. In spite of the virtual media blackout it faced, the book would launch his career as a public intellectual and political journalist. (In 1960, he would become one of the founders of the Latin American wire service Prensa Latina.) It is a classic case of a writer who, presented with a subject of pressing injustice, puts aside his other literary ambitions. The story of the "secret executions" of June 1956 came to Walsh by chance. At the time, by his own account, he was an avid reader of fantasy literature, a writer of detective stories, an aspiring "serious" novelist, and, last of all, a journalist. He had been staunchly anti-Peronist at the time of the 1955 coup that overthrew Perón, put off by Perón's zealous persecution of lawful dissenters and his admiration for Mussolini, after whose government Perón had modeled his own, right down to the establishment of a loyal band of privileged workers who acted as his street enforcers and unofficial thugs. By the same token, as a man of the left Walsh could not support the equally repressive stupidities of the military government that replaced Perón. This relative impartiality lent a moral authority to *Operation Massacre* that a more partisan report could not have possessed.

The irrefutable nature of Walsh's investigation is one of the reasons for the book's enduring power. In a country where state atrocities were routinely buried, where silence was a civic means of survival, where innocent citizens could be kidnapped and executed without leaving a trace and even their families kept in the dark—in this country *Operation Massacre* was a work of enormous importance. The book was, and remains, a warning and prophecy of what was to come, a cry to a judicial system that, with few exceptions, allowed and even encouraged the state's security forces to act with impunity.

Most important, it is a *document* that fully examines the events, the people, the mechanism of the murders, while identifying and holding accountable everyone involved. *Operation Massacre* is a true crime story, designed not to titillate or exploit but to instruct, to reveal and enlighten. It is built upon that rarest element of Argentine life at the time: facts. Facts were a form of sedition with their icy power that nothing—not opinion, passion, or rumor—could equal. Uttering, much less publishing, the facts in those days could be punishable by death.

And the facts are astonishing. On June 9, 1956, the evening of the failed coup attempt, twelve working class men gather at a mutual friend's house to watch a prize fight, have a few drinks, and play cards. Under orders from military personnel, the police storm the gathering, transport the twelve men to a half frozen suburban field, shoot them, and depart. Due to the hurried, careless discharge of the crime, some of the men remain alive, either wounded or lying motionless and unharmed in the field, left for dead.

As with all investigations of this scale, the story reveals itself to

Walsh in phases, through interviews with survivors, lawyers, prosecutors, police, and military participants. There are moments when *Operation Massacre* reads like a forensic mystery; and Walsh's talents as a detective novelist inform the story as it unravels, in increments, with its complicated timeline that is so crucial to determining what actually happened.

At one point, Walsh is forced to become part of the story himself, confirming the death of a victim to his parents who had been clinging to the hope that their son was still alive. In another instance, that illustrates to perfection the bizarre and perverse ethos that ruled the land, the police claim that one of their victims' "exhibited injuries"—by which they mean the gunshot wound to the face that they have inflicted on him—are "evidence of his active participation in the revolutionary movement." Another victim, after being left for dead, is arrested while wandering the streets and thrown into solitary confinement without medical attention. He only survives because the regular prisoners throw scraps of bread through the peep hole of his cell.

Yet, as atrocities in Argentina would go—and it is a mean and hellish game to compare them—the massacre of June 9, 1956, was "modest." It is, Walsh knows, the specifics, the particulars, the concrete evidence surrounding a crime that give it meaning, by the simple act of *proving that it happened at all*. It not only attests to and dignifies the individual suffering that has occurred, it also holds individuals responsible for that suffering. And this exposure, this threat of future justice, may be the only effective deterrent, the only point of restraint on those charged with carrying out the orders of state terror.

Prosecutions often occur decades after the crimes. They don't bring back the dead or change history. But they do affect the future. They lift the cloud of rage and unresolvedness that can hang over the psyche of a country for as long as the perpetrators run free. They force the state, and the general population, to acknowledge the ordeal of their compatriots. They air the truth and relieve an immeasurable weight of psychological repression. Crucially, they vindicate the loved ones of the disappeared who have been consigned to a state of silence and shame.

Socially speaking, victims are rarely regarded as heroes, no matter their courage. More often they become pariahs, unwelcome reminders of the public's collective guilt. Writing *Operation Massacre*, Walsh took the precaution of acquiring signed statements from survivors and witnesses. In doing so he has shown future generations of Argentines that, in the face of iron-clad facts, a form of justice and restitution is possible. The facts, put down by a brave committed writer, ensure that there will be no immunity for those responsible for state-sponsored terror.

2.

On June 20, 1973, seven months after I arrived in Argentina, Perón, who in absentia had assumed the proportions of a mythical, magical god, returned to the country. He was almost seventy now, still tall and erect, though his blooming reddened face showed the cost of the debaucheries of his well-heeled exile. Within minutes of Perón's landing at Ezeiza Airport in Buenos Aires, where three and a half million Argentines had swarmed to greet him, right-wing Peronists opened machine gun fire on the crowd, targeting members of the Montoneros, the militant left-wing Peronist group whose members and legions of sympathizers were there, en masse, to celebrate what appeared to be an unequivocal victory.

Nearly two hundred people were killed. Many more were injured in the stampede that followed the shooting. And with that, the alliance of enemies that had brought Perón back to Argentina shattered, as it was always destined to do. The Montoneros, whose guerrilla-style agitations had done much to pave the way for Perón's return, would soon go back underground, even with Perón in power. A flood of betrayals, kidnappings and drive-by assassinations from both sides followed, and the first stage of what the world would come to know as *La Guerra Sucia*—the Dirty War—began.

Operation Massacre had been a galvanizing text for the Montoneros during the dictatorships prior to Perón's return and, despite his strong misgivings about Peronism, Walsh would eventually join the group in the 1970s as a kind of elder, intellectual mentor and guide. As the terror escalated, Walsh came to believe that the Montoneros were the only representatives of the left with sufficient organizational skill and popular support to challenge the dictatorship. During the late 1960s and early 1970s, Montoneros had successfully tapped into the profoundly romantic nostalgia that working class and poor Argentines felt for Perón. Their strategy was to cast Perón's vague and elusive political pronouncements in a revolutionary light, and by doing so ideologically to nudge his supporters to the left. Employing the caudillo's own words, they couldn't be accused of disloyalty or distortion. The implication was that "true" Peronism belonged to the left.

Walsh urged the Montoneros to aspire to the establishment of a democratic government, with a stable judicial system, a functioning congress, freedom of the press, and open dependable elections. Of paramount importance to Walsh was the creation of a strong legal code consisting of humane, enforceable laws that punished political crimes and guaranteed the continuance of democracy. He disagreed with the Montonero leadership when they burrowed inexorably underground, becoming increasingly avant gardist, clandestine and cut off from the general population. By 1974, vicious street brawls between Montonero fighters and government forces were a constant feature of urban life. The explosion of bombs and gunshots throughout the night were normal. My own companion (and future wife) was arrested and almost killed after stumbling upon a surprise Montonero demonstration near the Congressional Plaza.* For tactical purposes, the Montoneros encouraged the government crackdown, believing that less militant sympathizers, having nowhere to turn and absorbing much of the brunt of the terror, would join them as fighters underground. This was not what happened. An airless blanket of paranoia and fear gripped the country, and the population, for the most part, withdrew, aiming simply to stay out of the way and survive.

3·

Walsh wrote his second most famous text on March 24, 1977. "Open Letter from a Writer to the Military Junta," it is called. The occasion for this letter was the first anniversary of the military junta that had overthrown Isabel Perón's government (Perón died in July 1974 while in office and his wife, Isabel, vice president at the time, assumed the top office). Fittingly, the letter is included in this book. Sharpened by Walsh's lucidly ethical prose, it is a kind of State of the Union, summing up the junta's accomplishment after one year in power.

Six months before he wrote the letter, Walsh's eldest daughter, a Montonero combatant, shot herself in the head after being trapped by a military ambush. Separately, Walsh's house was ransacked; numerous close friends—academics, unionists, intellectuals, writers—were kidnapped and, in the Kafkaesque parlance of the time, "went disappeared."** For Walsh, who had just turned fifty, there seemed to be nothing left to lose.

On the day Walsh posted the letter, fifteen thousand Argentines had disappeared, ten thousand political prisoners were being held

---

* For details see the essay "Love in the South" in my collection *Beg, Borrow, Steal: A Writer's Life* (Vintage 2010).
** Since the disappeared prisoner did not officially exist, there was no legal necessity to present him before a judge or account for him at all.

without trial or formal charges, four thousand were dead, and tens of thousands more had fled the country: what Walsh called "the raw numbers of this terror." During the next six years the terror would continue unabated and the number of victims would increase exponentially—thirty thousand dead is an oft-cited number, though a reliable count has yet to be established.*

The carnage was the grim natural extension of the executions Walsh had described twenty years earlier in *Operation Massacre*. By 1977, the details of those executions seemed almost quaint, especially Walsh's frustration about the impotence of the courts in dealing with the crime. By the mid 1970s, the judicial system had become a shell of its former self, existing only to rubber stamp government crimes.

Once torture became official policy, its techniques taught in military schools, there was no end to what it could entail: the rack, the drill, the blowtorch, and, in the case of at least one kidnapped Peronist, being skinned alive. During my companion's times in prison, in 1974, a young man died while being tortured in a room next to her cell. Business as usual in those nightmarish days.

But Walsh's letter is more than a list of abominations. He is acutely aware of the less obvious toll of terror—the psychological and moral stain that it spreads through victim and torturer and passive citizen alike, becoming an ineradicable part of the collective consciousness. "You have arrived at a form of absolute, metaphysical torture that is unbounded by time," Walsh writes, directly addressing the members of the junta. "The original goal of obtaining information has been lost in the disturbed minds of those inflicting the torture. Instead, they have ceded to the impulse to pommel human substance to the point of breaking it and making it lose its dignity, which the executioner has lost, and which you yourselves have lost."

No statement gives a more accurate or disturbing sense of this

---

* *National Geographic* magazine has estimated that the Montoneros and the People's Revolutionary Army, the other active guerrilla group, were responsible for about 6,000 casualties among the security forces and civilians.

ethos than that of an officer of the junta who declared, "The battle we are waging knows neither moral nor natural limits; it takes place beyond good and evil."

Following the tautology of terror, the definition of a "subversive" widened to a surreal degree. Officials, civilians, and Montoneros alike cloaked themselves in the righteous, heightened language of war that allows for no line of thought beyond itself. The president of the Sociedad Rural, the organization of large landowners whose support was critical to the junta's survival, felt perfectly justified in expressing his anger that "certain small but active groups keep insisting that food should be affordable." They too would be submitted to the blowtorch.

In fact, the economic hardships imposed by the junta amounted to another form of torture. Over the course of the junta's first year, Walsh points out, the consumption of food decreased by forty percent and the number of hours the average employee needed to work to cover his daily cost of living rose from six to eighteen. The annual inflation rate of 400 percent forced shopkeepers to raise prices from morning to afternoon. As I witnessed myself, many stopped accepting Argentine currency altogether, preferring US dollars, but settling for Brazilian cruzeiros (as they were called at the time) or even Bolivian pesos.

Walsh wrote the letter "with no hope of being heard, with the certainty of being persecuted, but faithful to the commitment I made a long time ago to bear witness during difficult times." The commitment began with the writing of *Operation Massacre* in 1956, and continued until his murder, the very day after he posted the letter and disseminated it to the local and foreign press. On March 25, 1977, Walsh was surrounded on a busy Buenos Aires street by a group of soldiers from the Navy School of Engineers, shot, and carried away to be finished off, much like the victims of June 9, 1956, whom he has memorialized in this classic book.

"Silencio Es Salud" read a huge banner strung across Buenos

Aires' most trafficked street during the bleakest days of the Dirty War. "Silence is Health"—a warning to a terrorized populace. Silence, in fact, is a dictatorship's greatest weapon. It is a warning that Walsh defied. In Argentina and in the rest of the world his work and life live on as a beacon of intellectual and political integrity and courage.

—Michael Greenberg

TRANSLATOR'S INTRODUCTION

The story is so good that it sounds like fiction: someone has survived an execution that no one even knew had taken place.

A writer who is passionate about detective novels and mysteries finds out about the survivor. The writer is also a journalist and finds a way to talk to the survivor. He learns from the survivor that policemen arrested him and a bunch of other men without telling them why, drove them out to a garbage dump, lined them up, and opened fire.

But there's more. There were more survivors. In fact, more men survived the execution than were killed.

The writer thinks he's found the scoop of his life.

In 1955, Juán Perón was halfway into his second elected term as President of Argentina. The country was divided: Perón had received great support from the labor movement, but developed enemies within the military, the Navy, and the Catholic Church. Those perceived as dissenters were increasingly persecuted, and a creeping fascism overtook the streets. Like many other intellectuals of his time, the twenty-eight-year-old Argentine writer Rodolfo Walsh was ready for a change. He lived with his wife and two young daughters in the city of La Plata, an hour southwest of Buenos Aires, and was considered by the literary community to have exceptional talent and promise. Two years earlier, his first book of short stories had received the Buenos Aires Municipal Literature Prize, chosen by the already well-known and highly respected Jorge Luis Borges and Adolfo Bioy Casares. Walsh also worked as a journalist, and as a translator and editor for the same small publisher that had put out his first book. Though he had been involved in an anti-imperialist, anti-Communist nationalist group as a teenager, he had drifted away from politics. Walsh was troubled by Perón's investment in foreign interests and the limitations imposed on the freedom of expression in Argentina, but he was far from being an activist.

On June 16, 1955, Navy jets bombed a rally in support of Perón that left hundreds dead. Perón remained in power for another three months until he was effectively ousted by a coup on September 21, 1955. The new regime called itself the Liberating Revolution, and Walsh was not alone in hoping and even believing that its prophetic name would prove true. He grew discouraged, though, as the new government began to take the shape of a dictatorship: less than six months after the coup, the Liberating Revolution enacted a decree that outlawed calling oneself a Peronist, sympathizing with Peronism in any way, mentioning the name of Perón or his late wife Evita, or reproducing any images of them.

While Perón was in exile, his supporters inside the military and on the streets began to organize. On June 9, 1956, Peronist loyalists in the army and their civilian supporters staged an uprising throughout the country. The Liberating Revolution crushed them at every turn in bloody skirmishes and decided to make an example of those who had rebelled. Martial law was instated at 12:32 a.m. on June 10, 1956, and a communiqué was released over State Radio at dawn announcing that eighteen civilian rebels had been executed in Lanús, a district in the southern part of the Province of Buenos Aires.

On the night of that Peronist uprising, Walsh was sitting at his usual café in La Plata playing chess. He had a deep voice and his eyes seemed small behind black-rimmed glasses. The game was suddenly interrupted by the sound of gunshots nearby. The military had taken over the streets in La Plata, too, not just Lanús. Walsh left the café and started to head home, thinking he should take the bus to avoid passing through a live fire zone. But the "irrepressible will" of his legs ("*la incoercible autonomía de mis piernas*") compelled him to keep walking. When he reached his house, he was met with soldiers in the bedrooms and on the roof who were using it as a base. From inside, standing by the window blinds, he heard a wounded soldier calling out from the street to his brothers in arms: "Don't leave me here alone, you sons of bitches."

> That is the moment when I understood what a revolution was . . . And I hated that revolution with all my might. As a reflex, I also hated all the previous ones, however just they may have been. I came to a deeper understanding of it in the tense hours that followed, seeing undisguised fear all around me in the almost childlike faces of the soldiers who didn't know if they were "loyalists" or "rebels," but knew that they had to shoot at other soldiers identical to themselves, who also didn't know if they were loyalists or rebels.

When Walsh bears witness to this young man who is convinced that he has been abandoned and is dying in the street, something in him shifts.

Still, after the uprising, Walsh's life goes on as before. It is only six months later, in December 1956, that he hears the phrase that would change his life: "*Hay un fusilado que vive*"—"One of the executed men is alive." It is the paradoxical beginning of a story that is too good to resist. He starts asking questions and finds out that the survivor was not from the failed coup in La Plata or the execution in Lanús, but from a separate, unannounced, secret execution that took place on the night of June 9 in a different district altogether. Years of writing detective fiction and obsessively reading through daily newspapers made him the perfect person to pursue the story, which only grew darker and more stirring the more he uncovered.

What Walsh finds out over the course of a year's worth of investigation is that the men who were taken out to be killed were a motley, civilian, working-class group. They ranged between twenty-one and fifty years old, and were all from the same neighborhood. Most of them lived with their families—they worked on the railroad or sold shoes or fixed refrigerators. Some of them had served in the military or worked on the docks. Two of them had six children each.

A handful of these men were known to be Peronists and some, not all, of them were aware of the Peronist uprising that was meant to take place that night. But when the police and armed guards barged into the two apartments in Florida, they didn't say why the men were being taken away or where they were going. The officers were following orders to arrest them from the Chief of Police of the Province of Buenos Aires. They loaded the men onto a bus, stopped at the local police department where they were submitted to interrogation for several hours, drove them out to a garbage dump, and tried, but failed, to execute them all. What distinguishes this execution from the Lanús execution is that it took place before martial law was instated. "And that is not execution," Walsh tells the reader. "It is murder."

After talking to the first survivor, Walsh writes up the story immediately and rushes to get it off to the press:

> I walk around all of Buenos Aires with it and hardly anyone wants to know about it, let alone publish it. You begin to believe in the crime novels you've read or written, and think that a story like this, with a talking dead man, is going to be fought over by the presses. You think you're running a race against time, that at any given moment a big newspaper is going to send out a dozen reporters and photographers, just like in the movies. But instead you find that no one wants anything to do with it.

Eventually he finds an underground publisher, "a man who's willing to take the risk. He is trembling and sweating because he's no movie hero either, just a man who's willing to take the risk, and that's worth more than a movie hero." What captivates Walsh is the courage of this man to publish potentially slanderous material about the Chief of Police of the Province of Buenos Aires. In the series of articles that would become *Operation Massacre*, Walsh gives accounts of the lives of the victims on the night of the uprising. In 1957, a small press called Ediciones Sigla published the articles as a book. It was met with critical acclaim, but Walsh was growing less interested in critical acclaim than he was in justice for the victims and their families.

Walsh became so consumed by what had happened to these men that he could not return to the life before; he carried the weight of their murder with him. He shares this weight with the reader through details. We know what the victims said to their wives before they left the house—"Till tomorrow," "I just have to run an errand and then I'll be back"—and whether they turned left or right when walking out the door. We know exactly how one man escaped the raid, what color cardigan the other was wearing that made him more visible to the guards under the headlights of the police van. We know the exact minute that the establishment of martial law was broadcast over State Radio, know what the victims were carrying in their pockets. We know what position their corpses were in when they arrived at the morgue. The book is built on detail upon detail.

As Ricardo Piglia notes in the Afterword to this book, Walsh "elevates the raw truth of the facts." He describes the lives of ordinary men with such considered and caring language that our sense of them is anything but ordinary. Here is Walsh's description of one man's youngest child and only daughter who is nine years old: "Dark-haired, with bangs and smiling eyes, her father melts when he sees her. There is a photo in a glass cabinet of her in a school uniform of white overalls standing next to a chalkboard." The details not only bring these people closer to the reader, they also offer the shape of the life that was lost.

Over the next twenty years, with the governing power of the country changing hands multiple times and with a personal need for justice spurring him on, Walsh became an activist. He supported the Cuban revolution and aided that government by cracking telex codes leading up to the 1961 Bay of Pigs invasion. He sympathized with and joined different Peronist groups, though he usually had his disagreements with them. He wrote more articles and books about true crimes in his own country—*The Satanowsky Case* (1958), *Who Killed Rosendo?* (1969)—and *Operation Massacre* was reprinted three times, each time with additions and revisions, a new introduction, or a provisional epilogue.

The stages of Walsh's personal journey are laid out most clearly in these texts and in the changes he made to the main text over the years. This journey is what differentiates Walsh and *Operation Massacre* most from Truman Capote and *In Cold Blood*, which appeared nearly a decade later and is often noted as a point of reference for understanding Walsh's work. Both books were considered groundbreaking in their literary treatment of true crimes that the writers had personally investigated and rendered in minute detail. But when Walsh wrote the articles that would become *Operation Massacre*, the men he incriminates—some of them wielding a great deal of discretionary power—had not been brought to justice, and never would be. His need to set the record straight is what makes him risk his life to tell the story, and what inspires him to keep going back to the original text year after year.

At the end of the introduction to the first, 1957 edition, Walsh writes: "I happen to believe, with complete earnestness and conviction, in the right of every citizen to share any truth that he comes to know, however dangerous that truth may be. And I believe in this book, in the impact it can have." As the years passed and the Chief of

Police was not convicted, Walsh began to lose heart. Neither the victims of "Operation Massacre" nor their families were compensated. In the epilogue to the 1964 edition, Walsh's tone has changed:

> I wanted one of the multiple governments of this country to acknowledge that its justice system was wrong to kill those men, that they were killed for no good reason, out of stupidity and blindness. I know it doesn't matter to the dead. But there was a question of decency at hand, I don't know how else to say it.
>
> [...]
>
> In 1957 I boasted: "This case is in process, and will continue to be for as long as is necessary, months or even years." I would like to retract that flawed statement. This case is no longer in process, it is barely a piece of history; this case is dead.
>
> [...]
>
> I am rereading the story that you all have read. There are entire sentences that bother me, I get annoyed thinking about how much better it would be if I wrote it now.

Would I write it now?

By the 1960s, Walsh was consumed by writing and activism. He had separated from his wife and, in 1967, he met Lilia Fereyra, the woman he would be with for the next decade. With civil protest in Argentina quashed again and again, Walsh became more politically active and gradually moved away from fiction as a genre. He believed he needed to write about true events and expose injustice occurring at this particular historical moment in this particular country. Even when he followed this course, however, there was no guarantee that any social good would come of his work. Walsh strikes a resigned note in the epilogue to the 1969 edition:

It was useless in 1957 to seek justice for the victims of "Operation Massacre," just as it was useless in 1958 to seek punishment against General Cuaranta for the murder of Satanowsky, just as it is useless in 1968 to call for the prosecution of those who murdered Blajaquis and Zalazar and are being protected by the government. Within the system, there is no justice.

In his excellent 2006 biography of Walsh, Eduardo Jozami writes that when writing *Operation Massacre*, Walsh used every journalistic means at his disposal to abandon literary fiction and to make the writing more accessible to working-class readers: the language is direct, there are very few abstract concepts, and the book is full of suspense.[*] These, of course, are means used in fiction as well. Still, Walsh insisted on the ideological premium that came with testimonial writing, writing based on true events. He retreated from fiction during the years of his heaviest political immersion, not producing one work of fiction between 1967 and 1972.

In 1970, the Montoneros, a militant Peronist group, kidnapped and murdered General Pedro Aramburu, who had been the de facto president during the June 9, 1956, failed Peronist uprising. The Montoneros cited the events of June 9, 1956—which they only knew about in such great detail thanks to *Operation Massacre*—as part of the justification for their actions. Walsh revised the fourth and final edition of the book, published in 1972, to reflect his opinions on Aramburu's murder—see Chapter 37 of this translation. Though he had his disagreements with the Montoneros, Walsh kept collaborating with them and eventually joined them in 1973. For him, they represented the most effective popular struggle for social justice at the time. His own true crime writings as well as his increased involvement in the armed Peronist resistance now made him a clear target in the eyes of the State.

---

[*]   Jozami, Eduardo. *Rodolfo Walsh: La palabra y la acción* (Buenos Aires: Grupo Editorial Norma, 2006), 151.

Walsh began writing for *Noticias*, a Peronist newspaper, and had established his own network of people whom he used as intelligence sources for his writings. After a Peronist victory in the national elections, Perón was invited back to Argentina. His many supporters, including Walsh, believed the change they had been hoping for was coming. But in the latter half of 1973, Perón's health began to fail him, and he died on July 2, 1974. Another military junta came into power and began to persecute Peronists once more, this time with a vengeance. The *Noticias* office was forced to close. Walsh started his own underground news agency called ANCLA ("Agencia de Noticias Clandestinas" or "Clandestine News Agency").

In 1957, a writer like Walsh could write a book like *Operation Massacre* and have it published and widely read, as controversial as it may have been. By 1977, there was no freedom of the press in Argentina, and the rule of law had been practically abolished. What was to be the most savage military junta in Argentina's history had been in power for a year. In his introduction to this book, Michael Greenberg describes the way in which more individuals suspected of subversive activities would disappear from the streets of Buenos Aires without a trace. Walsh walked around the city incognito, not acknowledging anyone he knew for fear of being caught. The final, chilling appendix to this book is Walsh's "Open Letter to the Military Junta," dated March 24, 1977. After listing pages of grievances against his oppressors, he concludes:

> These are the thoughts I wanted to pass on to the members of this Junta on the first anniversary of your ill-fated government, with no hope of being heard, with the certainty of being persecuted, but faithful to the commitment I made a long time ago to bear witness during difficult times.

The following day, after dropping the letter in the mail to mainstream newspapers in Buenos Aires, Walsh was on his way to a meeting with a fellow Montonero. The person he was supposed to meet was tortured until he surrendered the details of the meeting. Walsh was stopped in the street by one of the State's armed gangs and managed to get one shot off with the .22 caliber gun he carried for protection before they gunned him down. He was fifty years old, and to this day his body has not been found.

Walsh's effort to tell the story became a fight for human decency. The story became one of life and death and the physical reality of ordinary people being treated horrifically and dying in a shameful way, leaving entire families bereft. Exactly how much is lost in the arbitrary execution of a group of men? Walsh was able to contain his rage and disappointment and convey what happened on the night of June 9, 1956, with ferocious precision and a forensic attention to detail. This, to me, is heroic: write so well about everyday people being murdered under a cruel regime that everyday readers sixty-six years later will know what it felt like and maybe also give a damn.

Translating this book was an enormous honor and a great challenge for me. The book came to me by chance, as a gift from my friend Dante in Buenos Aires. The prologue is what really caught my attention and made me think I could possibly do this text justice in English: Walsh's sentences were notably short and direct, not circuitous and ambiguous in the way that often makes Spanish deceivingly difficult to translate well. It made sense to me that he had read the English-language crime writers, that he himself had translated from English and came from a family of Irish immigrants. There was something familiarly English about his Spanish. Walsh does, however, change his tense all the time, which can be disorienting in English, but is less so in Spanish. I tried to preserve these changes inasmuch as they reflected the urgency that was present in the Spanish: a sudden switch to the present tense brings the reader swiftly to the present of the text itself. Suddenly she is there, bearing witness to the events of the night of the crime. I had also to acknowledge the frequent changes of register in Walsh's language: there is certainly a colloquial nature to much of Walsh's prose, and to that end, I have tried to use contractions sparingly and carefully, only in instances where I believe they help to reflect the rhythm of the Spanish text more faithfully. But there is also a more formal dignity and rectitude to his writing:

> There had been, in fact, no grounds for trying to execute him. No grounds for torturing him psychologically to the limits of what a person can endure. No grounds for condemning him to hunger and thirst. No grounds for shackling and handcuffing him. And now, there were no grounds—only a simple decree, No. 14.975—for restoring him to the world.

Walsh travels between these registers with grace, imbuing these passages with a nobility that I tried to render in English. Along similar lines, I have tried to keep phrasing that I believe Walsh made intentionally impenetrable in Spanish nearly as impenetrable in English. Walsh was writing in 1957, after all, which meant that I was unfamiliar with certain expressions: What is a *multitudinario esquive de bulto*? Walsh uses the phrase to describe the reaction he is met with when he tries to publish the articles that would become *Operation Massacre*. Literally it means something like "a massive, swelling avoidance," but it's a colloquial expression that I chose to translate as "no one wants anything to do with it." No one was interested in publishing Walsh's yellowing pages, no one wanted to get too involved in his mess.

When I didn't know something and couldn't find any written evidence to help me, I would ask my mother, an Argentine who was born in the '40s, or my right hand in this entire operation, Pablo Martín Ruiz, born in the '60s in Argentina. Pablo checked over every single translated sentence at least twice with an eye for accuracy and political and historical context. I needed to understand where Walsh stood politically in order to translate his tone with integrity, especially when it came to the appendices, each one tracking a different current in Walsh's personal journey as an activist. Perhaps the most trying segments were in the third part of the book, which is composed primarily of abstruse legalese. I recruited my brother, a lawyer in the US Department of Justice, to check that my wording was as accurate as it could be, especially given the different justice systems and time periods involved.

I take my lead from Walsh in thanking those who helped make this translation possible: to my dear friend Dante for giving me Walsh's book as a gift, and to his mother, who took the time to find photographs for possible use in this edition. Thank you to Daniel Divinsky at Ediciones de la Flor and to everyone at Seven Stories Press. The writings of Eduardo Jozami, Michael McCaughan, and Luis Alberto Romero were especially useful to me. I am grateful to Ben for reading and keeping me to a higher standard of excellence. To my family, thank you for supporting me with your time, your attention, and your whole hearts, as always. *A Ileana, mi querida abuela, gracias por tu apoyo y tu amor siempre.* Pablo Martín Ruiz was my Enriqueta Muñiz: I simply could not have done this without him. Dan Simon was my Bruno and Tulio Jacovella, my Leónidas Barletta. But of course these comparisons are perverse: no one had to risk their lives so that this translation could be published, and for that I am truly thankful.

Daniella Gitlin
Translator
New York City, Spring 2013

PROLOGUE

News of the June 1956 secret executions first came to me by chance, toward the end of that year, in a La Plata café where people played chess, talked more about Keres and Nimzowitsch than Aramburu and Rojas, and the only military maneuver that enjoyed any kind of renown was Schlechter's bayonet attack in the Sicilian Defense.[1]

Six months earlier, in that same place, we'd been startled around midnight by the shooting nearby that launched the assault on the Second Division Command and the police department—Valle's failed rebellion.[2] I remember how we left en masse, chess players, card players, and everyday customers, to see what the celebration was all about; how, the closer we got to San Martín Square, the more serious we became as our group became smaller; and how, when I finally got across the square, I was alone. When I reached the bus station there were several more of us again, including a poor dark-skinned boy in a guard's uniform who hid behind his goggles saying that, revolution or not, no one was going to take away his gun—a handsome 1901 Mauser.

I remember finding myself alone once more, in the darkness of Fifty-Fourth Street, just three blocks away from my house, which I kept wanting to get to and finally reached two hours later amid the smell of lime trees that always made me nervous, and did so on that night even more than usual. I remember the irrepressible will of my legs, the preference they showed at every street for the bus station, returning to it on their own two or three times. But each time they went a bit farther before turning back, until they didn't need to go back because we had gone past the line of fire and arrived at my house. My house was worse than the café and worse than the bus station because there were soldiers on the roof and also in the kitchen and the bedrooms, but mainly in the bathroom. Since then I've developed an aversion to houses that face police departments, headquarters, or barracks.

I also haven't forgotten how, standing by the window blinds, I heard a recruit dying in the street who did not say "Long live the nation!" but instead: "Don't leave me here alone, you sons of bitches."

After that, I don't want to remember anything else—not the announcer's voice at dawn reporting that eighteen civilians had been executed in Lanús, nor the wave of blood that flooded the country up until Valle's death. It's too much for a single night. I'm not interested in Valle. I'm not interested in Perón, I'm not interested in revolution. Can I go back to playing chess?

I can. Back to chess and the fantasy literature I read, back to the detective stories I write, back to the "serious" novel I plan to draft in the next few years, back to the other things that I do to earn a living and that I call journalism, even though that's not what it is. Violence has spattered my walls, there are bullet holes in the windows, I've seen a car full of holes with a man inside it whose brains were spilling out—but it's only chance that has put all this before my eyes. It could have happened a hundred kilometers away, it could have happened when I wasn't there.

Six months later, on a suffocating summer night with a glass of beer in front of him, a man says to me:

—One of the executed men is alive.

I don't know what it is about this vague, remote, highly unlikely story that manages to draw me in. I don't know why I ask to talk to that man, why I end up talking to Juan Carlos Livraga.

But afterward I do know why. I look at that face, the hole in his cheek, the bigger hole in his throat, his broken mouth and dull eyes, where a shadow of death still lingers. I feel insulted, just as I felt without realizing it when I heard that chilling cry while standing behind the blinds.

Livraga tells me his unbelievable story; I believe it on the spot.

And right there the investigation, this book, is born. The long night of June 9 comes back over me, pulls me out of "the soft quiet seasons" for a second time. Now I won't think about anything else for almost a year; I'll leave my house and my job behind; I'll go by the name Francisco Freyre; I'll have a fake ID with that name on it; a friend will lend me his house in Tigre; I'll live on a frozen ranch in Merlo for two months; I'll carry a gun; and at every moment the characters of the story will come back to me obsessively: Livraga covered in blood walking through that never-ending alley he took to escape death, the other man who survived with him by running back into the field amid the gunfire, and those who survived without his knowing about it, and those who didn't survive.

Because what Livraga knows is that there was a bunch of them, that they were taken out to be shot, that there were about ten of them taken out, and that he and Giunta were still alive. That's the story I hear him repeat before the judge one morning when I say I'm Livraga's cousin so they let me into the court where everything is infused with a sense of discretion and skepticism. The story sounds a bit more absurd here, a little more lush, and I can see the judge doubting it, right up until Livraga's voice climbs over that grueling hill, to where all that's left is a sob, and he makes a gesture to take off his clothes so that everyone can see the other gunshot wound. Then we all feel ashamed, the judge seems to be moved, and I feel myself moved again by the tragedy that has befallen my cousin.

That's the story I write feverishly and in one sitting so that no one beats me to it, but that later gets more wrinkled every day in my pocket because I walk around all of Buenos Aires with it and hardly anyone wants to know about it, let alone publish it. You begin to believe in the crime novels you've read or written, and think that a story like this, with a talking dead man, is going to be fought over by the presses. You think you're running a race against time, that at any given moment a big newspaper is going to send out a dozen reporters and photographers, just like in the movies. But instead you find that no one wants anything to do with it.

It's funny, really, to read through all the newspapers twelve years later and see that this story doesn't exist and never did.

So I wander into increasingly remote outskirts of journalism until finally I walk into a basement on Leandro Alem Avenue where they are putting out a union pamphlet, and I find a man who's willing to take the risk. He is trembling and sweating because he's no movie hero either, just a man who is willing to take the risk, and that's worth more than a movie hero. And the story is printed, a flurry of little yellow leaflets in the kiosks: badly designed, with no signature, and with all the headings changed, but it's printed. I look at it affectionately as it's snatched up by ten thousand anonymous hands.

But I've had even more luck than that. There is a young journalist named Enriqueta Muñiz who has been with me from the very beginning and has put herself entirely on the line. It is difficult to do her justice in just a few sentences. I simply want to say that if I have written "I did," "I went," "I discovered" anywhere in this book, it should all be read as "We did," "We went," "We discovered." There were several important things that she got alone, like testimonies from Troxler, Benavídez, and Gavino, who were all in exile. At the time, I didn't see the world as an ordered sequence of guarantees and certainties, but rather as the exact opposite. In Enriqueta Muñiz I found the security, bravery, and intelligence that seemed so hard to come by.

So one afternoon we take the train to José León Suárez and bring a camera with us, along with a little map that Livraga has drawn up for us in pencil, a detailed bus driver's map. He has marked the roads and rail crossings for us, as well as a grove and an X where it all happened. At dusk, we walk about eight blocks along a paved road, catch sight of the tall, dark row of eucalyptus trees that the executioner Rodríguez Moreno had deemed "an appropriate place for the task" (namely, the task of shooting them), and find ourselves in front of a sea of tin cans and delusions. One of the greatest delusions was the notion that a place like this cannot remain so calm, so quiet and forgotten beneath the setting sun, without someone keeping watch over the history imprisoned in the garbage that glistens with a false tide of thoughtfully gleaming dead metals. But Enriqueta says "It happened here," and casually sits down on the ground so that I can take a picnic photo of her because, just at that moment, a tall sullen man with a big sullen dog walks by. I don't know why one notices these things. But this was where it happened, and Livraga's story feels more real now: here was the path, over there was the ditch, the garbage dump and the night all around us.

The following day we go see the other survivor, Miguel Ángel Giunta, who greets us by slamming the door in our faces. He doesn't believe us when we tell him we're journalists and asks for credentials that we don't have. I don't know what it is that we say to him through the screen door, what vow of silence, what hidden key, that gets him to gradually open the door and start to come out, which takes about half an hour, and to talk, which takes much longer.

It kills you to listen to Giunta because you get the feeling you're watching a movie that has been rolling and rolling in his head since the night it was filmed and can't be stopped. All the tiny details are there: the faces, the lights, the field, the small noises, the cold and the heat, the escape from among the tin cans, the smell of gunpowder, and panic. You get the feeling that once he finishes he's going to start again from the beginning, just as the endless loop must start over again in his head: "This is how they executed me." But the more upsetting thing is the affront to his person that this man carries within him, how he has been hurt by the mistake they made with him, because after all he's a decent man who wasn't even a Peronist, "and you can ask anybody, they'd tell you who I am." But actually we're not sure about this anymore because there appear to be two Giuntas, the one who is talking fervently as he acts out this movie for us, and the other one who is sometimes distracted and manages to smile and crack a joke or two, like old times.

It seems like the story could end here because there is no more to tell. Two survivors, and the rest are dead. I could publish the interview with Giunta and go back to that abandoned chess game in the café from a month ago. But it's not over. At the last minute Giunta mentions a belief he has, not something he knows for sure, but something he has imagined or heard murmured: there is a third man who survived.

Meanwhile, the great *picana* god and its submachine guns begin to roar from La Plata.[3] My story floats on leaflets through corridors at Police Headquarters, and Lieutenant Colonel Fernández Suárez wants to know what the fuss is all about. The article wasn't signed, but my initials appeared at the bottom of the original copies. There was a journalist working at the newspaper office who had the same initials, only his were ordered differently: J. W. R. He awakes one morning to an interesting assortment of rifles and other syllogistic tools, and his spirit experiences that surge of emotion before the revelation of a truth. They make him come out in his underwear and put him on a flight to La Plata where he's brought to Police Headquarters. They sit him down in an armchair opposite the Lieutenant Colonel, who says to him, "And now I'd like you to write an article about *me*, please." The journalist explains that he is not the man who deserves such an honor while quietly, to himself, he curses my mother.

The wheels keep turning, and we have to trudge through some rough country in search of the third man, Horacio di Chiano, who is now living like a worm underground. It seems as though people know us already in a lot of these places, the kids at least are following us, and one day a young girl stops us in the street.

—The man you're looking for —she tells us— is in his house. They're going to tell you he isn't, but he is.

—And you know why we've come?

—Yes, I know everything.

Okay, Cassandra.

They tell us he's not there, but he is, and we have to start pushing past the protective barriers, the wakeful gods that keep watch over a living dead man: a wall, a face that denies and distrusts. We cross over from the sunlight of the street to the shade of the porch. We ask for a glass of water and sit there in the dark offering wheedling words until the rustiest lock turns and Mr. Horacio di Chiano climbs the staircase holding onto his wife, who leads him by the hand like a child.

So there are three.

The next day the newspaper receives an anonymous letter that says "Livraga, Giunta, and the ex-NCO Gavino managed to escape."

So there are four. And Gavino, the letter says, "was able to get himself to the Bolivian Embassy and was granted asylum in that country."

I don't find Gavino at the Bolivian Embassy, but I do find his friend Torres, who smiles and, counting it out on his fingers, says, "You're missing two." Then he tells me about Troxler and Benavídez.

So there are six.

And while we're at it, why not seven? Could be, Torres tells me, because there was a sergeant with a very common last name, something like García or Rodríguez, and no one knows what's become of him.

Two or three days later I come back to see Torres and hit him pointblank with a name:

—Rogelio Díaz.

His face lights up.

—How'd you do it?

I don't even remember how I did it. But there are seven.

So now I can take a moment because I have already talked to

survivors, widows, orphans, conspirators, political refugees, fugitives, alleged informers, anonymous heroes. By May, I have written half of this book. Once more, roaming around in search of someone who will publish it. At about that time, the Jacovella brothers had started putting out a magazine. I talk to Bruno, then Tulio. Tulio Jacovella reads the manuscript and laughs, not at the manuscript, but at the mess he is about to get himself into, and he goes for it.

The rest is the story that follows. It was published in *Mayoría* from May through July of 1957. Later there were appendices, corollaries, denials, and retorts that dragged this press campaign out until April 1958. I have cut them all out, together with some of the evidence I used back then, which I am replacing here with more categorical proof. In light of this new evidence, I think any possible controversy can be set aside.

Acknowledgements: to Jorge Doglia, Esq., former head of the legal department of the Province's police, dismissed from his position based on the reports he gave for this case; to Máximo von Kotsch, Esq., the lawyer for Juan C. Livraga and Miguel Giunta; to Leónidas Barletta, head of the newspaper *Intenciones*, where Livraga's initial accusation was published; to Dr. Cerruti Costa, head of the late newspaper *Revolución Nacional*, which ran the first articles about this case; to Bruno and Tulio Jacovella; to Dr. Marcelo Sánchez Sorondo, who published the first edition of this story in book form; to Edmundo A. Suárez, dismissed from his position at State Radio for giving me a photocopy of the Registry Book of Announcers for the broadcast that proved the exact time when martial law was declared; to the ex-terrorist named "Marcelo," who took risks to get me information, and who was horribly tortured shortly thereafter; to the anonymous informant who signed his name "Atilas"; to the anonymous Cassandra who knew everything; to Horacio Maniglia, who gave me shelter; to the families of the victims.

Part One

THE PEOPLE

Next page: Mayoría *cover from May 27, 1957. Bottom left reads: "Lived and complete history of the innocent victims of the José León Suarez killings and of those who miraculously survived."*

MAYORÍA

SEMANARIO ILUSTRADO INDEPENDIENTE

NO NEGOCIA

Hay detrás de la 5100 otra California, esta vez inglesa?

Buenos Aires, 27 d...
Año I · Nº 8 · Precio de...

Empieza en esta edición

LA OPERACION MASACRE

Historia vívida y con...
víctimas inocentes de...
de José León Suárez...
salvaron milagrosam...

1. CARRANZA

Nicolás Carranza was not a happy man on the night of June 9, 1956. Protected by the shadows, he had just come into his house, and something might have been gnawing at him on the inside. We'll never really know. A man carries so many heavy thoughts with him to the grave, and the earth at the bottom of Nicolás Carranza's grave has already dried up.

For a moment, though, he could forget his worries. After an initial, surprising silence, a chorus of shrill voices rose to receive him. Nicolás Carranza had six children. The smaller ones might have hung on to his knees. The oldest, Elena, probably put her head just at her father's arm's reach. Tiny Julia Renée—barely forty days old—was asleep in her crib.

His wife, Berta Figueroa, lifted her gaze from the sewing machine. She smiled at him with a mix of sadness and joy. It was always the same. Her man always came in like this: on the run, in the night, like a flash. Sometimes he stayed the night and then disappeared for weeks. Every so often he would have messages sent her way: at so-and-so's house. And then she would be the one going to her meeting, leaving the children with a neighbor to be with him for a few hours racked with fear, anxiety, and the bitterness that came with having to leave him and wait for time to pass slowly without any word.

Nicolás Carranza was a Peronist. And a fugitive.

That's why, whenever he would be coming home secretly like he was that night and some kid from the neighborhood yelled "Hello, Mr. Carranza!", he would quicken his step and not answer.

—Hey, Mr. Carranza! —curiosity was always following him.

But Mr. Carranza—a short and stocky silhouette in the night—

would walk away quickly on the dirt road, raising the lapels of his overcoat to meet his eyes.

Now he was sitting in the armchair in the dining room bouncing his two-year-old, Berta Josefa, his three-year-old, Carlos Alberto, and maybe even his four-year-old, Juan Nicolás—he had a whole staircase worth of children, Mr. Carranza—on his knees. He rocked them back and forth, imitating the roar and whistle of trains run by the men who lived in that railroad suburban town, men like him.

Next he talked to his favorite, eleven-year-old Elena—she was tall and slim for her age with big grey-brown eyes—and shared only some of his adventures, with a bit of happy fairytale mixed in. He asked her questions out of a sense of concern, fear, and tenderness, because the truth was that he felt a knot form in his heart whenever he looked at her, ever since the time she was put in jail.

It's hard to believe, but on January 26, 1956, she was locked up for a few hours in Frías (in Santiago del Estero). Her father had dropped her off there on the twenty-fifth with his wife's family and continued on along his regular Belgrano line trip to the North, where he worked as a waiter. In Simoca, in the province of Tucumán, he was arrested for distributing pamphlets, a charge that was never proven.

At eight o'clock the following morning, Elena was taken from her relatives' home, brought to the police station, and interrogated for four hours. Was her father handing out pamphlets? Was her father a Peronist? Was her father a criminal?

Mr. Carranza lost his mind when he heard the news.

—Let them do what they want to *me*, but to a child . . .

He howled and wept.

And fled the police in Tucumán.

It was probably from that moment on that a dangerous glaze washed over the eyes of this man whose features were clear and firm, who used to be a happy nature, the fun-loving best friend to his own kids and to everyone's kids in the neighborhood.

They all ate together on the night of June 9 in that working-class neighborhood of Boulogne. Afterward, they put the kids to bed and it was just the two of them, he and Berta.

She shared her sorrows and her worries. Was the railway going to take away their home now that he was out of work and on the run? It was a good brick house with flowers in the garden, and they managed to fit everyone there, including a pair of women factory workers they had taken in as lodgers. What would she and the children live off of if they took her house away?

She shared her fears. There was always the fear that they would drag him from his home on any given night and beat him senseless at some police station, leaving her with a vegetable for a husband. And she begged him as she always did:

—Turn yourself in. If you turn yourself in, maybe they won't beat you. At least you can get out of jail, Nicolás . . .

He didn't want to. He took refuge in harsh, dry, definitive statements:

—I've stolen nothing. I've killed no one. I am not a criminal.

The little radio on the shelf in the sideboard was playing folk songs. After a lengthy silence, Nicolás Carranza got up, took his overcoat from the coat stand, and slowly put it on.

She looked at him again, her face resigned.

—Where are you going?

—I have some things to take care of. I might be back tomorrow.

—You're not sleeping here.

—No. Tonight, I'm not sleeping here.

He went into the bedroom and kissed his children one by one: Elena, María Eva, Juan Nicolás, Carlos Alberto, Berta Josefa, Julia Renée. Then he said goodbye to his wife.

—Till tomorrow.

He kissed her, went out to the sidewalk, and turned left. He crossed B Street and walked just a few paces before stopping at house number thirty-two.

He rang the doorbell.

2. GARIBOTTI

The young men are wild and there may be some aggression in the air at the home of the Garibottis in the working-class neighborhood of Boulogne. The father, Francisco, is the archetype of a man: tall, muscular, with a square and firm face, mildly hostile eyes, and a thin mustache that flows well over the corners of his mouth.

The mother is a beautiful woman, even with her tough, common features. Tall, strong, with something contemptuous about her mouth and eyes that do not smile.

There are six children here as well, just like at Carranza's, but that's where the similarities end. The five oldest ones are boys who range from Juan Carlos, who is about to turn eighteen, to eleven-year-old Norberto.

Delia Beatriz, at nine years old, somewhat softens this otherwise intensely male environment. Dark-haired, with bangs and smiling eyes, her father melts when he sees her. There is a photo in a glass cabinet of her in a school uniform of white overalls standing next to a chalkboard.

The whole family appears on the walls. Yellowing, far-off snapshots of Francisco and Florinda—they are young and laughing in the park—ID photos of the father and the kids, even some fleeting faces of relatives and friends, have all been glued to a big piece of board and stuck inside a frame. Just as at the Carranzas', the inescapable "portrait artists" have been here as well and, beneath a double "bombé" frame, have left a wealth of blues and golds that attempt to portray two of the young boys, though we can't figure out which ones.

This passion for decor or mementos reaches its peak in the predictable print of Gardel all in black, his hat nearly covering his face, his foot resting on a chair as he strums a guitar.

But it is a clean, solid, modestly furnished house, a house where a working man can live decently. And the "company" charges them less than one hundred pesos in rent.

This may be why Francisco Garibotti doesn't want to get into any trouble. He knows the union is not doing well—the military has gotten involved, friends have been arrested—but all of that will pass some day. One needs to be patient and wait it out.

Garibotti is thirty-eight years old, with sixteen years of service to the Belgrano Railway under his belt. Now he works the local line.

That afternoon he left work around five and came straight home.

Of his two sons, he might favor the second eldest. He has his father's name: Francisco, only with the extra middle name, Osmar. This sixteen-year-old young man with a serious look in his eye is all set to start working for the railroad as well.

There is a true camaraderie between the two of them. The father likes playing the guitar while his son sings. This is what they're doing that afternoon.

It gets dark early on these midwinter June days. It's already night-time before they even bother to notice. Mother sets the table for dinner. A frying pan crackles in the kitchen.

Francisco Garibotti has nearly finished his dinner already—he ate steak and eggs that night—when the doorbell rings.

It's Mr. Carranza.

What's Nicolás Carranza come for?

—He came to take him away. And they brought him back to me a corpse —Florinda Allende would later recall with resentment in her voice.

The two men talk for a while. Florinda has stepped back into the kitchen. She senses that her husband is feeling an itch to go out on this particular Saturday night, and she plans to fight for her rights, but on her own turf, without the neighbor in the room.

Francisco comes in after a moment.

—I have to head out —he says, not looking at her.

—We were going to go to the movies —she reminds him.

—You're right, we were. Maybe we can go later.

—You said you'd go out with me.

—I'll be right back. I just have to run an errand and then I'll be back.

—I can't imagine what errand you need to run.

—I'll explain later. The truth —he tries to make himself clear, anticipating her reproach— is that I'm also a little tired of this guy . . . and all his ideas . . .

—Doesn't seem like it.

—Look, this is the last time I'll give him the time of day. Wait for me a little while.

And as though to prove that he is only going out for a minute, that he has every intention of coming back as soon as he can, he gets to the door and, just as he finishes putting on his overcoat, yells out:

—If Vivas comes by, tell him to wait. Tell him I'm going to run an errand and I'll be back.

The two friends set out. They walk a few blocks along Guayaquil, a long street, and turn right, heading toward the station. They take the first local bound for the barrio of Florida. It's only a few minutes away by train.

No one can testify as to what they talked about. We can only speculate. Maybe Garibotti repeated Berta Figueroa's advice to his friend: that he turn himself in. Maybe Carranza wanted to put him in charge of something in case he didn't make it back home. Maybe he knew about the uprising in the making and mentioned it to him. Or maybe he simply said:

—Let's go to a friend's place to listen to the radio. There's going to be some news . . .

There could also be more innocent explanations. A card game or the Lausse match that would be on the radio later.[4] Something like that may have happened. What we do know is that Garibotti has left without really feeling like it, and intended to come back soon. If he ends up not going back later, it's because they have managed to conquer his curiosity, his interest, or his inertia. He was unarmed when he left, and would at no point have a weapon in his hands.

Carranza is also unarmed. He will let himself be arrested without any sign of resistance. He will let himself be killed like a child, without one rebellious movement. Begging uselessly for mercy until the final gunshot.

They get off in Florida. They turn right and cross the railroad tracks. They walk six blocks along Hipólito Yrigoyen Street. They cross Franklin. They stop—Carranza stops—in front of a country house with two small light blue wooden gates that lead directly into a garden.

They go in through the right gate. They walk through a long corridor. They ring the bell.

From this point on we won't have any verifiable accounts of Garibotti. As for some account of Carranza before the final, definitive silence—we still have to wait for many hours to pass.

And many incomprehensible things, too.

3. MR. HORACIO

Florida is twenty-four minutes from Retiro on the F. C. Belgrano line. It's not the best part of the Vicente López district, but it's also not the worst. The municipality skimps on waterworks and sanitation, there are potholes in the pavement and no signs on the street corners, but people live there despite all that.

Six blocks west of the train station lies the neighborhood where so many unexpected things are going to happen. It exhibits the violent contrasts common to areas in development, where the residential and the filthy meet, a recently constructed villa next to a wasteland of weeds and tin cans.

The average resident is a man between the ages of thirty and forty who has his own home with a garden that he tends to in his idle moments, and who has not finished paying the bank for the loan that allowed him to buy the house in the first place. He lives with a relatively small family and works either as a business employee or a skilled laborer in Buenos Aires. He gets along with his neighbors and proposes or agrees to initiatives in support of the common good. He plays sports—typically soccer—covers the usual political issues in conversation and, no matter what government is in charge, protests the rising costs of living and the impossible transportation system without ever getting too excited about it.

This model does not allow for a very wide range of variation. Life is calm, no ups and downs. Nothing ever really happens here.

During the winter, the streets are half-deserted by the early evening. The corners are poorly lit and you need to cross them carefully to avoid getting stuck in the mud puddles that have formed due to the lack of drainage. Wherever you find a small bridge or a line of stones laid down for crossing, it's the neighbors who have put it there. Sometimes the dark water spans from one curb all the way to another. You can't really see it, but you can guess it's there using the reflection of some star or the light of the waning lanterns that languish on the porches into the wee hours. San Martín Avenue is the only place where things are moving a bit: a passing bus, a neon sign, the cold blue glare of a bar's front window.

The house that Carranza and Garibotti have walked into—where the first act of the drama will unfold, and to which a ghost witness will return in the end—has two apartments: one in front and one in back. To get to the back one, you need to go down a long corridor that is closed in on the right by a dividing wall and on the left by a tall privet hedge. The corridor, which leads to a green metal door, is so narrow that you can only walk through it in single file. It's worth remembering this detail; it carries a certain importance.

The apartment in back is rented out to a man who we'll come back to at the last moment. The apartment in front is where the owner of the whole building, Mr. Horacio di Chiano, lives with his family.

Mr. Horacio is a dark-skinned man of small stature with a mustache and glasses. He is about fifty years old and for the last seventeen years he has worked as an electrician in the Ítalo. His ambitions are simple: to retire and then work awhile on his own before truly calling it quits.

His home exudes a sense of peaceful and satisfied middle class. From the set furniture to the vague phrases that run across decorative plates on the walls—"To err is human, to forgive divine" or some innocent, bold claim, "Love makes the time pass, time makes love pass"—to the devotional image placed in a nook by his wife or by their only child, Nélida, a quiet twenty-four-year-old girl. The only thing of note is a certain abundance of curtains, pillows, and rugs. The lady of the house, Pilar—white-haired and mild-mannered—is an upholsterer.

This Saturday is identical to hundreds of other Saturdays for Mr. Horacio. He has stayed on duty at work. His job consists of resolving clients' electrical problems. At five o'clock in the afternoon he gets his last call, this one from Palermo. He heads that way, fixes the problem, and comes back to the main office. By then it is already nighttime. At 8:45 p.m. he lets the Balcarce office know by phone that he's leaving and begins to make his way home.

There is nothing new about this routine. It has been the same for years and years. And the world is not any different when he gets on the Belgrano line train at Retiro station. The evening papers don't boast any major headlines. In the United States, they've operated on Eisenhower. In London and Washington, they're talking about Bulganin's take on disarmament. San Lorenzo beat Huracán in a game leading up to the soccer championship. General Aramburu takes one of his regular trips, this time to Rosario. The city official appointed by the de facto government gushes with lyricism when receiving him: ". . . the time has come to work in peace, to be productive in peace, to dream in peace and to love in peace . . ." The President responds with a phrase that he will repeat the following day, but under different circumstances: "Do not fear the fearful. Freedom has won the game." Later on he gives the journalists who are with him some fatherly advice on how to tell the truth. Nothing new, really, is happening in the world. The only things of interest are the calculations and commentary leading up to the big boxing match for the South American title that's taking place tonight in the Luna Park.

Mr. Horacio happens to come home at the same time as his neighbor, who lives fifty meters down the very same Yrigoyen Street. It's Miguel Ángel Giunta. They stand there talking for a moment. There is no real friendship between the two—they have known each other for less than a year—but they do share a cordial neighborly relationship. They tend to take the same train in the mornings. Mr. Horacio has invited him into his home more than once. Until now Giunta hasn't had the opportunity to accept, but tonight the offer is made again:

—Why don't you come watch the fight after dinner?

Giunta hesitates.

—I can't promise anything. But maybe.

—Bring your wife —insists Mr. Horacio.

Actually, that's why Giunta is wavering. When stepping out that afternoon, he had left his wife feeling a bit ill. If he finds that she's feeling better, he might come. This is how the two men leave it. Then each of them hurries into his own house. The temperature has begun to drop. The thermometer reads -4°C and will keep dropping.

It is 9:30 p.m. At that moment, thirty kilometers from here, in Campo de Mayo, a group of officers and NCOs led by colonels Cortínez and Ibazeta, set the tragic June uprising in motion.

Mr. Horacio and Giunta don't know this. Most of the country doesn't know it either and won't know it until after midnight.

State Radio, the official voice of the Nation, is playing Haydn.

4. GIUNTA

Giunta, or Mr. Lito as they call him in the neighborhood, comes back from Villa Martelli, where he has spent the afternoon with his parents.

Giunta is not even thirty years old. He's a tall man, elegant, blond, and clear-eyed. Effusive and expressive in his gestures and his language, he has a healthy dose of wit to him, skeptical irony, even. But what you come away with is a sense of solid honor, of sincerity. Of all the witnesses who survive this tragedy, no one else will be as convincing or have as easy and natural a time proving his innocence, showing it to be concrete and almost tangible. Talking to him for an hour, hearing him remember, seeing the indignation and the memories of horror gradually emerging from inside him, making themselves visible in his eyes and even making his hair stand on end, is enough to set aside any skepticism.

For fifteen years Giunta has been working as a shoe salesman in Buenos Aires. He picked up two minor skills at his job that are worth mentioning. First, he practices a certain "psychology" method that sometimes lets him guess his clients'—and by extension others'—wishes and intentions, which are not always obvious. Second, he has an enviable memory for faces, sharpened over the years.

He does not suspect—as he is dining in the peaceful house that he bought with his own sweat, as he is surrounded by the affection of his loved ones—that hours later these skills will help him escape the grimmest experience of his life.

5. DÍAZ: TWO SNAPSHOTS

Meanwhile, people are filing into the apartment in back. There will be up to fifteen men there at one point, playing cards around two tables while talking or listening to the radio. Some will leave and others will join. In some instances it will be difficult to determine the precise chronology of these comings and goings. And not just the chronology. Even the identity of one or two of them will ultimately remain blurry or unknown.

We know, for example, that at around 9:00 p.m. a man named Rogelio Díaz shows up, but we don't know exactly who brings him or why he comes at all. We know he is an NCO (a sergeant who served as a tailor, according to some) who retired from the Navy, but we don't know why he retired—or why he was retired. We know he lives very nearby, in Munro, but we don't know if it is just proximity that explains his presence here. We know he is married with two or three children, but later on no one will be able to tell us his family's exact whereabouts. Is he involved with the revolutionary movement? Maybe. But maybe not.

The one exact detail, the only one that everyone who remembers seeing him can agree upon, is his physical appearance: a burly man from the provinces, very dark-skinned, of unidentifiable age ("You know, with darker people, it's hard to tell a person's age . . ."). He is a cheerful, chatty guy who gets all worked up playing Rummy one minute, and then, once everyone's already afraid of him, will be completely different the next, snoring happily and loudly on a bench in the San Martín Regional Office, as though he didn't have the smallest care in the world. A man's entire life can be summed up in these two snapshots.[*]

6. LIZASO

The image we have of Carlitos Lizaso is sharper, more urgent, and more tragic. This tall, thin, pale young man, reserved and almost

---

[*] When I first mentioned Díaz in my articles for *Revolución Nacional*, his existence and survival were more of a conjecture, which later I could fortunately prove true. The person who had mentioned him to me could only remember his last name, and wasn't even sure of that much. After questioning a rather sizable number of secondary witnesses, I deduced that a Sergeant Díaz did indeed exist. Curiously, no one could remember his first name and nearly everyone thought he was dead. That was until I found a list of Olmos prisoners in a weekly magazine where a certain "Díaz Rogelio" appeared. My informants then remembered that Rogelio was his Christian name. While this book was being published in the magazine *Mayoría*, I gathered the following additional information about him: he was in fact a sergeant from Santiago del Estero who served as a tailor and was in the Navy's Fourth Infantry Battalion (in the North Basin) in 1952, before being transferred to Santiago River's Naval Academy.

timid, is twenty-one years old. He comes from a big family in the district of Vicente López.

Politics has always been a major topic of discussion in his house. Mr. Pedro Lizaso, the father, was a member of the Radical Civil Union at one time.[5] He then became a Peronist sympathizer. In 1947 he is named City Commissioner for a short time. Later on, something inside him takes a turn in the other direction: by 1950, he has distanced himself from Peronism and will keep distancing himself more and more as time goes on; he is practically in the opposition when the September revolution comes about.

—We had the secret hope that everything would change, that any good that was left would be saved and the bad would be destroyed —a friend of his would later say.— But then . . .

Then we already know what happens. A wave of revenge overtakes the country. Mr. Pedro Lizaso, old, sick, and disillusioned, goes back to the opposition.

These changes are reflected in his two sons. In September 1955, when the revolution shakes everyone to their core and those who aren't fighting are glued to their radios, listening to the official news as well as the news filtering in less frequently from the opposition— what an extraordinary thing to think about! No one would end up shooting them for doing that—someone asks Carlos:

—Who would you fight for?

—I don't know —he replies, unsettled.— For no one.

—But if they made you, if you had to choose.

He thinks for a moment before responding.

—For them, I think —he finally replies.

"Them" are the revolutionaries.

Since then, there's been a lot of water under the bridge. Carlos Lizaso seems to have forgotten about such dilemmas. From the outside, this is what his life looks like: He has dropped out of high school to help out at his father's auction house. He works hard, has a knack for earning money, hopes to move up in the business, and is well on his way despite his young age. In his moments of rest, he distracts himself by playing chess. He is a strong player who has had some success in several youth tournaments.

It isn't hard to reconstruct every one of his moves on the afternoon of June 9. First he goes to see his sister. Later on he heads to his girlfriend's house and stays with her for about an hour. It's past nine o'clock when he says goodbye and leaves. He takes the bus and gets off in Florida. He walks a few blocks, stops in front of the house with the light blue gates, ventures into the long corridor . . .

What does he know about the rebellion that's taking place at that exact moment? Here again, contradiction and doubt arise: On the one hand, he is a calm, thoughtful young man. He doesn't carry any weapons and wouldn't even know how to use them. He was exempted from military service and has never had a simple revolver in his hands.

On the other hand, we can guess what his thoughts are when it comes to politics. A detail confirms this.

After he leaves, his girlfriend finds a piece of paper with Carlos's handwriting on it in her house:

"If all goes well tonight . . ."

But all will not go well.

7. WARNINGS AND PREMONITIONS

There is one man, at least, who seems to see it coming. He will pass by Lizaso's house once, twice, three times, to look for him, to take him away, to steal him from death, even though the latter extreme hasn't yet crossed anybody's mind. And it will all be futile.

This man—who will later turn to terrorism and go by the name "Marcelo"—plays a curious role in the events. He is a friend of both the Lizaso family and some of the other main characters. He feels like a father to Carlitos, an affection that time and misfortune will turn sour. This man knows what's going on. That is why he's afraid and why he wants to take the young man with him. But he will keep finding him entertained, engaged, chatting, and he'll let himself be deterred by the same promise again and again:

—I'll leave in ten minutes . . .

"Marcelo" isn't happy with this. Before leaving for the last time, he turns to the man who he considers responsible for the confusing situation that seems to be developing in the apartment. He knows him. He takes him aside and they speak softly.

—Do any of these people know anything?

—No. Most of them don't know anything.

—So what are they doing here?

—What do I know . . . They're going to listen to the fight.

—But you, sir —"Marcelo" insists, now irritated— why are you letting them stay here?

—You want me to throw them out? I'm not the owner here.

The conversation becomes unpleasant. "Marcelo" sharply interrupts it.

—Do what you want. But that guy there —he tilts his head towards Lizaso, who is standing a ways away, talking with a group of people— you don't take him anywhere, you hear me?

The man shrugs his shoulders.

—Don't worry. I'm not going to take him anywhere. And besides, at this point, nothing's going to happen tonight.

8. GAVINO

"At this point, nothing's going to happen tonight," Norberto Gavino tells himself again. That piece of news should have been broadcast on the radio a while ago already. For a moment, he thinks "Marcelo" is right. But then he brushes it off. If nothing's happening, then no one's in danger. Many of them have simply stopped by, people he doesn't even know; it'd be ridiculous to say: "Get out, I'm about to start a revolution."

Because there's no question that Gavino, despite being out of the loop and not knowing what to expect, *is* a part of the uprising.

Gavino is about forty years old and has an average but athletic build. He was once an NCO of the National Gendarmerie and later started selling plots of land. Sharp, short-tempered, and prone to bragging (as well as to the dangerous missteps that it can lead to in a life like his), Gavino has been conspiring for some time now, and at the beginning of May, an upsetting incident sealed him on this path. His wife, completely unaware of what her husband was up to, was thrown in jail as a hostage. Gavino found out that they would only set her free when he turned himself in. From that moment on, he thought only of revolution.

He had been on the run ever since, and believed military authorities and the police were after him. With very good reason. Everything that happened that night, the press that came out about it in the days that followed, and other pieces of evidence confirm this.* He couldn't come up with a better way to avoid the siege than to take refuge in his friend Torres's apartment.

And that's where he was now waiting, nervously, for the news that he would never hear.

9. EXPLANATIONS IN AN EMBASSY

This brings us to the character that plays a large part in the tragedy—Torres, the tenant who lives in the apartment in back.

Juan Carlos Torres lives two or three different lives.

---

* In mid-1958, Gavino wrote to me from Bolivia to express his dissatisfaction with the brief portrait of him here, which I sketched based on the testimony of other witnesses. He also denies responsibility for the death of Lizaso, but I never suggested that the responsibility was his to bear. It seems clear that Lizaso knew something about Valle's uprising, and went there that night of his own accord.

To the owner of the building, for example, he is an ordinary tenant who pays his rent on time and doesn't cause any problems, though sometimes he does disappear for a few days and, when he comes back, doesn't say where he's been. To his neighbors, Torres is an easygoing, fairly popular guy who likes to have people over for barbecues and gatherings where nobody talks about politics. To the police, in the period after the uprising, he is a dangerous, elusive, vainly and tirelessly sought-after individual . . .

I found him, finally, many months later, taking asylum in a Latin American embassy, pacing from one side to the other of his forced enclosure, smoking and gazing through a large window at the city, so near and so inaccessible. I went back to see him several times. Tall and thin, with a large head of black hair, a hooked nose, and dark, penetrating eyes, he gave me the impression, despite being holed up in there, of a resolute, laconic, and extremely cautious man.

—I don't have any reason to lie to you —he said.— Whatever damning thing you manage to get out of me I'll say is false, that I don't even know who you are. That's why I don't care if you publish my real name or not.

He smiled without animosity. I told him I understood the rules of the game.

—There was no reason to shoot those men, —he then went on.— Me, okay, I'll give you that, since I was "there" and they found some papers in my house. Nothing more than papers, though, no weapons like they later said. But I escaped. And Gavino also escaped . . .

He paused. Maybe he was thinking about those who hadn't escaped. About those who had nothing to do with it. I asked him if there had been talk of revolution.

—Not even remotely —he said.— For those who were really involved, namely Gavino and me, all we had to do was give each other one look to communicate. But neither he nor I knew if we were even going to act, or where. We were waiting for a sign that never came. I found out what was going on when Gavino asked me for the key to the apartment because the police were after him. We were friends, so I gave it to him. It's possible that someone else who was in on it had come by wanting to know more.

His tone turned somber.

—The tragedy was that other guys from the neighborhood also showed up, guys who saw people gathering at the house and came in to hear the fight or play cards like they always did. People were always coming into my house, even if they didn't know me. Two undercover cops were there that night and no one even noticed. That guy Livraga, the one the papers are talking about—the truth is that I didn't know him, don't even remember having seen him. The first time I saw him was in a photograph.

A heavy question hovered between us. Juan Carlos Torres went ahead and answered it.

—We didn't tell them anything —he said sorrowfully— because the reality was that, up until that point, nothing had happened. As long as we didn't get any concrete news, it was still a night like any other. I couldn't warn them or tell them to leave because that would've raised suspicions, and I tend not to talk more than necessary.

"A few minutes more, and every one of them would have gone home and nothing would've happened."

A few minutes more. In this case, everything will revolve around a few minutes more.

10. MARIO

Mario Brión lives at 1812 Franklin Street. It is a house with a garden, almost at the corner, less than a hundred meters from the fateful house.

On the afternoon of June 9, Brión is thirty-three years old. He is a man of medium height, blond, mustached, and starting to bald. A certain melancholy, perhaps, exudes from his oval face.

A serious young man and a hard worker, the neighbors say. We gather that his has been a normal life, with no bright highlights or dazzling adventures. At the age of fifteen he becomes an office clerk while staying in school, takes courses in English (which he will come to speak with a certain fluency), and graduates from high school with a commercial degree. He seems to have set a life plan for himself with clear stages that he goes about completing one by one. He uses his savings to buy a plot of land, build a house. Only then does he decide to get married, to his first girlfriend. Later on they have a son: Daniel Mario.

From his father, a Spaniard who learned to make a living in tough trades, he has inherited a wide-ranging love of reading. It's surprising to find Horace, Seneca, Shakespeare, Unamuno, and Baroja in his library next to the cold collections on accounting. There are also those books of inevitable American provenance, all of varied titles that could be summed up in one: *How to Succeed in Life*. These books suggest, more than the dubious results that they promise, what Mario's aspirations were: to work, to advance in life, to protect his family, to have friends, to be appreciated.

He would not have had to do much to achieve all of this. His company had offered him a position as head of his section. He made good money: his home did not lack any comforts. Whatever useful initiatives there were in the neighborhood came from him alone. A small paved road that joins the corner of his house with San Martín Avenue is a reminder of this. He is the one who collected the money, he is the one who gathered the neighbors to work on Sundays and holidays.

Mario Brión—people say—is a happy guy who is kind to everyone and a bit shy. He neither smokes nor drinks. The only things he does for fun are go to the movies with his wife or play soccer with his friends from the neighborhood.

That night, he has eaten his dinner late, as usual. Afterward he leaves to buy the paper. This, too, he always does. He likes to read the paper, in an armchair, while listening to a record or some program on the radio. On the way, he runs into a friend or an acquaintance. We won't know who it was.

—They want me to come hear the fight —he announces to his wife, Adela, when he returns.— I don't know if I should go . . .

He's indecisive. In the end he makes a decision. After all, he had also been thinking of tuning into the fight.

He gives a kiss to his son Danny—who is already four years old—and says goodbye to his wife.

—I'll come back as soon as it's over.

Despite the cold, he doesn't put on an overcoat. He wears only a thick white cardigan.

He walks to Yrigoyen Street and enters the long corridor. A last-minute witness will see him standing next to the radio receiver, smiling and with his hands in his pockets, a bit isolated, a bit removed from the other groups that are talking and playing cards.

11. "THE EXECUTED MAN WHO LIVES"

At number 1624 on Florencio Varela Street, in the Florida district, stands a beautiful California-style house. It could be the home of a lawyer or a doctor. It was built by Mr. Pedro Livraga, a quiet man getting on in years, with his own two hands. In his youth he was a building laborer and later on, through the gradual mastery of the job, ended up as a contractor.

Mr. Pedro has three children. The oldest daughter is married. The two sons, on the other hand, live with him. One of them is Juan Carlos.

He is a thin man of average height and ordinary features: grey-green eyes, brown hair, and a mustache. He is a few days shy of turning twenty-four.

His ideas are entirely commonplace and shared by other people in town: they are generally correct regarding concrete and tangible things, and more nebulous and random in other arenas. He has a reflective, even calculating temperament. He will think a great deal about things and not say more than is necessary.

This doesn't take away from a certain instinctive curiosity he has, a deep impatience that manifests itself not so much in his smaller acts, but rather in the way he goes about adjusting to the world. He dropped out of high school after finishing his freshman year. Then, for several years, he was a clerk at the Aviation Authority. Now he works as a bus driver. Later on, once he is already "brought back from the dead," he will join his father in construction work.

He is a fine observer, but he might trust himself too much. Over the course of the extraordinary adventure that he is about to experience, he'll catch some things with such exceptional precision that he'll be able to draw up very exact diagrams and maps. Other things he will get wrong, and he will be stubborn about sticking to his mistakes.

He will prove to be lucid and calm in the face of danger. And once the danger has passed, he will show a moral courage that should be noted as his main virtue. He will be the only one among the survivors or the victims' family members who dares to come forward and demand justice.

Does he know anything, on that afternoon of June 9, about the rebellion that will take place later on? He has come home before his shift is over, which could seem suspicious. But it turns out that the bus he drives—number five of all the buses that run along the 10 line in Vicente López—has broken down on him, and the company will confirm this detail.

Does he know anything? He will flatly deny that he does. And he will also add that he doesn't have a record of any kind—criminal, legal, professional, or political. This claim will also be proven and confirmed.

But despite all that, does he know anything? Many people in Greater Buenos Aires know about it, even if they aren't thinking of taking part. Still, of the numerous testimonies we collected, there is not one that suggests Livraga was involved or informed.

It is after ten o'clock at night when Juan Carlos leaves his house. He turns right and goes down San Martín Avenue, heading towards Franklin, where there is a bar he often goes to. It's cold and the streets are not very busy.

A certain indecision overtakes him. He doesn't know whether to stay and play a game of pool or go to a dance that he promised he would attend.

Chance decides for him. Chance that appears in the form of his friend, Vicente Rodríguez.

12. "I'M GOING TO WORK . . ."

He is a tower of a man, this Vicente Damián Rodríguez, a thirty-five-year-old man who loads cargo at the port and, heavy as he is, plays soccer, a man who retains something childlike in his loudness and his crankiness, who aspires to more than he is able to do, who has bad luck, who will end up chewing on the grass of a barren field, asking desperately for them to kill him, for them to finish killing him since the death that he is gulping down won't get done flooding him through the ridiculous holes that the Mauser bullets are leaving in him.

He would have liked to be something in life, Vicente Rodríguez. He is teeming with great ideas, great gestures, great words. But life is fierce with people like him. Just having a life will be a constant uphill struggle. And losing it, a never-ending process.

He is married, has three kids and loves them, but of course they need to be fed and sent to school. And that poor house that he rents, surrounded by that thick, dirty wall with that stretch of uncultivated land where the chickens do their pecking, is not what he imagined it would be. Nothing is as he imagined it would be.

He never manages to properly transfer the sense of power that his vigorous muscles give him to the objective world around him. At one time, it's true, he is active in his union and even serves as a representative, but later all of that falls apart. There's no union, no representatives in his life anymore. That's when he understands that he is nobody, that the world belongs to doctors. The sign of his defeat is very clear: in his neighborhood, there is a club, and in that club, a library; he will come here in search of that miraculous source—books—that power seems to flow from.

We don't know if he even gets a chance to read the books, but what will remain of Rodríguez's passing through this cannibalistic time that we are living in—aside from the misery in which he leaves his wife and children—is an opaque photograph with a blurred stamp on it that simply says "Library."

Rodríguez has left his house—4545 Yrigoyen Street—around nine o'clock. And he has set out on the wrong foot. To his wife, he says:

—I'm going to work.

Is it an innocent lie to cover up one more outing? Is he hiding something more serious, namely his plan to take part in the movement? Or is he really going to work? It's true that more than an hour has passed since he left the house, but the street that he's walking along leads to the station. From there he can get on the train that takes him to the port in twenty-five minutes where he might ask for an extra shift at work.

It's hard to tell. In this case, just as in others. On the one hand, Rodríguez is in the opposition, a Peronist. On the other, he is an open, talkative man who finds it very difficult to keep quiet about something important. And he hasn't said anything to his wife, whom he has been married to for thirteen years. Not even insinuated it. He has simply told her: "I'm going to work," and has said goodbye in the usual way, without any trace of impatience or anxiety.

Then again, it's worth considering his behavior later on. He is completely passive when they take him to be killed in the assault car. A survivor who knew him well will later observe:

—If the Big Guy had wanted to, he could've messed those thugs up in a heartbeat . . .

It could be that he never thought they were going to kill him, not even at the last minute, when it was obvious.

The two friends chat for a moment. Livraga had lent him a suitcase a few days back to carry equipment for the soccer club where they both play.

—When are you coming by to get it? —Rodríguez asks him.

—Let's go now, if you want.

—While we're at it, we can listen to the fight.

A lot of people are talking about this fight. At eleven o'clock the champion, Lausse, who just finished a triumphant run in the United States, will fight the Chilean Loayza for the middleweight South American title.

Livraga is a boxing enthusiast and has no trouble accepting the offer. They head to Rodríguez's house. We don't know what excuse Rodríguez is thinking of giving his wife, and it doesn't matter anyway, because he won't have the chance. Fifty meters away from his house, he stops in front of the building with the light blue gates, sees there is a light on in the back apartment, and says:

—Wait for me a minute.

He goes in, but comes back right away.

—We can listen to the fight here. They have the radio on. —And he clarifies:— They're friends of mine.

Livraga shrugs his shoulders. It makes no difference to him.

They enter the long corridor.

13. THE UNKNOWNS

Is there anyone else in the back apartment? Carranza, Garibotti, Díaz, Lizaso, Gavino, Torres, Brión, Rodríguez, and Livraga are all there for sure. "Marcelo" has been by three times and won't be back. Some friends of Gavino came by but have also left early.

We know at the very least of one neighbor, an acquaintance of Brión's who has come to hear the fight like he has; at the last minute, though, he feels sick, leaves, and saves himself.

The parade does not end there. Around a quarter to eleven, two strangers show up who—if what was about to happen were not so tragic—make the scene ripe for a comedy. Torres thinks they are Gavino's friends. Gavino thinks they are Torres's friends. Only later will they learn that these men are cops. They stay a few minutes, moving between groups, investigating the situation. When they leave, they will report that there are no weapons on site and that the coast is clear.

It's a necessary precaution because the site is configured in such a way that, from the metallic door that grants access to the apartment, a man armed with a simple revolver could control the entire corridor. He could make it difficult for several whole minutes for any potential enemy to enter. With a machine gun, the position could be held for hours.

Yet when the police—who at that same moment are inspecting a bus at the Saavedra Bridge stop—arrive, no one will show even the slightest resistance. Not a single shot will be fired.

But is there anybody else, aside from those already mentioned? It will be hard to find a witness who remembers everyone; those who would be able to are either missing or dead. We can only guide ourselves with clues. Torres, for instance, will say that there were two more men. He knew that one of the men was an Army NCO. As for the second man, he didn't even know that much.

Other indirect testimonies also mention the NCO. And they specify: sergeant. The descriptions are confusing and divergent. It seems he got there at the last minute . . . No one knows who brought him . . . Hardly anyone there knew him . . . Someone, though, will see him again, or will believe he sees him, hours later, at the moment when he gets hit with a bullet and collapses.

And the second man? We don't even know if he existed. Or what his name was, or who he was. Or if he is alive or dead.

With respect to these two men, our search came to a dead end.

It's a few minutes to eleven. The radio is broadcasting the under-cards of the boxing match. The group playing cards falls silent when the commentator announces the presence of Lausse the champion and Loayza the Chilean in the ring.

In the meantime, Giunta has arrived at the apartment in front at around ten-thirty. A perfect calm reigns over Mr. Horacio's house. Señora Pilar talks to them for a few minutes before turning in. Her daughter Nélida is preparing *mate* for the guest while Mr. Horacio turns on the receiver.

If he happens to tune in to State Radio, the official voice of the Nation, he will find that they have just finished playing a Bach concert and that at 10:59 p.m., they begin playing a Ravel concert . . .

At around the same time, twenty men have just finished gathering at Florida's Second Precinct to carry out a mysterious operation.

When Officer Pena finds out who is leading the men, he thinks: *Something big.*

The word revolution has not yet been uttered. Certainly not on Radio Splendid, where you can hear the tense voice of Fioravanti, the commentator relaying the first moves of the match, over the buzzing of the crowd.

It's a short and violent fight, and by the second round the out-come seems practically decided. It lasts less than ten minutes in total. Somewhere in the middle of the third round, the champion knocks Loayza out for the count.

The owner of the house and Giunta looked at each other with smiles of satisfaction.

Giunta was drinking a glass of gin and getting ready to go. From the bedroom, Señora Pilar asked her husband for a hot water bottle. Mr. Horacio went to the kitchen, filled up the bottle, and was com-ing back with it when they heard violent knocks on the door. They sounded like blows made with the butt of a gun or a rifle.

The shout sounded out in the silence of the night:

—Police!

Part Two

THE EVENTS

Next page: Walsh's first article for Mayoría. *The title reads "'Operation Massacre' by R. J. Walsh: a book that can't find a publisher." Pictured in the photos are Nicolás Carranza and Francisco Garibotti, both of whom were killed in the José León Suárez execution.*

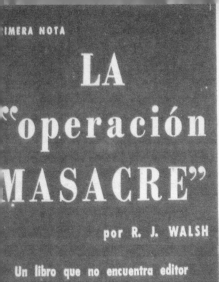

LA "operación MASACRE"

por R. J. WALSH

Un libro que no encuentra editor

utor del largo relato que amos a publicar en este o, y que se prolongará te varios más, explica en roducción cómo concibió , mejor dicho, como sin- necesidad de investigar, o, los hechos configura- r el "caso Livraga" y de r, después, el resultado investigaciones.

primero, pudo hacerlo, a de todo. La policía no lo pedirlo. Lo segundo, no. ro, producto de sus inves- nes, no encontró quien lo a. Y, así, subtítulo éste: BRO QUE NO ENCUEN- EDITOR.

lector se preguntará: ¿Es lo que aquí se dice? Eso le a preguntar: ¿Es serio? y ¿Son ciertos los he- que se narran? En cuanto r, Rodolfo J. Walsh está erado unánimemente uno dos o tres mejores es- de relatos policiales en ra lengua. Su libro "Va- nes en Rojo", editado en a Aires por Hachette, ob- el Premio de Literatura de nicipalidad de Buenos Ai- n 1953 (repetimos, el pre- Literatura, y no uno de policiales, porque las de Walsh están sólida- arquitecturadas desde el de vista artístico e igual- mente escritas, en un len- terso y fluido, circuns- que eleva sus cuentos encima de la común litera- policial que se publica en y revistas). Y hace muy cuando Donald Yeats, sor de la Universidad de igan, decidió traducir dos os argentinos para la int Detective Magazine", de vista llevaba la firma de Walsh.

cuanto a la segunda pre- , ¿Son ciertos los hechos se narran? juzgue el lec- tor mismo a través de la irre- batible prueba anexa al relato. Por nuestra parte, tan pocas dudas nos caben, que nos aven- turamos a consignar un formal vaticinio: al término de esta publicación, si antes no ocu- rren hechos muy graves, más de un alto personaje del actual elenco gubernativo tendrá que rendir cuentas de sus actos en la noche del 9 al 10 de junio de 1956 tras las rejas de la cárcel. Lo decimos pesando muy bien nuestra responsabilidad de pe- riodistas libres.

Y, ahora, a jugarse por la verdad y la justicia. Que ha- blen los hechos, con la autori- dad de las pruebas y la magia irresistible de la pluma que, en cinematográfico ritmo, va pre- sentando unos y otras.

INTRODUCCION

LA primera noticia sobre la masa- cre de José León Suárez llegó a mis oídos en la forma más ca- sual, el 18 de diciembre de 1956. Era una versión imprecisa, propia del lugar —un café— en que la oí formulada. De ella se despren- día que un presunto fusilado duran- te el motín peronista del 9 y 10 de junio de ese año sobrevivía y no estaba en la cárcel.

La historia me pareció cinema- tográfica, apta para todos los ejer- cicios de la incredulidad. La misma impresión causó a muchos, y eso fué una desgracia. Un oficial de Marina, por ejemplo, a quien relaté los he- chos antes de publicarlos, los ca- lificó de "Novela por entregas".

La incredulidad, sin embargo, pue- de ser apenas la máscara de la sa- biduría. Suele ser tan ingenuo el incrédulo absoluto como el que todo lo cree; pertenecen en el fon- do a una misma categoría psico- lógica.

Pedí más datos. Y al día siguien- te conocí al primer actor importan- te del drama: el doctor Jorge Do- glia. La entrevista con él me im- presión vivísima. (?) El Doglia, un abogado de 32 años, tu- viera los nervios destrozados por una lucha sin cuartel librada duran- te varios meses desde su cargo de Jefe de la División Judicial de la Policía de la Provincia, contra los "métodos" policiales de que era tes- tigo. Pero su sinceridad me pareció absoluta. Me refirió casos pavoro- sos de torturas con picana y ciga- rrillos encendidos, de azotes con go- mas y alambres, de delincuentes co- munes —por lo general "linyeras" y rateristas sin familiares que pu- dieran reclamar por ellos—, muer- tos a corderrazos en las distin- tas comisarías de la provincia. Y to- do esto bajo el régimen de una Re- volución Libertadora que muchos argentinos recibieron esperanzados porque creyeron que iba a terminar con los abusos de la represión poli- cial.

Doglia había combatido valerosa- mente contra todo eso, mas ahora lo asaltaba el desaliento. Dos meses antes había denunciado las torturas y las masacres ante un Servicio de Informaciones. Pero allí un buró- crata que bien podría pasarse el resto de sus días estudiando en los textos elementales las normas pa- ra cultivar al informante —princi- pio que suponemos básico de todo Servicio similar— no encontró nada mejor que delatarlo. En vez de pro- tegerlo, pusieron en peligro su vi- da, sujeta desde entonces a las más directas amenazas.

Una denuncia similar presentada por Doglia ante el Ministerio de Gobierno de la Provincia terminó en una acumulación de papel erudi- to, un expediente donde, con pro- sa digna de Gracián —en sus malos momentos—, un señor subsecretario llegó a la conclusión de que algo había, pero no se sabía qué. A es- tas horas el expediente seguirá cre-

un Tribunal Militar, y reclamo sería atendido. se cumplió puntualmen zos de febrero de 1957. está por verse. Todo lo que resuelva la Su de la Nación, ante la planteado el conflicto nal.

En cuanto al fusilado te, conseguí esa noch dato concreto: se llama los Livraga.

En la mañana del 20 tuve en mis manos la demanda judicial pr Livraga. Más tarde bar que la relación de allí se hacía era exac cial, aunque con algur siones e inexactitude Pero todavía era de matográfica. Parecía rectamente de una p

Y, sin embargo, es ya un hecho. No se podía ser enteramen mas era un hecho q que decía haber sid forma irregular e il taba ante un juez de denunciar "a quien sable" por tentativa y daño.

Pero había algo rito se mencionaba sobreviviente, un tal brindaba una posibi de verificar los hec dos. Ya estábamos a tancia de aquí! rum gido en un café tre ras antes.

Esa misma tarde demanda estuvo en ñor Leónidas Barle "Propósitos", y tam rectores de otros s sumamente "oposit

Nicolás Carranza, el ferroviario, y Francisco C... amigo, dos de las infortunadas víctimas del terr...

ciendo, acumulando fojas, polvo y frases declamatorias. Pero en resu- men, nada. En resumen, lentitud e inepcia, cuando es evidente que se trataba de un asunto que importa- ba resolver pronto y bien. Esto es el servicio que prestan al actual Go- bierno algunos funcionarios.

En el periodismo no depositaba Doglia una excesiva confianza. Pre- sumía que los diarios oficiales no iban a ocuparse de un asunto tan escabroso, y por otra parte no de- seaba que los órganos de oposición lo explotaran con criterio político.

Tampoco esperaba demasiado en la Justicia, ante la que acababa de presentarse como demandante el fu- silado sobreviviente. Doglia vatici- nó desde el primer momento: 1)

firieron la auto... critican en los... grandes. Barletta prometió nada. S difusión de es perjudicar la m ligación judicial. lo más urgente re te una adecuada del demandante de otros testigos sideraba en pelig

Cuatro días m del 24 de diciem taba en la casa posito".

El 21, entre la contacto direct estudio de un tal von Kelsch...

14. WHERE IS TANCO?

Mr. Horacio is so taken aback that he doesn't even manage to put down the hot water bottle. He runs, turns the key in the lock, and before he can unhook the chain, the door is pushed in violently from the other side, the bolt jumps, and he is shoved, surrounded, mobbed by the throng of policemen and individuals armed with weapons big and small, who in a few seconds flood all the rooms of the house, and whose voices are soon heard in the patio and the corridor that leads to the back. Everything happens at the speed of lightning.

The one in charge is a tall, heavyset, dark-haired, mustached man with a striking sense of authority. He brandishes a .45 caliber pistol in his right hand. He shouts in a deep, husky voice that makes him sound drunk at times. He is wearing light pants and a short, olive green jacket: it is the uniform of the Argentine Army.

Mr. Horacio has taken a step back, terrified. He manages only to put his hands up, still holding onto the hot water bottle that at this point is burning his fingers. The leader of the group knocks it out of his hand with a smack.

—Where is Tanco? —he shouts.

The head of the household looks at him, not understanding. It is the first time he has heard the name of the rebel general whose dramatic escape from the wall in front of the firing squad people will only hear about a few days later. The leader of the group pushes him aside and walks up to face the other one, to face Giunta.

Giunta is simply petrified. He is still in his chair, open-mouthed, eyes enormous, unable to move. The leader approaches him and deliberately, delicately, puts the gun to his throat.

—Don't be smart with me! —he says to him in a deep voice.— Put your hands up!

Giunta puts his hands up. Then he hears that mysterious question for a second time, the one that keeps being repeated like a nightmare. Where is Tanco. *Where is Tanco?*

His stunned silence earns him a blow that nearly knocks him off his chair. We will see this left-handed punch—which is protected by the menacing weapon that the right hand is brandishing—again. It seems to be a favorite of the man who is using it.

The scene was electrifying and it happened fast. What follows happens just as fast and in the form of a crackling of commands:

—Grab that old guy and this other guy and take them out to the car!

They don't even have time to object. They are taken out and thrust into a Florida precinct car, a Plymouth. A red bus and a light blue police van with a mobile radio are parked on the same sidewalk.

In the meantime, it seems that a man has escaped from the patio of the building—Torres—and someone else—Lizaso—has tried to do the same and failed.

The patio belongs to the apartment in front, but is connected in a roundabout way to the back through a little door. The little door opens into the corridor, the one with the privet hedge.

The whole episode is confusing and no two versions of it are alike. A consolidation of all the different versions suggests that Torres, accompanied by Lizaso, was walking to Mr. Horacio's apartment, taking the same route as usual, to ask if he could use the phone, which he did quite regularly. It was then that they heard and maybe saw the police arriving.

Torres doesn't hesitate. The fence around the patio is not very high. He jumps it in one try and flees through the neighboring buildings. In his frenzied dash, he jumps over hedges and roofs, rips his clothes, seriously wounds his hand and neck—he'll never know how—zigzags across blocks and blocks, finally gets on a bus and, bleeding and exhausted, finds shelter. In a way, he was the first survivor.

There are three versions of Carlitos Lizaso's story. The first is that he was able to reach a nearby piping plant where the night watchman would not let him hide, which in turn led to his capture. The second is that he was caught in the patio after the fence collapsed under his weight. The last is that he did not even try to escape. The only thing we know for sure is that he was arrested.

In the meantime, the same astounding and savage scene has taken place in the back apartment. The police encounter no opposition when they enter. No one budges. No one protests or even resists. The guard Ramón Madialdea will state later that "a gun with a pearl handle" was confiscated here. That weapon (if it existed) was the only one in the house.

They order them onto the street, one by one. The leader of the group is waiting for them there, quick to shout at them again, punching and kicking them as they load them onto the bus. He hammers Livraga in the stomach with the barrel of the gun, yelling:

—So you were going to start a revolution, huh? With that face?

He said the same thing to Carlitos Lizaso. He begins asking everyone their names. You can tell by his gesture of disdain—the "Come on, move!" that he uses to push them toward the bus—that most of them mean nothing to him. But Gavino's name is like a revelation to him. His face lights up with joy.

He grabs him forcefully by the neck and in one swift movement inserts the barrel of the gun in his mouth.

—So you're Gavino! —he howls.— So you're . . . !

His finger trembles on the trigger. His eyes are radiant.

—Tell me where you've hidden him —he orders sternly.— *Where is Tanco!* Now, right away, because I'll kill you, I'll kill you right here! It's no skin off my back!

The barrel of the gun clatters between Gavino's teeth. A trail of blood flows from his split lip. His eyes are glazed over with fear.

But he doesn't tell him where Tanco is. Either he is a hero, or he hasn't the slightest idea where the rebel general is . . .[*]

They tell Giunta and Di Chiano to get out of the car and make them get on the bus too. At the last minute, three more men who have been arrested nearby get on as well. One is the night watchman at the piping plant. Another is a driver who happened to be passing by. And the third is a young man who was saying goodnight to his girlfriend at her house . . .

The bus—the fortieth one on the 19 line—sets out with its usual driver, Pedro Alberto Fernández, whom they detained for their use forty-five minutes ago. The prisoners don't know where they are going or why—except for maybe one or two of them—they are being taken.

But one of them will manage to hear a revealing part of a conversation between the guards.

"That one," the one leading the operation, the Army man dressed in uniform, the even-handed dealer of kicks and blows, the one whom everyone addresses respectfully as "sir," while referring to him by a more familiar nickname from a distance—that man was the chief of the Police Department of the Province of Buenos Aires, (RET) Lieutenant Colonel Desiderio A. Fernández Suárez.

∾

Señora Pilar and her daughter believe they are living a nightmare that will not end. The house is still being invaded by men searching

---

[*] The reconstruction of this scene is based on indirect testimonies. Months later, in a signed statement that is in my possession, Gavino himself confirmed it with these words ". . . most of us were beaten, especially the undersigned, by the Chief of Police, who hit my head, mouth, and left pectoral, so many times that I fell to the floor where he and several guards started to kick me, screaming loudly, tell me where Tanco is or I'll kill you. When they got tired of beating me, the Chief picked me up by my hair, pulling a bunch of it out, and said: So you're the famous Gavino, tonight we're executing you. Then he went through my pockets and took my ID and about five hundred pesos, which were never returned to me."

the furniture and the drawers, interrogating them, and shouting at the top of their lungs. More commands come in from outside, sharp as bullets.

Amid all of this, though, they happen to witness a strange incident. The Chief of Police goes back, picks up the phone, and speaks in an altered voice. They manage to catch only a few snippets of the conversation and the name of a woman:

—. . . A total success . . . Amazing . . . It looks like they started something down south too . . . Tell Cacho to take care of herself . . . Yes, a total success . . .

After the conversation has ended, he joins the others in searching the house. Nélida tries to step away from the bedroom where the Chief of Police is looking for revolutionary schemes among her undergarments, or maybe for Tanco himself. But he makes her come back, "so that later she doesn't say something's missing."

The first phase of "Operation Massacre" has passed quickly. It is barely 11:30 p.m. At that exact moment, State Radio, the official voice of the Nation, cuts Ravel's music short and starts playing Igor Stravinsky's 6489/94 recording.

15. VALLE'S REBELLION

Far from there, the real uprising is now raging furiously.

In June of 1956, the Peronists that had been overthrown nine months earlier staged their first serious attempt to regain power through a revolt led by military officers, with some active civilian support.

The proclamation signed by Generals Valle and Tanco explained the root of the uprising by giving an exact description of the state of things. The country, it claimed, "is living under a harsh and merciless tyranny"; people are being persecuted, imprisoned, and exiled; the "majority party" is being excluded from public life; people are living under the "totalitarian monstrosity" of Decree 4161 (which prohibited even mentioning Perón); the Constitution has been abolished so as to get rid of article 40, which prevented "the surrender of public services and natural resources to international capitalism"; the aim is to subject workers to "the will of capitalism" through starvation, and "to have the country regress to its most ruthless colonial period by handing over its most basic economic resources to international capitalism."

Stated in 1956, this was not just accurate: it was prophetic. Valle's proclamation was unusual in its lack of hypocrisy. It did not make the usual pleas for Western and Christian values or any jabs at communism, but it also did not overlook the attack on unions by "elements known for agitating in the service of ideologies or international interests."

Compared to this analysis, the policy portion of the proclamation was weak. It sacrificed, perhaps inevitably, ideological content for emotional impact. In short, it proposed a considered return to Peronism and Perón by transparent means: elections within no more than 180 days, with all political parties participating. The economic policy of the platform, unsurprisingly, contradicted its previous criticism by assuring that there would be "full guarantees for foreign capital that is either already invested or will be invested," etc.

The proclamation illustrated the two elements that characterized Peronism in those early days of the resistance: first, it had a clear ability to perceive the ills that it suffered due to its being the popular majority party; second, it was remarkably ambiguous when it came to diagnosing the causes, to turning itself into a true revolutionary movement, and to leaving campaign slogans and pretty words to the enemy once and for all.

Of course Valle acted, and gave his life, which means more than words ever could. Understanding his actions is easier today than it was ten years ago; it will be even easier in the future. Valle's figure will continue to grow and take the place it deserves in the people's memory, together with the conviction that his movement's success would have saved the country the shameful phase that followed, this second *década infame* that we are now living in.[6]

The story of the uprising is short. Less than twelve hours pass between the time that the operations begin to when the last rebel group is defeated.

In Campo de Mayo, the rebels—led by colonels Cortínez and Ibazeta—have taken control of both the NCO academy infantry group and the services group of the first armored division. The occupation of the NCO academy fails after a short shoot-out, though, and the attack is left isolated.*

At eleven o'clock at night, a group of NCOs revolt in the Army Mechanics School, but have to retreat after a shoot-out.

In Avellaneda, in the surrounding area of the Second Military Region Command, rebels and policemen engage in two or three skirmishes. The police arrest some of the rebels. Next they burst into the Industrial School and surprise Lieutenant Colonel José Irigoyen, who is with a group trying to set up a command there for Valle and a secret transmitter. The repression is devastating. Eighteen civilians and two military officers are sent to a summary court-martial in the Lanús District Police Department. Six of them will be executed: Irigoyen, Captain Costales, Dante Lugo, Osvaldo Albedro, and two brothers, Clemente and Norberto Ros. Leading this operation is the second-in-command at the district police department, Lieutenant Commander naval pilot Salvador Ambroggio. Chief Inspector Daniel Juárez is the one administering the coups de grâce at will. For the purposes of intimidation, the government announced at daybreak that eighteen people had been executed.

In La Plata, a bomb thrown at a shoe store downtown appears to be the sign the rebels are waiting for. In the Seventh Regiment, Captain Morganti calls the company under his command to action.

---

* A detailed account of the operations and the repression that followed can be found in the book *Martyrs and Executioners* by Salvador Ferla, published in 1964.

Groups of civilians take over the telephone exchanges. Astounded passersby along the main streets see a number of Sherman tanks go by, followed by troops in armored trucks that are headed at full speed to the Second Division Command and the police station. There are barely twenty guards, not well-armed, at the station. Not even the police chief or second-in-command are there: the former is inspecting Mr. Horacio di Chiano's furniture in Florida, and the latter is leading the repression in Avellaneda and Lanús.

The most spectacular battle of the entire attempt at rebellion is about to begin. Around a hundred thousand shots will be fired, according to an unofficial calculation. There will be a half-dozen killed and some twenty wounded. But the rebel forces, whose superiority in terms of military equipment at first seems overwhelming, will not come away with even the most fleeting success.

Ninety-nine out of every hundred people in the country are unaware of what's going on. In the very same city of La Plata, where the shooting continues incessantly all night long, there are many who keep sleeping and only find out about it the following morning.

At 11:56 p.m. State Radio, the official voice of the Nation, stops playing Stravinsky and puts on the marching song that they usually use to end their programming. The voice of the announcer bids his listeners goodnight until the following day at the usual time. At midnight the broadcast is interrupted. All of this is confirmed on page fifty-one of State Radio's registry book of announcers that was in use at the time and is signed by the announcer Gutenberg Pérez.

Not a word has been uttered about the subversive events of the night. Not even the slightest allusion has been made to martial law, which, like any law, must be declared and publicly announced before coming into effect.

Therefore, at midnight on June 9, 1956, nowhere in the Nation's territory is martial law in effect.

But it has already been applied. And it will be applied later to men who were arrested before it was instated, and without the excuse—like the one they had in Avellaneda—that they had been caught with weapons in hand.

16. "WATCH OUT, THEY COULD EXECUTE YOU . . ."

Meanwhile, the bus filled with prisoners picked up in Florida has headed southwest. It leaves the district of Vicente López and enters that of San Martín. The behavior of the guards escorting them is proper, which is to say indifferent. Some of the prisoners talk to each other.

—Why do you think they've taken us? —one asks.

—What do I know . . . —another answers.— Probably for playing cards.

—Something doesn't smell right. The big guy said something about a revolution.

Mr. Horacio and Giunta are the most baffled of all. Because they weren't even playing cards. Gavino, who doesn't know them but could enlighten them, keeps quiet. Dazed and disheveled, wiping the blood away from his lip, he does know why they have been taken.

They arrive in San Martín and, leaving behind the station and the main square, stop in front of a building on Nueve de Julio Street with armed guards at the door. Some have already figured out where they are. They are at the District Police Department. The trip has lasted less than twenty minutes.

They stay seated in the bus for twenty minutes, maybe even half an hour more before they are told to get off. They see people leaving the nearest movie theater. Passersby look at them curiously. There are no signs of unrest anywhere.

At 12:11 a.m. on June 10, 1956, State Radio surprisingly resumes its broadcast on the official station, airing a selection of light music for the next twenty-one minutes. It is the first official sign that some-thing serious is happening in the country.

In the meantime, the fateful house in Florida comes to claim two unexpected victims. Julio Troxler and Reinaldo Benavídez stop by looking for a friend who they think is there. They do nothing more than walk down the corridor and ring the bell at the back apart-ment—which is strangely silent and dark—before the door suddenly opens and a sergeant and two guards appear, pointing their guns at them.

Though surprised, Julio Troxler hardly bats an eye. He is a tall, athletic man who will demonstrate an extraordinary calm at every turn that night.

Troxler is twenty-nine years old. Two of his brothers are in the Army, one of whom carries the rank of major. He himself might feel a certain military calling, which he channels poorly, seeing how he ends up joining the Police Department of the Province of Bue-nos Aires. He is strict and austere, but still, he does not tolerate the "methods"—the brutality—that he is expected to employ, so he resigns when Peronism is in full bloom. From then on, he throws his discipline and his ability to work into technical studies. He reads as many books and magazines as he can find on specializations that interest him—motors, electricity, refrigeration. He actually begins to do quite well for himself with a refrigerator repair shop that he sets up in Munro.

Troxler is a Peronist, but he doesn't talk much politics. Those who tried to describe him suggested that he is an extremely laconic and pensive man who resists arguments at all costs. One thing's for sure: he is familiar with the police and knows how to deal with them.

The description we can give of Reinaldo Benavídez is even more superficial. Average height, around thirty years old, he has an hon-est and pleasant face. At that time he is co-running a grocery store in Belgrano and living with his parents. Something incredible is going to happen to Benavídez, something that, even on this night of extraordinary events and experiences, seems as though it was taken from some outrageous novel. But we'll come back to that.

By an extraordinary coincidence—which will come up again later—Julio Troxler knows the sergeant who is facing him and pointing his gun at him. That may be why they have both stood still for a moment, observing each other.

—What happened? —Troxler asks.

—I don't know. I've got to take you both with me.

—What do you mean you've got to take me with you? Don't you remember me?

—Yes, sir. But I've got to take you with me. I have my orders.

The sergeant steps away for a moment. He goes to the apartment in front to ask for instructions over the phone. The two detained men are left alone with the guards. It's true that they are unarmed, but if they set themselves to the task, they may be able to overpower them and escape. Hours later, in more difficult, nearly impossible circumstances, both of them will act with exceptional decisiveness and sangfroid. At the moment, they are calm. Clearly they don't suspect anything too serious.

And they let themselves be taken away, just like that.

All police stations have been in a state of alarm since earlier in the day. In his office at Florida's Second Precinct, Captain Pena has tuned in the receiver.

At precisely 12:32 a.m., State Radio interrupts the chamber music to announce, across all the stations in the country, that a communiqué from the Presidential Press Secretary's Office will be read, declaring two decrees.

The dramatic announcement is as follows:

"Since the situation caused by elements that are disruptive of public order is forcing the provisional government to adopt appropriate measures with calm energy to ensure public tranquility in the whole territory of the Nation and to continue to meet the goals of the Liberating Revolution,[7] it is decided that the provisional President of the Argentine Nation, exercising his Legislative Power, declares as law:

"Article Number 1 – Let martial law be in effect throughout the entire territory of the Nation.

"Article Number 2 – The current decree-law will be endorsed by his Excellency the Provisional Vice President of the Nation and by the ministers: secretaries of the State, the Airforce, the Army, the Navy, and the Interior.

"Article Number 3 – Pro forma.

"Signed: Aramburu, Rojas, Hartung, Krause, Ossorio Arana and Landaburu."[8]

The second decree, taking into account the fact that martial law "constitutes a measure whose application the public must be made aware of," lays out the rules and circumstances according to which the law will be put into practice.

The captain has just finished listening to the announcement when they bring him the two prisoners. Just like the sergeant, the captain is surprised to see Troxler, whom he knows and likes.

—What are you doing here?

Troxler smiles, shrugging his shoulders, and explains what happened without making a big deal of it. It must have been a mistake . . . They talk for a few minutes. Then the captain gets a phone call.

—They want you at the Department —then he adds:— Hey, watch out, they could execute you . . . They declared martial law just a minute ago.

The two of them laugh.

But the captain is worried.

17. "CHEER UP"

12:45 a.m. They have let the prisoners off the bus at the District Police Department. They take them down a long corridor and lead them into an office on the left where there are a number of park benches, green ones, that the men start to sit on. The building appears to be under renovation. The walls of the room have been recently painted, and some of the painting materials are still around.

At first they don't pay attention to the prisoners, who are tossing around all kinds of speculations. Livraga sits down next to his friend Rodríguez and the first thing he does is ask:

—Big Guy, are you involved in anything?

Rodríguez shrugs his shoulders.

—I know just as much as you do.

Giunta and Mr. Horacio are perplexed. What intrigues them the most is that question they've heard repeated several times: Where is Tanco?

The three who were picked up on the streets, not at home, are falling to pieces in their explanations and regrets. One tirelessly repeats that he went to have dinner with some friends and on his way home, they grabbed him. Another was standing at the door of his girlfriend's house saying goodnight . . . The night watchman at the piping plant, an elderly man who still has his rubber boots on, is mumbling in an unintelligible Italian.

Mario Brión is thinking about his wife, who doesn't know anything and must be waiting for him: he has never come home so late.

Does Carlitos Lizaso remember that message he left for his girlfriend? "If all goes well tonight . . ."

Garibotti is sorry he listened to his friend Carranza, who is sitting next to him, quiet and dejected. Who knows now when they are going to let them go, maybe at daybreak or at noon the next day . . . Carranza himself is remembering Berta's words: "Turn yourself in, turn yourself in . . ." Well, now he has been turned in. They might let the other guys go, but him . . . As soon as they look at his record, he'll be done for. Maybe he's thinking of that day he ran away from the officers in Tucumán. No one is watching the door and, even though the corridor is long, there is no one in sight.

Maybe with a little bit of luck . . . But no, Berta's right. It's time for him to turn himself in and for them to do whatever they want with him. They're not going to kill him, that's for sure, not for some pamphlets and some conversations . . .

Gavino's worried. They're not going to let him go, either, now that they've got him. And he knows very well why they've got him. He'll get a year or two in jail until a new government comes to power and he is granted amnesty. Perhaps they'll send him to the south. Well, maybe it's better this way . . . maybe now they'll let his wife go . . . and not kill him on a night like this. He wonders if the rebellion . . .

Just then an officer appears and, addressing the two or three closest to him, asks:

—Fellas, are you political prisoners?

When he is met with hesitation in response, he adds:

—Cheer up. The rebellion broke out and we don't have contact with La Plata anymore.

La Plata is the only place where the fighting is going according to plan. The leader of the uprising, Colonel Cogorno, launches an attack on the Second Division Command and the Police Headquarters throughout the night. The attacking forces include the Seventh Regiment's company, three tanks under Major Pratt's command, and two or three hundred civilians.

The tanks position themselves to face Police Headquarters, but for some inexplicable reason only manage to blast the building two times. There are twenty-three men inside: afterward there will be thirty-five.

The shootout—which involves everything from small arms to heavy machine guns—is extremely violent, but the attackers can't manage to organize a proper assault. Maybe they're waiting for something that never actually happens. What we know for sure is that Colonel Piñeiro, fighting on the inside, makes it through the whole night.

The Second Division Command, two blocks away from Headquarters, is comparatively much more protected: it has about fifty men and a heavy machine gun set up in a dominant strategic position—on Fifty-Fourth Street, between Third and Fourth—so that they can stave off the advancing troops of the Seventh Regiment.

Among the men who are defending the Government with weapons in hand, we will mention one who did not make the papers.

His name is Juan Carlos Longoni. He is (was) a police inspector, a thin, stone-faced guy with a tough look in his eyes, a man of few words. He is laid off during the time of Peronism, but they take him back in 1955. He comes to be assistant to the head of the Judicial Division, Doglia, Esq. . . .

That night Longoni is asleep at home when he hears the first shots. He gets up and, still dressing himself, steps out to the street. He hails a cab and asks to be taken to the war zone. In the thick of the shooting, the cab driver is so frightened that he faints. Longoni leaves him in Medical Care, goes on alone, and manages to join the Commando Unit. He asks for a gun and a combat position. They hand him a Falcon and let him choose whatever position he wants. He fights all night long.

That is the man that the Chief of Police of the Province will lay off—laid off again!—seven months later for supporting Doglia in his complaints regarding this case—the case of the prisoners who were still awaiting their uncertain fates in the San Martín District Police Department.

18. "CALM AND CONFIDENT"

1:45 a.m. The radio is also on in the office of Chief Inspector Rodolfo Rodríguez Moreno, chief of the San Martín District Police Department. The declaration of martial law has been replayed at 12:45 a.m., 12:50 a.m., 1:15 a.m., 1:35 a.m. Now they are broadcasting it again.

About fifteen minutes ago, the Office of the Vice President of the Nation released the Communiqué No. 1, which, for the first time, lets the country know some details about what is happening.

> On behalf of the provisional president —the text reads— let it be known to the people of the Republic that at 11:00 p.m. on Saturday, uprisings erupted among some military units in the Province of Buenos Aires.
> The Army, the Navy, and the Airforce, with support from the National Gendarmerie, the Coast Guard, and the Police immediately commenced operations to subdue the attempt at rebellion.
> The rule of martial law has been decreed in the entire territory of the Republic.
> We suggest that the people remain calm and confident in the power and strength of the Liberating Revolution.
> Signed: Isaac F. Rojas, Rear-Admiral, Provisional Vice President.

One of the prisoners has asked permission to go to the bathroom; on the way, the guard escorting him lets him in on what's happening.

There is anxiety among the group when this man comes back with news that definitively confirms all the signs, suspicions, and fears that have been accumulating since eleven o'clock the previous night, when they heard the word "revolution" uttered for the first time from the mouth of the Police Chief himself. Gavino looks pale.

—When? —he insists.— When?

—Just now, it sounds like —they reply.

Gavino lets out a sigh of relief. He knows they can't do anything to him. He was arrested before martial law was instated so he couldn't have violated it.

Mario Brión has a terrible feeling.

—Who knows, they could kill us anyway . . .

Everyone looks at him askance. There is a pause. Then several of them talk at once:

—I went to have dinner at some friends' house, and on my way back . . . on my way back . . .

—Is saying goodnight to your girlfriend against the law? I didn't do anything, I don't know anything, they have to let me go . . .

In the impenetrable Italian of the old night watchman, a word stands out now, punctuating his speech at regular intervals, "*revoluzione . . . revoluzione . . .*"

Suddenly two policemen armed with carbines tell everyone to be silent. A change has come over the entire enormous building— it is hardly noticeable, but sinister. The guards' attitude, which until now has been carefree, has turned sour and surly. Voices that were ringing out in the corridor on and off dissolve into occasional echoes. Then, prolonged silences.

Unaware of everything, spilled over a bench, like some great black Neptune, Sergeant Díaz is snoring loudly. His wide thorax expands and collapses at an easy rhythm. Sleep coats his face with an expressionless mask.

The rest begin to look at him with annoyance, then horror.

19. MAKE NO MISTAKE . . .

2:45 a.m. Rodríguez Moreno's got a bad feeling. Why did these poor bastards have to come to him, of all people? And yet, there is some mysterious justification, some nod to destiny in the fact that this particular mission is going to fall to him.

Rodríguez Moreno is an imposing, difficult man with a rocky and troublesome history. Tragedy follows him like a doting dog. Even before 1943, he was apparently involved in a horrifying event as chief of the Mar del Plata precinct, according to a number of sources. A hobo is brutally beaten in a cell one night and then thrown on a beach, completely naked in the dead of winter. He dies from the cold. They end up prosecuting Rodríguez Moreno and even send him to jail in Dolores. But then he is released. Because he was innocent, say his defenders. Because of political reasons, say his critics. The episode remains murky and forgotten.

And now this. Later, toward the end of 1956, there will be talk of a similar episode again in Mar del Plata, where he has been transferred to serve as Chief of the District Police Department. A Chilean pickpocket dies from being bashed around in a cell. Does it have anything to do with Rodríguez Moreno? They say it doesn't . . . But disaster follows him. At the start of 1957 he led an operation in which an officer was killed, riddled with bullets from a machine gun fired by his fellow officers. An unfortunate incident, is how the papers put it.

Next to him on that night of June 9 is his second-in-command, Captain Cuello. There are a number of contradictory accounts of this short, nervous man as well.

—We're going to take your statements —Rodríguez Moreno orders.

The prisoners start to line up single-file in two groups. One group goes to the Chief's office. The other, to the clerk's office.

Juan Carlos Livraga is unsettled. He doesn't want to believe that his friend Vicente Rodríguez has screwed him over, but an awful suspicion keeps rolling around in his head. That's why, when Rodríguez returns from giving his statement, Livraga gets up in a hurry and goes in before he is even called. He wants to be interrogated by the same person, to find out what his friend has said, to protect himself with his friend's testimony.

The interrogation is long and thorough. They ask him if he knew anything about the rebellion. He says he didn't. He tells a long detailed story of how he arrived at the house in question. He stresses that he only went there to hear the fight. A clerk condenses everything into a pair of typed lines.

He is shown a pile of white and light blue armbands with two letters printed on them: P.V.[9] They ask him if he has seen them before. He says he hasn't. The typist adds another line.

They show him a revolver. They ask if it's his.

The question shocks Livraga. The gun is not his, but what's strange is that they don't know whose it is.

They add two or three more lines to his statement. The long piece of paper curves over the roller and falls behind the machine. Livraga notices that several statements precede his on the sheet. The way he is oriented, facing the typist, he can still manage to make out a few upside-down lines. He calms down when he sees: "Rodríguez . . . accident . . . friend . . . fight . . . doesn't know . . ." Rodríguez has given the same information. Other testimonies are similar. Giunta, who never forgets a face, is questioned by a "chubby, curly-haired officer with a handlebar mustache."

Gavino knows perfectly well that they are not going to believe him if he says he was also at Torres's apartment by accident. He tries to find someone who will back him up. Carranza agrees. They both state that they are Peronist sympathizers who expected there would be an uprising and went to hear the news on the radio.

—What were you doing in that house? —they ask Di Chiano.

—What would I be doing . . . It's my house.

—What were you doing?

—I was with my family, listening to the radio.

—Nothing else?

—Nothing else.

Ever since Troxler and Benavídez arrived, they have been kept in a different office so as not to be mixed with the others. Their testimonies are shorter. After all, they did nothing more than ring a doorbell.

—What are you going to do with us? —one of them asks.

—I think they're sending you to La Plata —is the vague reply.

At 2:53 a.m., the Office of the Vice President of the Nation, Rear-

Admiral Rojas, reads Communiqué No. 2 out loud, reporting that the rebellion in the Army Mechanics School has been quashed and the battle at the NCO academy at Campo de Mayo is being quelled. The message is broadcast across all the radio stations in the country.

"Make no mistake —he concludes.— The Liberating Revolution will no doubt achieve its goals."

3:45 a.m. The interrogations have ended. Two officers stand up to talk near the door.

—If this thing turns around, we can just let these guys go . . . —one of them says, turning his head towards the men.

But the thing doesn't turn around. On the contrary. The shooting dies down in La Plata. The rebels understand how impossible it would be to take over Police Headquarters or the military command: they have lost the race against time. People scram and desist when a naval airplane sends out a flare. This is only a small glimpse of what will happen when daybreak sets the flight of government machines in motion. At the Río Santiago Shipyard, the Marines are enlisted. The Chief of Police has finally joined the effort himself and brought backup.

The prisoners at the District Police Department, nervous and drowsy, are shaking on the benches. The cold is brutal. Since three o'clock, the thermometer has been at 0°C. At this point, it looks like they are not going to transfer them from here tonight. Some try to curl up and sleep for a bit.

That's when they start calling them up again, one by one. The first one to come back says they took everything he had on him: his money, his watch, even his keys. He shows everyone the receipt he was given.

Some manage to take precautions. Livraga, for instance, who has forty pesos, hides thirty in one of his socks. They give him a receipt for "A White Star watch, a key ring, ten pesos, and a handkerchief." (Officer Albarello signs it.)

Benavídez is given a receipt for "Two-hundred-and-nineteen

pesos and forty-five cents, identity papers, and various items." Giunta's reads fifteen pesos, a handkerchief, and cigarettes.

The one who has the most money is Carlitos Lizaso. Several witnesses saw him leave Vicente López that afternoon with more than two thousand pesos in his wallet. There was even someone who told him not to carry such a large sum on him. At the District Police Department, they log the amount at only seventy-eight pesos.

Could he have done what Livraga did? Maybe. What we know for sure is that those two thousand pesos will disappear completely, in one pocket or another. Only a small part of the booty collected that night—money, watches, rings—will return to its owners.

The atmosphere among the prisoners is getting heavier and heavier. One thing's for sure: no one is thinking of letting them go.

20. EXECUTE THEM!

4:45 a.m. It seems as though Rodríguez Moreno is trying to buy more time. He probably doesn't think of killing ten or fifteen unlucky saps as a very pleasant way to spend his evening. He is personally convinced that more than half of them have nothing to do with anything. And he even has doubts about the rest. He has a tense exchange with the Chief of Police, who has already arrived in La Plata. The orders are strict: execute them. The alternative: be subject to martial law himself. It sounds like they are even talking about sending him an envoy with troops.

At 4:47 a.m., they broadcast Communiqué No. 3 from the Office of the Vice President of the Republic:

"Campo de Mayo has surrendered. La Plata is practically contained. In Santa Rosa, the cavalry regiment has been enlisted to defeat the last rebel group. Eighteen civilian rebels who tried to attack a precinct in Lanús have been executed."

The Marine Corps and the Police Academy lift the siege on

Police Headquarters. The rebels disperse. Fernández Suárez arrives at the Government House, where Colonel Bonnecarrere has had no choice but to listen to the nearby shooting all night long, and they walk together toward Police Headquarters. They are walking up the wide staircase that looks onto Rivadavia Square when Fernández Suárez turns to a subordinate and, so that everyone can hear him, gives the order:

—*Those prisoners in San Martín should be taken out to a field and executed!*

Apparently that's not enough. Fernández Suárez has to take the radio transmitter into his own hands.

Rodríguez Moreno receives the command. It is incontestable. So he makes his decision.

21. "HE FELT HE WAS COMMITTING A SIN"

At the last minute, three of them get lucky: the night watchman, "the man who went to have dinner," and "the man who was saying goodnight to his girlfriend." They are pulled aside, given back their identity papers and personal items, and set free.

Rodríguez Moreno will later say that they had been included in the order for execution but he released them "of his own accord."

They make the rest of them go outside. An assault car is parked in front of the Department, one of those blue trucks that are open on both sides and have wooden seats that cut across the middle. A police van waits a few meters back. Next to it, a small man in a raincoat is nervously rubbing his hands together. It's Captain Cuello.

The prisoners receive the order to get on the truck. There is still one who asks again:

—Where are they taking us?

—Don't worry —is the cunning response.— We're transferring you to La Plata.

Nearly everyone has gotten on. Just then a strange scene comes to pass: it's Cuello who impulsively shouts out of the blue:

—Mister Giunta!

Giunta turns around, surprised, and walks toward him.

There is an almost pleading tone to Cuello's deep, steady voice now.

—But, Mr. Giunta . . . —he moves his arms a bit, his hands clenched— but you . . . you were in that house? You really were?

Giunta realizes all of a sudden that he is asking him to say no. He just needs a syllable to let him go, to fix the situation somehow. Cuello's face surprises him: it's tense, he's squinting a little, and a muscle twitches uncontrollably in one of his cheeks ("He knew I was innocent. He *felt he was committing a sin* by sending me to my death," Giunta will later say, in his typically striking language).

But Giunta can't lie. Or rather: he doesn't know why he has to lie.

—Yes, I was there.

The policeman brings his hand to his head. It's a gesture that lasts a fraction of a second. But it's strange . . . Then he pulls himself together again.

—Okay —he says dryly.— Go.

Giunta will not forget the scene. Without even noticing, he will continue to build upon it in his mind over the course of many more minutes. He has already conditioned himself, unknowingly prepared himself for what could happen. He has the professional habit of observing faces, studying their reflexes and reactions. And what he just saw in Cuello's face is still shapeless and nebulous, but worrisome nonetheless.

All of them have now gotten on. And again, the same enigma: How many were they in total? Ten, according to Livraga's calculation. Ten, Mr. Horacio di Chiano will repeat. But they have not been counted. Eleven, Gavino will say. Eleven, both Benavídez and Troxler will estimate.* But it's clear that there are more than ten of them, and more than eleven, because in addition to those five, there's Carranza, Garibotti, Díaz, Lizaso, Giunta, Brión, and Rodríguez. Twelve at least. Giunta will calculate twelve, a number confirmed by Rodríguez Moreno who, nevertheless, also mentions somebody "with a foreign name that sounded like Carnevali who later found asylum at an embassy." Twelve or thirteen, Cuello will claim. But Juan Carlos Torres will say that, based on indirect testimonies, there were fourteen. And the Chief of Police of the Province, months later, will also speak of fourteen prisoners in Florida. If there were two extra men, one of them must have been the anonymous NCO that Torres mentions.

And the guards? There are thirteen of them, according to one testimony. Based on information obtained from another source, they seem to be under the command of a corporal by the name of Albornoz, of the district of Villa Ballester. Is he the one Livraga will later see under extraordinary circumstances? We don't know.

There is one thing that truly stands out: the policemen are armed with Mausers alone. Given the kind of operation that they are carrying out and the circumstances under which they are doing so, it is nearly incomprehensible. Is this about some sort of opportunity, an "out" that Rodríguez Moreno is consciously or unconsciously going to give the prisoners? Or is it that there aren't any machine guns in the District Police Department? There is no easy solution to this riddle. What's certain is that, thanks to this fortunate circumstance—and to other equally strange ones that we'll later encounter—half of those condemned to die will make it out alive.

---

* In his statement, Gavino lists the prisoners by name, including "N. N., a young man, approximately thirty-five years old, blond and mustached," who must have been Giunta. But he leaves out Mario Brión. In contrast, the joint statement of Troxler and Benavídez (which is also in my possession) lists "Mario N." but leaves out Giunta. The explanation that occurs to me is this: Gavino, Troxler, and Benavídez didn't know Brión or Giunta from before. These latter two share certain physical similarities. Seeing them from one moment to the next in the semi-darkness of the truck, the men came to identify one with the other, combining two people into just one.

But they don't know that they are condemned, and this outrageous cruelty ought to be highlighted in the list of aggravating and mitigating factors. They have not been told that they are going to be killed. What's more, until the very last moment, there will be those who try to deceive them.

The guards draw the canvas curtains that enclose the body of the police car, and the truck heads northwest. They are followed by the van holding Cuello, Rodríguez Moreno, and Officer Cáceres, along 9 de Julio Street and its continuation, Balcarce Street, which turns into Route 8. They cover 2100 meters—about fifteen somewhat populated blocks—before exiting at the first open lot, which is about a thousand meters long. From there the road veers off to the west.

The prisoners don't have the opportunity to observe these topographical details. They are traveling as though in a cell, in nearly total darkness. All they can see is the rectangle of paved road that the windshield up front lets through.

It is bitingly cold. The temperature stays at 0°C. Those who suffer the most are Giunta, who is wearing just a jacket, and Brión with his white cardigan. They are sitting face to face on the left, Brión on the first double seat with his back to the driver, and Giunta in the second, looking forward. One of the clasps of the curtain that covers the doorframe is broken, and the fabric flaps against the truck with sharp blows, letting in a gust of freezing wind that cuts like a knife. They both turn to hold the curtain down and talk softly.

—I think they're going to kill us, Mr. Lito —Brión says.

Giunta is still mulling over what happened with Cuello, but tries to console his neighbor.

—Don't think about those things, Mr. Mario. Didn't you hear them say they were taking us to La Plata . . .

If they could see anything, they would realize that they are getting farther and farther away from their alleged destination. Next to Giunta is Mr. Horacio. He also believes they are being taken to La Plata. In front of Mr. Horacio is Vicente Rodríguez, quiet and pensive. Gavino is sitting next to Carranza. He is afraid, while Carranza is trusting. The one who is also trusting, confident, even optimistic in all of this, is Juan Carlos Livraga. He is a bus driver who knows the roads, he should realize that they're not taking them where they say they are. Still, he notices nothing.

In the back seats are Lizaso, Díaz, Benavídez, Troxler . . . Troxler is tense, alert, trying to look out for the slightest indication that might let him know where he is. He is very familiar with the guards and used to dealing with them and giving them orders. Why don't any of them want to look him in the eye? Julio Troxler must have noticed something in their behavior that made him so suspicious.

The truck drives back into a populated area. On the left is a thousand-meter stretch unevenly scattered with houses. Then houses appear on the right as well. The road cuts diagonally across lots and streets for another thousand meters. And suddenly it widens and splits into two. Troxler almost jumps up in his seat. He has just figured out where they are. They are at the intersection of Route 8 and the Camino de Cintura highway.[10] So, not only are they not going to La Plata, they are going in the opposite direction. And Route 8 leads to Campo de Mayo. And in Campo de Mayo . . .

One particular incident interrupts his conclusions. The driver is feeling sick. He stops the truck, gets off, and looks like he's vomiting. There is an exchange with those in the van.

One of the prisoners—it's Benavídez—offers to help.

—If you want, I can drive —he says, completely innocently.— I know how to drive.

They don't pay attention to him. The driver gets back on. They set out again.

"And in Campo de Mayo . . ." Troxler thinks to himself. But he is wrong. Because the assault car turns at a clear right angle onto the Camino de Cintura, it's heading north!

It is incomprehensible.

22. THE END OF THE JOURNEY

It really is incomprehensible. What is Rodríguez Moreno thinking? Continuing west on Route 8, there is a four- or five-kilometer lot about ten blocks away, a true barren land in the night where there is even a bridge over a river—the perfect setting for what's about to happen. And yet, they turn north towards José León Suárez and enter a semi-populated area where there are only wastelands, each about three or four blocks long.

Is it stupidity? Is it early remorse? Is it possible that he doesn't know the area? Is it an unconscious impulse to seek out witnesses for the crime that he is going to commit? Does he want to give the condemned men a "sporting" chance, to leave them to fate, to luck, to each one's individual shrewdness? Does he mean to absolve himself this way, by handing over each one's fate to destiny? Or does he want the total opposite: to calm them down so it will be easier to kill them?

At least one of them is not calming down. It's Troxler. He has finally managed to get one of the guards to look him in the eye and keep his gaze. But this anonymous guard does something else as well. He gives him a swift, deliberate, unmistakable blow with his knee. A sign.

So Troxler *already knows*. But he decides to play a wild card, to force a decision or at least put the others on their guard.

—What's going on? —he asks loudly.— Why are you touching me?

A look of panic flashes in the policeman's eyes. He is already regretting what he's done. The corporal looks at him suspiciously.

—No reason, sir —he stammers.— It was an accident.

The truck has come to a halt.

—Six of you, get off! —orders the corporal.

Mr. Horacio is the first to step out, from the right side of the truck. Rodríguez, Giunta, Brión, Livraga, and one more person follow, each guarded by an officer. They can see their surroundings for the first time. They are on an asphalt road. There are fields on either side of it. Just in front of where they got off, there is a ditch filled with water and, behind that, a wire fence. The location, despite everything, is nearly perfect.

But then a commanding voice rises again from the police van parked behind them:

—No, not here. Further up!

They get them back on the truck and resume the journey. Troxler has taken up his distressed, mute post once again. He is now trying to catch the gaze of the other prisoners, to coordinate with them, to get their attention and rally for a frantic, surprise attack. But it's useless. The others seem stunned, resigned, bewildered. They still don't believe, can't believe . . . Only Benavídez seems to respond to him. He is just as alert, tense, and anxious.

The truck carries on for three hundred meters more before stopping one last time, this time definitively. The seven-kilometer trip has taken almost thirty minutes.

The same prisoners get off. Carranza and Gavino as well. Maybe Garibotti and Díaz. Troxler will later confirm that Benavídez, Lizaso, and the anonymous NCO stay in the truck with him.[*] Other testimonies are confusing, divergent, still contaminated by the panic.

To the right of the dark and deserted road, there is a small paved road that peels off and leads to a German Club.[11] On one side of the street there is a row of eucalyptus trees that cut tall and bleak against the starry sky. On the other side, a wide wasteland extends out to the left: a slag dump, the sinister garbage heap of José León Suárez, tracked through with waterlogged trenches in winter, infested with mosquitoes and unburied creatures in summer, all of it eaten away by tin cans and junk.

---

[*]   Or perhaps it was "Mario N.," that is to say Brión, whose last name Troxler didn't know. But other survivors confirmed that Mario got off with them. The contradiction—typical of such situations—remains unsolved until today.

They make the prisoners walk along the edge of the wasteland. The guards push them along with the barrels of their rifles. The van turns onto the street and shines its headlights on their backs.

The moment has come . . .

23. THE SLAUGHTER

. . . The moment has come. It is signaled by a short, remarkable exchange:

—What are you going to do to us? —one of them asks.

—Keep walking! —they reply.

—We are innocent! —a number of them shout.

—Don't be afraid —they answer.— *We're not going to do anything to you.* WE'RE NOT GOING TO DO ANYTHING TO YOU!

The guards steer them like a terrified herd toward the garbage dump. The van comes to a stop, shining its headlights on them. The prisoners seem to be floating in a glowing pool of light. Rodríguez Moreno steps out, gun in hand.

At this moment, the story ruptures, explodes into twelve or thirteen nodules of panic.

—Let's make a run for it, Carranza —Gavino says.— I think they're going to kill us.

Carranza knows it's true. But the slightest hope that he's mistaken keeps him walking.

—Let's stay . . . —he murmurs.— If we run, they'll shoot for sure.

Giunta is walking sluggishly, looking back with one arm raised to his brow to shield his eyes from the blinding glare.

Livraga is stealthily making his way over to the left. Step by step. Dressed in black. Suddenly, it's like a miracle: the headlights leave him alone. He has stepped outside their range. He is alone and almost invisible in the dark. Ten meters ahead, he can make out a ditch. If he's able to reach . . .

Brión's cardigan shines in the light, an almost incandescent white.

In the assault car, Troxler is sitting with his hands resting on his knees and his body leaning forward. He looks out of the corners of his eyes at the two guards who are watching the nearest door. He's going to jump . . .

Facing him, Benavídez is looking at the other door.

Carlitos, bewildered, can only muster a whisper:

—But how . . . They're going to kill us like this?

Vicente Rodríguez is walking slowly along the rough and unfamiliar terrain below. Livraga is five meters away from the ditch. Mr. Horacio, who was the first to get off, has also managed to make his way ever so slightly in the opposite direction.

—Halt! —a voice commands.

Some of them stop. Others take a few more steps. The guards, on their part, start to retreat, taking some distance, the bolts of their Mausers in hand.

Livraga doesn't look back, but hears the turn of a crank. There's no time to make it to the ditch. He's going to throw himself on the ground.

—Forward, line up side by side! —shouts Rodríguez Moreno.

Carranza turns around, his face contorted. He drops to his knees before the firing squad.

—For my children . . . —he weeps.— For my chil . . .

Violent vomiting cuts his plea short.

In the truck, Troxler has pulled the bow and arrow of his body taut. His jaw is almost touching his knees.

—*Now!* —he howls and hurls himself at the two guards.

He holds a rifle in each hand. And now they are the ones afraid and begging:

—Not the guns, mister! Not the guns!

Benavídez is already up and grabs Lizaso by the hand.

—Let's go, Carlitos!

Troxler brings the heads of the two guards together and throws each one in a different direction, like dolls. He leaps up and is swallowed by the night.

The anonymous NCO (or is he an apparition?) is slow to respond. He tries to get up too late. A third guard is aiming his rifle at him from the front end of the vehicle. A shot is heard. The NCO lets out an 'Aaah!' and sits back down, just as he was. Only dead.

Benavídez jumps. He feels Carlitos' fingers slipping away from his own. In a state of desperate helplessness, he realizes he has lost him, that the boy has been buried beneath three bodies that are holding him down.

The policemen on the ground hear the shot behind them and hesitate for a fraction of a second. Some turn around.

Giunta doesn't wait any longer. He runs!

Gavino does the same.

The herd begins to separate.

—Shoot them! —screams Rodríguez Moreno.

Livraga throws himself headfirst to the ground. Farther ahead, Di Chiano also takes a dive.

The shots thunder in the night.

Giunta feels a bullet whiz by his ear. He hears a commotion behind him, a low moaning and the thump of a body falling. It's probably Garibotti. An amazing instinct tells Giunta to drop to the ground and not move.

Carranza is still on his knees. They put a rifle to the nape of his neck and fire. Later they riddle his entire body with bullets.

Brión has little chance of escaping with that white cardigan that shines in the night. We don't even know if he tries.

Vicente Rodríguez has dropped to the ground once already. Now he hears the guards running toward him. He tries to get up, but can't. He has tired himself out in the first thirty meters of his escape and it isn't easy to move all one hundred of his kilos. By the time he gets going, it's too late. The second round of shots takes him out.

Horacio di Chiano rolled over twice and froze, playing dead. He hears the bullets destined for Rodríguez whistle overhead. One cuts very close to his face and covers him in dirt. Another rips through his pants without wounding him.

Giunta stays glued to the ground for about thirty seconds, invisible. Suddenly he leaps up like a hare and starts to zigzag. When he senses the shots coming, he throws himself back on the ground. Almost instantaneously, he hears the astounding whir of the bullets again. But by now he is far away. He is nearly safe. When he repeats his maneuver, they won't even see him.

Díaz escapes. We don't know how, but he escapes.* Gavino runs for two or three hundred meters before stopping. At that moment, he hears another series of explosions and a terrifying shriek that tears through the night and seems to last forever.

—May God forgive me, Lizaso —he will later say, weeping, to one of Carlitos' brothers.— But I think that was your brother. I think he saw everything and was the last to die.

Up above the bodies stretched out in the garbage dump, where the caustic smoke of the gunpowder still burns in the glow of the headlights, a few groans hang in the air. A new burst of bullets seems to put an end to them. But then Livraga, who is still frozen and unnoticed in the spot where he fell, hears the bloodcurdling voice of his friend Rodríguez, who says:

—Kill me! Don't leave me like this! Kill me!

And now they do show him mercy, and they execute him.

24. TIMES STANDS STILL

Horacio di Chiano is not moving. His mouth is wide open, his arms

---

* "With respect to Díaz . . . the declarants do not remember at what point he got off the truck, but what they know for sure is that when they got off, he wasn't there anymore; it's very possible that . . . he may have gotten off when one of the guards wasn't looking . . ." Joint declaration of Benavídez and Troxler.

bent at his sides, his hands on the ground beneath his shoulders. By some miracle, he hasn't broken the glasses that he is wearing. He has heard everything—the shots, the screams—and isn't thinking anymore. His body is the domain of a fear that penetrates him to his very bones: all of his tissues are saturated with fear, in every cell a heavy drop of fear. *Don't move.* All the wisdom that mankind has accumulated can be condensed into these two words. Nothing exists aside from this atavistic instinct.

How long has he been this way, playing dead? He doesn't know anymore. He'll never know. He only remembers that at a certain moment he heard the bells of a nearby chapel ringing. Six, seven times? It's impossible to say. Maybe he dreamt those slow, sweet, sad sounds that were falling mysteriously from the darkness.

Ringing out endlessly all around him are the echoes of the horrific carnage, the rushing of prisoners and guards, the explosions that terrorize the air and reverberate in the mountains and nearby country houses, the gurgling of dying men.

At last, silence. Then the roar of an engine. The van starts up. It stops. A gunshot. Silence once more. The engine starts humming again in an intricate nightmare of stops and starts.

In a moment of clarity, Mr. Horacio understands. *The coup de grâce.* They are going from one body to the next and killing off those who show any signs of life. And now . . .

Yes, now it's his turn. The van comes closer. The ground beneath Mr. Horacio's glasses vanishes into chalky specks of light. They are shining a light on him, aiming at him. He can't see them, but he knows they are aiming at the back of his neck.

They are waiting for some sign of movement. Maybe not even that. Maybe they'll shoot him regardless. Maybe they think the very fact that he's not moving is strange. Maybe they'll figure out what is already obvious, namely that he isn't wounded, that he's not bleeding at all. A terrible nausea rises up from his stomach. He manages to stifle it with his lips. He wants to shout. Part of his body—his wrists resting like crowbars on the ground, his knees, the tips of his feet—would like to make a crazed run for it. The other part—his head, the nape of his neck—keeps telling him: don't move, don't breathe.

What does he do to stay still, to hold his breath, to keep from coughing, to keep from howling out of fear?

But he doesn't move. And neither does the light. It guards him, it watches him, like a game of patience. In the semicircle of rifles that surround him, no one says a word. But no one shoots. Seconds, minutes, years pass like this . . .

And the shot does not come.

When he hears the engine again, when the light disappears, when he knows that they are moving away, Mr. Horacio starts to breathe, slowly, slowly, as though he were learning to do it for the first time.

Closer to the paved road, Livraga has also stayed still but, unfortunately for him, in a different position. He is lying with his face up to the sky, his right arm stretched out and back and his chin resting on his shoulder…

He not only hears but also sees much of what is happening: the flashing bullets, the running guards, the exotic *contradanza* of the van that is now pulling back slowly in the direction of the road.[12] The headlights begin veering to the left, toward him. He closes his eyes.

Suddenly he feels a burning tickle, an irresistible stinging in his eyelids. Wild violet figurines dance in an orange light that penetrates his eye sockets. An unstoppable reflex makes him blink beneath the blazing stream of light.

The command strikes like lightning:

—Get that one, he's still breathing!

He hears three explosions go off at point-blank range. With the first one, a spurt of dust shoots by his head. Next he feels a searing pain on his face and his mouth fills with blood.

The guards don't bend down to check if he's dead. It is enough for them to see that ripped up and bloodied face. So they walk away believing that they have delivered the coup de grâce. They don't know that this bullet (and the one that got his arm) are the first ones to actually hit him.

The dismal assault car and Rodríguez Moreno's van retreat to where they came from.

"Operation Massacre" has ended.

25. THE END OF A LONG NIGHT

The fugitives dispersed into the field of the night.

Gavino has not stopped running. He jumps over puddles and ditches, gets to a dirt road, sees houses at a distance, takes unfamiliar streets, stumbles onto a railroad track, follows it, gets to the vicinity of the Chilavert station on the Mitre line, miraculously finds a bus, gets on it . . .

He is the first to seek asylum in a Latin American embassy while martial law is in full force. The terrible affair had ended for him.

Not so for Giunta, who had a never-ending nightmare waiting for him. The moment he reached a more populated area, he sought refuge in the front yard of a house. Inside there was light and movement. Nearly the entire neighborhood of José León Suárez had been awakened by the shooting.

The petrified fugitive had no sooner stepped into the garden when a window opened and a woman appeared, shouting:

—Don't even dare, don't even dare! —and added, turning halfway around, seeming to address the man of the house:— Take him out! He got away!

Giunta doesn't wait to hear anything more. He must think the world has gone mad tonight. Everyone wants to kill him . . .

He clears the fence with one jump and resumes his desperate sprint. Now he is avoiding the more trafficked areas, walking deliberately along dirt roads.

But there is one encounter he can't escape. Standing on the corner are three young men who watch with curiosity as he goes by. His voice faltering, he tells them some part of what happened and asks for money, even just a few coins to take some means of transportation to get away from this hell. He finds a softer heart among these nightwalkers: one gives him a peso, another gives him a ten-peso bill.

Like Gavino, Giunta makes it to Chilavert station. It's likely that neither of them know that Chilavert was the name of another executed man, one who fell in the Battle of Caseros . . .

He goes to the window and asks for a ticket.

—Where to? —asks the clerk.

Giunta looks at him, amazed. He hasn't the slightest idea. He doesn't even know where he is. He must be quite a sight, this man whose eyes are popping out of their sockets, whose hair is standing on end, whose face is covered in sweat on this freezing night, who is asking for a ticket and doesn't know his destination.

—Where to? —the clerk repeats, looking at him curiously.

—Wherever . . . Where does this line go?

—Retiro.

—That's it. Retiro. Give me a ticket to Retiro.

He gets the ticket. He leans against a wall. He closes his eyes and breathes deep. When he opens them again, there are three strangers looking at him on the platform, just looking at him . . .

All three of them seem to have their eyes fixed on the same spot. Giunta lowers his head and discovers his muddy shoes, his pants torn up from the getaway.

But now the train is arriving. He jumps on. The strangers get on behind him. Giunta starts to walk through the train cars. Two of the men have sat down. But the third is following him, nearly stepping on his heels.

Giunta acts with remarkable clarity of mind: he slows down his step so that the man is practically touching him, and then sits down all of a sudden—or rather, he drops like a rock—in the first seat that he finds on the right.

The stranger sits down as well. In the same row of the empty car, in the seat on the left.

Giunta doesn't look at his pursuer. He fixes his gaze on the dark window in an effort to make out the movements of the image reflected in it. He almost jumps up from his seat. Because the Stranger—could it be a coincidence?—is doing the same thing, watching him in his own window.

Will this night never end? Giunta is in despair. The train leaves Villa Ballester behind. The stranger keeps cunningly observing him. They reach Malaver. A few minutes later they are in San Andrés.

Once more, Giunta's instincts work in his favor. He decides in a flash. He waits for the train to start moving again, to pick up some speed. Then he jolts up, runs to the door, pulls it open in one go, walks down the platform steps, and throws himself off . . .

It's a miracle he doesn't kill himself. As soon as he puts pressure on his foot, the ground forces him to take giant leaps that he has never had to in his life. In his discombobulated puppet dash—ten meters, twenty meters—he brushes against a privet hedge that leaves long scratches on one arm. But the train is far away by now, lost like a glowworm in the dark.

And Giunta is—or believes he is—safe.

∽

Julio Troxler has hidden himself in a nearby ditch. He is waiting for the shooting to end. He sees the police cars drive away. Then he does something incredible. *He goes back!*

He goes back, dragging himself stealthily and calling out quietly to Benavídez, who escaped from the assault car with him. He doesn't know if he survived.

He gets close to the bodies and starts turning them over one by one—

Carranza, Garibotti, Rodríguez—looking at their faces in search of his friend. Pain grips him when he recognizes Lizaso. He has four holes in his chest and one in his cheek. But he doesn't find Benavídez.*

The bodies were still warm. He probably doesn't see Horacio di Chiano, who continues to play dead not too far from there. He understands that there is nothing left to do there, and starts walking in the direction of José León Suárez.

He is almost at the station when he sees Livraga coming towards him, teetering and covered in blood. At the same moment, an officer from the nearby police station was making his way towards the wounded man, shouting: "What's going on? What's going on?"

—They executed us . . . they fired some shots at us —Livraga mumbled, among other insults and unintelligible mutterings.

The officer held him under his armpits and helped him walk towards the station. Along the way, they passed by Troxler.

For the third time this evening, the former police officer was recognized by one of his old colleagues.

—Hey Troxler! How's it going? —the other guy shouts, passing by.

—Good, you know . . . —he replies.

He is about to keep walking when he sees a truck with Army soldiers approaching. As always, Julio Troxler does the most natural thing: he heads to a short line of early risers who are waiting for a Costera bus and joins it. He doesn't plan on boarding the bus—besides, he doesn't even have five cents on him—but he knows he will attract less attention there.

It seems fated. Because the truck stops just in front of the line.

---

* Troxler recounts that ". . . he found Carlos Lizaso along the way . . . in the place where the truck had been, in a supine position, with half of his body on the road and the rest of it in the ditch alongside it . . . he checked to make sure he wasn't still alive . . . he crossed the road and, on the path that leads to the German Club, found Rodríguez in the middle of the street next to a large puddle of blood, then Carranza, and, on the right side . . . another corpse that he couldn't identify . . ."

Without stepping out, an officer yells:

—Fellas, you haven't heard any shots, have you?

The question seems addressed to everyone, but it's Troxler that the officer is looking at, it's him that he is addressing, for a very simple reason: he is the tallest in line.

Troxler shrugs his shoulders.

—As far as I know . . . —he says.

The truck takes off. Troxler leaves his place in line and starts to walk. He doesn't have any money for the bus; a basic sense of prudence stops him from asking a stranger for money, or even for permission to call his friends . . .

He's exhausted and frozen cold. He hasn't eaten anything since the night before. He walks eleven hours straight through Greater Buenos Aires, which has morphed into a desert without water or shelter for him, a survivor of the massacre.

It is six o'clock in the evening when he reaches a safe haven.

26. THE MINISTRY OF FEAR

The "coup de grâce" that they delivered to Livraga went straight through one part of his face to another, crushing his nasal wall and his teeth, but missed his vital organs. His youth and his athleticism served him immeasurably: he never lost consciousness even though his face was swelling up and he was in a great deal of pain. The intense cold of the frost seemed to keep him awake.

He hears a new round of shots. It is probably the execution of Lizaso, the only one that seemed to have been formally carried out. Some evidence allows us to assume that the guards had him restrained up until the last minute, that they lined the squad up in front of him and fired according to regulation. The unlucky young man did not get the chance to even think of fleeing. Or, what's more likely: at the crucial moment, he preferred to face his executioners courageously. What we know is that he was facing them when they fired at him, right in the middle of his chest.

Livraga hears the police cars driving away and waits. He is still not moving. Only when several minutes have passed does he try to get up. He rests his right arm on the ground; it has another bullet wound in it.

Now an endless torment begins: fear and physical suffering will follow one after the other and eventually become one. There will be a moment when Livraga will regret having survived.

He manages to get up. He walks. He makes his way to the garbage dump where he saw Giunta escape and looks for him. There is something foolish and pathetic about this search. It's as though he cannot believe in anyone in this world anymore, as though the only person he can trust is the man who has been through the same experience. (Much later on he will find Giunta at last—in Olmos.)

After a long detour through open fields, he returns to the main road. He is leaving a trail of blood behind him. He approaches a village. There are several lights. He sees a train station sign: José León Suárez. Someone tries to ask him something, but he keeps going without answering. He is exhausted. He's going to fall down. Somebody manages to take him in his arms.

It's a police officer.

At that moment, the thought of an unending nightmare must have occurred to Livraga: the cycle of being arrested, executed, arrested, executed again . . .

Yet, he had finally found himself with a human being.

The officer—whom we have already seen greeting Troxler—did not even ask him why he was wounded. He hurried him onto a jeep, put a guard by his side to look after him and, placing himself in front of the wheel, set out in a mad race to the nearest hospital.

They passed the bodies on the way. The officer stopped the car in its tracks and ordered the guard to step out and investigate.

—They're dead —the guard announced.

The policeman turned toward Livraga.

—Tell me the truth, man, what happened?

Instead of answering, Livraga vomited up a mouthful of blood. The policeman didn't hesitate any longer. Leaving the guard standing on the road, he hit the accelerator.

27. AN IMAGE IN THE NIGHT

Mr. Horacio doesn't know how long he was playing dead. Half an hour? An hour? His sense of time was completely altered. All he knows is that he did not leave the spot where he'd fallen until it started to get bright out. That was probably at around seven-thirty. On June 10, the sun rose at 7:57 a.m.

He lifted his head and saw the field covered in white. Along the horizon, he could make out a solitary tree. Nine months later he was surprised to find out that it was not just one tree; rather, the branches of several trees at the far end of an undulating terrain were creating this optical illusion. Incidentally, the detail proved to this writer—if I still harbored any doubts—that Mr. Horacio had been there. The only place from which that strange mirage can be observed is the site of the execution.*

On one side of the "phantom tree," at the edge of the town of José León Suárez, he spotted the chapel whose bells he had heard ringing when they were about to deliver the coup de grâce . . .

He stood up and made a great effort to start running in that direction. He was numb. The cold was brutal. At 8:10 a.m. the temperature was -3°C.

---

* I had been very intrigued by this topographical trace that Mr. Horacio kept mentioning and that I had never managed to observe during my three or four visits to the garbage dump. That was until I went with him one day. Soon enough, after the two of us had looked for it for a good while, *I saw it*. It was fascinating, worthy of a Chesterton story. Moving fifty paces in any direction, the optical effect would disappear, the "tree" would split into many trees. At that moment I knew—it was an unusual kind of proof—that I was at the scene of the execution.

Along the way he came to a muddy ditch that was impossible for him to get past. He had to grab a sheet of corrugated metal from a pile of garbage and place it across like a bridge.

Leaving the wasteland behind, he went into town. He walked about eight blocks. He thought it was only two. He saw a bus heading down a cross street. He thought it was red. It was yellow. He thought it was the number 4. It was the number 1.

He got on.

—Where does this go? —he asked, just like Giunta.

—To Liniers.

In a small pocket of his pants he had salvaged a small sum of money from the ravenousness of the police. He was able to pay for his ticket. It sounds like a fairytale: they gave him a ticket with a palindromic number on it . . .

He got off in Liniers. He walked into a bar. He ordered a coffee. They were still warming up the machine so there wasn't any. He went to another bar. They gave him a double espresso and a double shot of sugar cane spirits there.

Only then did he feel like his soul was returning to his body.

∽

How did Sergeant Díaz escape? We can only speculate. What we know for sure is that, two months after the massacre, he was still alive, hidden in a house in Munro. That's where the police commissioner of Boulogne arrested him. He was sent to Olmos. He is the only survivor I was never able to reach.

And the "NCO X"? Did he exist? Who was the man that Troxler and Benavídez saw being shot dead in the truck? One of the twelve whom we already know of, but who was a stranger to them? The mystery remains to this day.

Without a doubt, the massacre left five dead, one critically wounded, and six survivors.

∾

The sun had come up over the dreadful scene of the execution. The corpses were scattered along the main road. Several had fallen into a ditch, and the blood in the stagnant water seemed to transform it into an unbelievable river floating with strands of brain matter. A good while later, they emptied one truck of tar there and another of lime . . .

There were Mauser cartridges everywhere. For many days after the fact, the boys of the neighborhood sold them to curious visitors. Faraway houses were left with marks from stray bullets.

The first to stop by the road that morning were unsuspecting townspeople on their way to work. After that, word spread through the town and a horrified, sullen crowd began to congregate around the atrocious sight.

Completely absurd accounts of what had happened were circulating in hushed voices.

—They were students —one person declared.

—Yes, they were going to attack Campo de Mayo . . . —said another.

Most were silent. The men took off their hats, a woman crossed herself.

Then everyone saw a new, long and shiny car coming along the road. It stopped suddenly in front of the group and a woman peeked her head out the window.

—What's going on? —she asked.

—These people . . . They've been executed —they responded.

She made an ironic gesture.

—Very well done! —she remarked.— They should kill all of them.

An astonished silence settled over the crowd. Then something traced the form of a parabola in the air and crashed onto the polished bodywork of the car in a cloud of dirt. After the first clump made contact, there was another, and then came the deluge. Howling and furious, the crowd surrounded the car. The driver managed to floor it.

The dead bodies were left out in the open until ten in the morning. At that point an ambulance came and took them to the San Martín polyclinic, where they were flung carelessly into a warehouse. Rodríguez was riddled with bullets; Garibotti had just one bullet wound, in his back. Carranza had many, including in his legs . . .

The night watchman at the depot was accustomed to the sight of dead bodies. When he arrived that afternoon, though, there was something that deeply shocked him. One of the executed men had his arms out by his sides and his head leaning on one shoulder. He had an oval face, blond hair, the beginnings of a beard, a melancholic expression, and a trail of blood coming from his mouth.

He was wearing a white cardigan. It was Mario Brión and he looked like Christ.*

The man stood there dazed for a moment.

Then he folded Brión's arms across his chest.

28. "THEY'RE TAKING YOU AWAY"

The police officer drove Livraga to the San Martín polyclinic, where he received his first treatments. Juan Carlos did not lose consciousness: for hours, doctors and nurses heard him repeat his story. Afterward they took him to the recovery room on the third floor.

The nurses, risking their jobs—and maybe even more: martial law was still in effect—protect the wounded man in every way imaginable. One secretly calls Juan Carlos' father and tells him to come see his son immediately because he is "unwell." Another hides his clothes; she knows Livraga is telling the truth and assumes that his

---

*   The night watchman's exact words to Mario's father many months later.

sweater with the bullet hole in its sleeve can be used as evidence. Yet another hides the receipt from the San Martín District Police Department, which would later serve as the introductory document for the criminal proceedings.

Juan Carlos' mother has just been operated on and is in a different hospital; they don't tell her the news. Mr. Pedro Livraga, on the other hand, goes to see his son immediately, accompanied by two cousins and Juan Carlos's brother-in-law. These four individuals sign a statement in the polyclinic's numbered registry book declaring that they have seen Juan Carlos alive and that his state, although certainly serious, does not in any way imply a fatal outcome.

This was a good precautionary measure to take because that afternoon or that night—for Livraga time has turned into the mere progression of pain—a corporal from the local police department comes in to keep watch and, finding himself faced with Livraga, looks once at him and then keeps staring, as if he doesn't want to believe that he is alive.

The policeman's face looks somewhat familiar to Livraga. He can't be sure, but he thinks he has seen him before. Could it be Corporal Albornoz who was in charge of the firing squad? It's not such an important question.

But the corporal—a dark-skinned man—has a big mouth. He talks to the nurses:

—They're going to take this one in again. Don't tell him, poor guy.

The nurses tell him. And the torture begins again.

The policeman, in the meantime, is looking for something. *The receipt.* He asks for Livraga's clothes. They don't give them to him. He gets angry and pointedly asks for the little piece of paper, which provides proof of the crime. No one knows anything.

No one except for Pedro Livraga who, upon returning to his house that night, mysteriously finds it in the pocket of his overcoat.

And he holds onto it until six months later when it reaches the hands of the judge.

Meanwhile, Juan Carlos' life is hanging by a very thin thread. There is no doubt that the local police want to get rid of him, the witness. But first they need to solve the "small" problem of the other survivors, who are being savagely pursued. If they can catch all of them, they will execute them again, taking the greatest precautions . . . But if even one escapes their clutches, it will be useless to get rid of the rest of them.

Livraga is no longer resisting, no longer protesting. When they put him on a stretcher that night and a nurse says to him in tears: "They're taking you away, kid," he's already given up. *So much suffering just to die.*

They roll him out covered in a sheet, like they would a dead man. They load him onto a jeep and take him away.

∽

In San Andrés, Giunta took a bus that brought him to his brother's house in Villa Martelli, where he found refuge and released some anxiety by telling his incredible story.

That night he slept at his parents' house and on Monday, June 11, he went to work. He thought his odyssey had ended. But when he went back to Florida that afternoon, his wife told him that the police had been by looking for him. She told them he was at his parents' house.

Giunta who, up until that moment had conducted himself with the utmost clarity, now does something stupid. He wants to come forward and explain his situation.

He went to his parents' place to turn himself in. He knew they were waiting for him there and he actually didn't even make it inside because they stopped him first.

What happened next constitutes an entire chapter in the history of our barbarity.

First they took him to the precinct in Munro, and from there to the District Police Department. They locked him in some sort of kitchen. An armed guard came in with him, sat Giunta down in a corner, and pointed a gun at him for the entire time.

—Take even one step and I'll blow your brains out! —he would repeat every so often.— Talk and I'll blow your brains out! Make even one move and I'll blow your brains out!

His vocabulary was rather limited, but convincing. Still, now and then he would provoke him:

—Go ahead, make a move. That way I can shoot you.

The prisoner did not attempt even the slightest gesture. Now and again, the guard seemed to get tired and would place his gun back in its holster. But soon enough he would go back to his entertaining game.

They were deliberately pushing him toward madness. When changing shifts, the guards would speak softly in a way that made their conversations sound confidential, but loudly enough for the prisoner to hear them:

—He's "getting out" tonight . . . —one of them would murmur.

—*Wherever* is he going? —the other would answer, chuckling.

—No one survives twice.

Aside from one sandwich, they gave him nothing to eat for hours at a time. When he wanted to sleep, he had to lie down on the freezing tile floor. The shouting outside interrupted his painful sleep.

—Caaareful, he's getting awaaay! Shut all the windows!

They seemed to be provoking him to run. It actually wouldn't have been so hard. He wasn't in a real cell. Giunta would not let himself be tempted.

Maybe they were trying to get him to kill himself. At one point they moved him to a different room on the second floor with a window facing the courtyard.

—Don't you think about trying to escape through there —an officer said to him, pointing at the window that was within reach.— Because even if you don't die from the fall . . . Anyway, that's just my opinion.

From the very start, they had been trying to recover the receipt they had issued him in the very same Department at dawn on the tenth. When their threats failed, they tried to seduce him. A young officer was trying to persuade him logically:

—Look, your situation has been cleared up, but we need that receipt. All you have to do is hand it in and you'll be a free man.

Giunta kept saying he didn't have it, and he was telling the truth. He had burned the receipt.

After two or three days of being locked up, he received a visit from Cuello, the second-in-command of the Department who had made a vague attempt to save him from execution. He couldn't believe his eyes. He thought he was seeing a ghost.

—But how did you do it? —he kept repeating.— *How did you do it?*

Giunta was so out of sorts at this point that he tried to apologize for running away. He explained that it had been an instinctive reaction, to escape death; the truth was that he hadn't meant to . . . Yes, he hadn't meant to offend them.

When they transferred him to San Martín's First Precinct on the seventeeth of June, he was a shell of a man, on the brink of insanity.

29. A DEAD MAN SEEKS ASYLUM

Had Benavídez died? His friends, according to Troxler's story, had hopes of finding him alive. Those hopes were dashed on the morning of June 12.

All the newspapers published a communiqué from the government with the official list of "men executed in the region of San Martín." And Reinaldo Benavídez was on it.

Benavídez himself must have been the most surprised to find out, seeing how he had survived . . .*

---

* ". . . from the site of the crime, he headed northwest and, after about five hundred meters, he went up to a bus driver who made a stop in that region and, asking the man for money, boarded the vehicle . . ." Troxler and Benavídez's

And yet, the explanation was very simple. It can be found in the blind irresponsibility that, from start to finish, has been behind this secret operation that was labeled as an execution.

You just have to read the list of men executed in San Martín to understand that the government did not have the slightest idea who its victims were.

They assumed Benavídez, who had been enjoying a clean bill of health ever since his escape from the garbage dump in José León Suárez, was dead. On the other hand, Brión, who had been killed, was not mentioned at all. They called Lizaso "Crizaso" and Garibotti "Garibotto."

It's hard to believe that they were able to make so many mistakes in a list of barely five names—names that corresponded to five people who were officially executed by the government, no less.

The odd thing is that none of these macabre mistakes have been corrected, even after I reported them. So, officially, Benavídez is still dead. Officially, the government never had anything to do with Mario Brión.

But on November 4, 1956, the newspapers reported that the previous day, Reinaldo Benavídez had gone into exile in Bolivia.

Yes, the very same.

The "dead man."

∾

The families of the victims were not spared any trouble, humiliation, or uncertainty.

One of his brothers had a feeling that Lizaso was going to meet his tragic end based on things he had heard; he walked from precinct to precinct in search of concrete news. At seven o'clock on the morning of June 12, when the news was already in the papers—

statement, dated the ninth of May, 1957, in La Paz, Bolivia, addressed to the author of this book.

and had been announced by Radio Mitre the night before—he went to the San Martín District Police Department. They had the cold-blooded cynicism to tell him that they didn't know Carlitos and to send him out to the Bureau of Investigation on what they knew was a wild-goose chase. From there he was sent to the Military District. And from there to Campo de Mayo, where the Head of the Military Camp came to speak with him:

—The only thing I can tell you for sure —he informed him— is that no civilians have been executed here.

He went to Florida's Second Precinct, then to the Army Department. No one knew anything. At the Government House, General Quaranta refused to see him.[13] Finally an Air Force officer, Major Valés Garbo, took pity on him and, with a few booming commands over the phone, succeeded in getting the police thugs to let go of the innocent kick that they were getting out of all this.

∞

In Florida on the night of the eleventh, a police squad went to Vicente Rodríguez's house to retrieve the murdered dockworker's ID booklet. His wife, who still did not know anything, received a summons from the Department on the twelfth for the following day.

At the District Police Department, they made her wait for an hour before an officer tended to her. She had not read the papers. She asked again about her husband, asked if he was in jail . . . That's when the officer looked her up and down.

—Are you illiterate? —he asked disdainfully.

Let it be noted: when tormenting a poor woman, there are advantages that literacy can offer.

—Many men were executed —the trained officer said in closing.— *Among them, your husband.*

They took her by van to the San Martín polyclinic. That is where Vicente's body was. She asked if she could take him with her to hold a wake for him. They told her she could not.

—Come back with a coffin. From here you go straight to the cemetery. Oh, and it has to be before Friday. If not, you won't find him here.

She came back with a coffin. And they went straight to the cemetery. With a police escort. It was only after the last clump of dirt had fallen that the last policeman withdrew.

∾

In Boulogne, where Carranza and Garibotti lived, the process was similar, only with one strange variation. The man in charge of retrieving all the ID booklets was tall, heavyset, and dark-skinned; he had a mustache and a deep, husky voice. He wore light pants and a short, olive green jacket: the uniform of the Argentine Army.

He was not brandishing a .45 caliber pistol in his right hand anymore.

At 7:00 p.m. on Monday, the eleventh, he stepped out of a jeep in front of Garibotti's house.

—I've come to collect your husband's booklet —he said to Florinda Allende, without introducing himself.

—It's not here —she replied.

—Look for it. It should be here.

He entered the house.

One of the railroad worker's sons, Raúl Alberto (thirteen years old), was sitting on the fence.

—Are you Garibotti's son? —the driver of the jeep asked him.

—Yes.

—The guy they killed?

The boy didn't know anything about it . . .

The dead man's booklet did not turn up. The tall, heavyset man crossed the street and knocked on the door at Carranza's house. Berta Figueroa did not yet know the fate of her husband or the whereabouts of the booklet.

—I don't know anything. He's the one who should have it.

—Look for it, ma'am, it has to be here because *he says it's here* —the military-police officer insisted.

Berta let him in and went looking for the ID.

Fernández Suárez stood looking at the large portrait of Nicolás Carranza that was hanging on the wall.

He was surrounded by Carranza's children looking at him shyly, their eyes wide and full of curiosity.

—Was that your dad? —the man asked Elena—the same "tall man" whose order was responsible for the fact that, though she didn't know it yet, the little one no longer had a dad.

—Yes —she responded.

—How many brothers and sisters do you have?

—Five —the girl answered.

—And you're the oldest?

—Yes.

Just then, Berta Figueroa returned with the booklet.

—Is my husband in jail? —she dared, anxiously, to ask.

—I don't know, ma'am —the Chief of Police of the Province of Buenos Aires replied in a hurry.— I don't know anything.

And from the jeep he added, with a voice huskier than before:

—They've asked for the booklet over in La Plata. It's for a procedural matter.

∽

On the afternoon of June 10, a young man was walking, deeply worried, toward Franklin Street in Florida. A woman he didn't know stopped him along the way.

—Are you related to Brión? —she asked.

—I'm his brother —he replied.

—Don't worry —she then said.— Horacio and Mario are okay.

And before he could ask anything more, the stranger left in a hurry.

It was the first piece of news he had received since Mario's disappearance the night before. All the events that followed would work to refute it, but this mysterious encounter would fuel—even in the face of hard evidence—the cruelest and most irrational hopes.

A brother-in-law of Mario's found out straightaway that he had been arrested and went to the District Police Department to ask after him. There—according to a third party—something strange happened.

—What did your brother-in-law look like? —asked the officer on duty.

—He was . . . —Just as Mario's relative had begun to explain, he caught the man's gaze and exclaimed in shock:— Actually, he looked just like you . . . !

Upon hearing these unexpected words, the officer apparently broke down and started to cry.

Mario's body was at the San Martín polyclinic, which is where his father went to retrieve him. They let him see his son for not more than a few seconds. One moment they were folding back the sheet that covered him, and the next they were wrapping him up again.

Months later, Mr. Manuel Brión received a mysterious phone call.

—Are you the father of Mario? —a voice asked.

—Yes . . .

—I want to talk to you about your son.

—Who are you?

—I'm a sailor. I've just returned from the south. I'll wait for you tonight next to the big wall of the Mechanics School . . .

He named a time and an exact location.

An unspeakable fear prevented the old man from making it to the meeting. But from that day forward he began to doubt what he had seen in the morgue at the polyclinic. Only the words of the night watchman at the depot, which we have already mentioned here, grounded him in the cruel reality of the situation.*

---

* The murder of Mario Brión was reported for the first time by me in *Revolución*

30. THE TELEGRAM GUERRILLA

Meanwhile, a silent battle was being fought for the life of Juan Carlos Livraga.

With Police Inspector Torres driving the jeep, Livraga is taken from the polyclinic to Moreno's First Precinct, where they throw him into a cell naked, without food or medical assistance. They don't list him in the registry book. Why would they? They are probably waiting to catch the other fugitives so they can execute him again, this time more carefully. Or they want him to die off on his own.

But his relatives will not rest. One of them manages to reach Colonel Arribau. There is strong evidence suggesting that this officer's intervention is what prevented Livraga from suffering another execution.

Mr. Pedro Livraga decides to appeal directly to the Pink House.[14] At 7:00 p.m. on June 11, the following registered telegram is sent from Florida, addressed to his Excellency the President of the Nation, General Pedro Eugenio Aramburu, the Government House, Buenos Aires, and received at 7:15 p.m.:

> IN MY CAPACITY AS FATHER JUAN CARLOS LIVRAGA EXECUTED THE 10TH AT DAWN ON ROUTE 8 BUT WHO SURVIVED BEING TENDED TO THEREAFTER SAN MARTIN POLYCLINIC FROM WHERE HE WAS MOVED SUNDAY AROUND 8 O'CLOCK NOT KNOWNING NEW WHEREABOUTS I ANXIOUSLY REQUEST YOUR HUMAN INTERVENING TO PREVENT BEING EXECUTED AGAIN ASSURING YOU THERE HAS BEEN CONFUSION AS HE IS UNCONNECTED TO ANY MOVEMENT. REGISTERED. PEDRO LIVRAGA.

Nacional on February 19, 1957. To write this indictment, I made contact with his family members, who still didn't want to accept that it was all over. Unfortunately, the inquiries that were made confirmed his death.

The reply arrives quickly. Telegram No. 1185—sent from the Government House on June 12, 1956, at 1:23 p.m., received at 8:37 p.m., and addressed to Mr. Pedro Livraga, Florida—reads:

IN REFERENCE TO TELEGRAM DATED THE 11TH I REPORT
YOUR SON JUAN CARLOS WAS WOUNDED DURING SHOOTING
ESCAPED THEREAFTER WAS ARRESTED AND IS STAYING AT
MORENO PRECINCT. HOUSE MILITARY CHIEF.

Juan Carlos' family hurries to the Moreno precinct. And there again they pull the old police trick: Juan Carlos—say the same clerks who just saw him thrown into a cell—has never been there before. It's pointless for Mr. Pedro Livraga to show them the telegram from the president's office: Juan Carlos isn't there. They don't know him. They instill what they say with a professional air of innocence. Later, in front of the judge, the commissioner will say that no visitors came to see him . . .

His family moves heaven and earth. To no avail. The young man does not turn up and at this point no one has any news from him. With the slow passing of each day, Mr. Pedro begins to get used to the harsh idea. Everyone in Florida assumes his son is dead.

But Juan Carlos is not dead. Remarkably, he survives his infected wounds, his excruciating pain, the hunger, the cold, the damp Moreno dungeon. At night he is delirious. Night and day do not even really exist for him anymore. Everything is a shimmering bright light where the ghosts of his fever move about, often taking on the indelible forms of the firing squad. When they happen to leave him some leftover food out of pity by the door and he drags himself toward it like a small animal, he realizes that he can't eat, that his shattered teeth still harbor searing promises of pain inside the shapeless and numb mass that is his face.

And so the days go by. The bandage they gave him at the hospital is rotting, falling off by itself in infected little bits. Juan Carlos

Livraga is the Leper of the Liberating Revolution.

We should not have anything to say in defense of the then-commissioner of Moreno, Gregorio de Paula. It's useless for a man to try to hide behind "orders from on high" when those orders include the slow murder of another unarmed and innocent man. But he must have been holding onto some shred of mercy when he arrived at the cell that night carrying a blanket at the tips of his fingers— until then, it had been used to cover the precinct dog—and let it fall over Livraga, saying:

—This isn't allowed, kid . . . There are orders from the top. But I'm bringing it to you as contraband.

Beneath this blanket, Juan Carlos Livraga felt strangely twinned with the animal it had previously sheltered. He was now, more than ever, the leprous dog of the Liberating Revolution.

∾

In his cell at San Martín's First Precinct, Giunta hears continuous laughter that seems to be coming from far away, rolling around the hallways, and suddenly exploding right next to him. It is he who is laughing. He, Miguel Ángel Giunta. He checks this by bringing his hand to his mouth and stifling the hysterical flow of laughter as it gushes all of a sudden from inside him.

He has had to repress it more than once this way, through reason, saying out loud:

—Hush. It's me. I need to keep it together . . .

But then the whirlwind pulls him in again. He talks to himself, laughs, cries, rambles and explains, and falls again into the well of terror where Rodríguez Moreno's silhouette is tall against the eucalyptus in the night, a gun shining coolly in his hand, and men are taking one, two, three paces back to aim their rifles. Then there's the unforgettable and perverse buzzing of the bullets, the band of fugitives, the plop! of a bullet penetrating the flesh and the shrill ahhh! of a man running full-speed who drops to the ground, just two steps behind him. Giunta jostles his head between his hands and mumbles:

—It's me, I'm okay, it's me . . .

But every murmur he hears in the hallways renews his agony. "They're coming to take me away," he thinks. "Now they're going to execute me again."

Sleep, at last, redeems him. It is bitterly cold, but somehow he manages to sleep on the wooden trundle bed without covers. At midnight he is woken by the cries of people being tortured, people being "given the machine."

No one, however, is focused on him. They don't even talk to him. Over the course of the eight days that he stays in the cell, they don't bring him even one plate of food or a glass of water. It's the ordinary prisoners, the ones going out for their regular walks, who save him from death by starvation. They throw pieces of stale bread and food scraps through the cell's peephole that the prisoner then scoops up eagerly from the floor. To ease his thirst, they think up an emergency procedure. They insert the spout of a kettle into the hole and the survivor feels for the falling stream of water with his mouth.

His family, meanwhile, has no news of him. The police play the fun game of blind man's bluff: from the District Police Department, they send them to the prison in Caseros, from Caseros to the penitentiary in Olmos, from Olmos to La Plata Police Headquarters, from La Plata to the precinct in Villa Ballester, from Villa Ballester to the San Martín District Police Department . . . a week of anxiety passes before they finally find out the truth: Miguel Ángel is at San Martín's First Precinct.

They go to see him, but are only allowed in the next day. They get there just in time—his wife, his elderly father, his cousin, his brother-in-law—to witness a pitiful scene. They have hardly had time to embrace him before he is taken away: they bring him out into the street, shackled and with an armed escort, and steer him toward the railway station. The pleas of his family—proper middle-class people for whom the mere idea of walking the streets handcuffed is worse than death—are of no use. There they go, this strange bunch, along the main roads of the city of San Martín at midday: the "frightening" prisoner, the armed thugs, and the crying family members who trail behind them. People gaze at this spectacle, astonished.

Thin, bearded, with a faraway look in his eyes, a ghost of himself, Miguel Ángel Giunta was taken to the penitentiary in Olmos on June 25. There, life would begin to change for him.

31. THE REST IS SILENCE . . .

The telegram addressed to Mr. Pedro Livraga, Florida, said:

> STATE OF HEALTH OF YOUR SON GOOD IN OLMOS LA PLATA.
> HE CAN BE VISITED ON FRIDAY 9 TO 11 OR BETWEEN 13 AND 17
> HRS. ONLY PARENTS, SONS OR SIBLINGS CARRYING THEIR AP-
> PROPRIATE IDENTITY PAPERS. COL. VICTOR ARRIBAU.

It was telegram number 110, and it had been sent from the Government House at 7:30 p.m. and received at 8:37 p.m. It was Monday, July 2, 1956.

Juan Carlos was still in Moreno. But it was clear already that his fate was being decided by the Pink House and not La Plata Police Headquarters. On Tuesday the third, they transferred him to Olmos. And his parents—who had assumed he was dead—anxiously counted down the days until Friday.

At last they saw him. They found it hard to recognize him: he had lost ten kilos, his face erased by bandages. That said, ever since his arrival at the penitentiary, he had been treated humanely and given appropriate medical attention. His health had actually improved considerably during these few days.

Giunta was also recovering from his anxious depression. At first, he'd been suffering a great deal from being grouped with the ordinary prisoners. That's when he decided to speak with the director of the penitentiary and recount his strange odyssey to him. The director—a kindhearted man who was later replaced—looked pensive.

—Many have come to me with that kind of story —he finally replied.— But they're not always true. If what you're saying is true, we'll see what can be done . . .

He ordered for him to be transferred to the political prisoner block. Giunta felt better there. The prisoners included communist and nationalist militants, union leaders, even a journalist, and with them at least he could talk, even if he wasn't interested in debates about politics or labor.

Afterward, Livraga arrived. Giunta didn't remember him. Juan Carlos, on the other hand, had held onto a crisp image of Livraga. The experience they shared brought them closer together. At first, Livraga had preferred to stay with the ordinary criminals: he still feared for his life and thought he had a greater chance of going unnoticed among them. Later his worries subsided and he asked to be moved to the other block.

Among the prisoners, one La Plata lawyer's name kept coming up: von Kotsch, Esq. They mentioned cases of prisoners who had been set free thanks to his intervention. Máximo von Kotsch, Esq., a thirty-two-year-old attorney actively affiliated with the *Radical Instransigente* Party, did indeed devote his well-known dynamism to the defense of detained union members.[15] Among them were the numerous oil workers tortured by the Province of Buenos Aires Police. Giunta and Livraga asked to speak with him, and von Kotsch, Esq., listened with awe to the story of what happened in the early morning hours of June 10 in the outskirts of José León Suárez. He agreed to defend the two survivors at once and, given the lack of a judicial process—they were at the disposal of the Executive Power—and of any real reasons that might justify their imprisonment, requested that they be set free.

On the night of August 16, 1956, the prisoners of the political block were getting ready for bed when they heard a guard's voice order:

—Quiet, people! —and then:— If I call your name, come out with all your things.

A shiver ran through the block. Some would be set free, others would stay. Everyone listened eagerly while those whose names were called gathered their things together in a frenzy.

—. . . Miguel Ángel Giunta . . . —the guard rattled off,— Juan Carlos Livraga . . .

They were the last two on the list. They looked at each other in disbelief. They embraced. Then the same thought occurred to them simultaneously. Maybe it was a ruse to kill them. But there, leaning against a column outside the prisoners' block, was von Kotsch, Esq., waiting for them. He was smiling. Giunta says he will never forget that moment.

That same night, the lawyer took them to La Plata's Police Headquarters to get their release papers approved. In Giunta's box for "Grounds," there was an expressive line of typed dashes.

There had been, in fact, no grounds for trying to execute him. No grounds for torturing him psychologically to the limits of what a person can endure. No grounds for condemning him to hunger and thirst. No grounds for shackling and handcuffing him. And now, there were no grounds—only by virtue of a simple decree, No. 14.975—for restoring him to the world.

∽

Giunta and Livraga owed their freedom and even their lives not only to the efforts of von Kotsch, Esq., but to a happy circumstance.

They were not, as they previously thought, the only surviving witnesses of "Operation Massacre." The Province of Buenos Aires Police had tried to catch the other fugitives and recover all the evidence, mainly the receipts issued by the San Martín District Police Department. If they had accomplished that, it is likely that everything—both people and things—would have disappeared in one final, silent act of carnage. But their attempt had failed and "Operation Massacre," even without Giunta and Livraga, was going to be widely publicized both here and abroad.

Gavino sought asylum in the Bolivian embassy before the last echoes of the executions had stopped ringing out. He was carrying the receipt with him when he left for that country.

Julio Troxler and Reinaldo Benavídez could not be arrested either. In mid-October, they took refuge in the same embassy, and on November 3, an airplane took them to La Paz. On October 17, a tall and dark-skinned man walked calmly to the entrance of the embassy at 500 Corrientes Street. Two policemen dressed as civilians hurtled themselves onto him and even got a hand on him. But they were too late: Juan Carlos Torres, the tenant of the apartment in back, had just escaped Fernández Suárez's clutches and was now on foreign ground. In June 1957 he, too, left for Bolivia.

Mr. Horacio di Chiano was in hiding for four months before returning timidly to his house in Florida. The terrifying experience had left him deeply scarred. They had wanted to kill him at close range. For countless seconds, beneath the headlights of the police van, he had waited for the coup de grâce that never came. He had not committed a crime, but he was on the run. He had lost his job after seventeen years of service and now he was squandering his savings to support his family. He will never understand anything about what happened.

Livraga and Giunta went back to work. Livraga helped his father laying bricks; Giunta returned to his old job.

Sergeant Díaz was not completely spared the fury that was

unleashed that night in June. He was held prisoner for many months in Olmos.

In the cemeteries of Boulogne, San Martín, Olivos, and Chacarita, modest crosses serve as reminders of the fallen: Nicolás Carranza, Francisco Garibotti, Vicente Rodríguez, Carlos Lizaso, Mario Brión.

In Montevideo, soon after hearing the news, Mr. Pedro Lizaso, Carlitos's father, passed away. In his final days he was heard repeating, over and over again:

—It's my fault . . . It's my fault . . .

At the end of 1956, Vicente Damián Rodríguez would have fathered his fourth child. His wife, hopeless and consumed by misery, resigned herself to his loss.

The massacre left sixteen children without fathers: Carranza's six, Garibotti's six, Rodríguez's three, and Brión's one. These little children who, for the most part, were doomed to a life of poverty and resentment, will know one day—they already know—that the "liberating" and "democratic" Argentina of June 1956 was on a par with Nazi hell.

That is where the ledger stands.

In my view, though, what best symbolizes the irresponsibility, the blindness, and the disgrace of "Operation Massacre" is a little piece of paper. A rectangle of official paper, twenty-five centimeters long by fifteen centimeters wide. It is dated several months after June 9, 1956, and, after being run by all the local province police stations—including that of the Province of Buenos Aires—it is issued in the name of Miguel Ángel Giunta, the surviving executed man. His name and ID number appear over the background of a white and light-blue-colored shield. Above, it reads: Argentine Republic – Ministry of Interior – Federal Police. And then, in larger letters, four words: "*Certificate of Good Conduct.*"

Part Three
THE EVIDENCE

Next page: The line of eucalyptus trees that Giunia could see from the site of the execution.

32. THE GHOSTS

Rodríguez Moreno was an exhausted and bewildered man when, at six o'clock in the morning on June 10, he informed La Plata Police Headquarters by radio that the order for execution had been carried out. Would he mention that more than half the prisoners had escaped? He opted to keep quiet.

At Headquarters, no one was sleeping. They asked for a list of the executed men. And now Rodríguez Moreno really had no choice but to send the list of the five dead.

—And the others? —bellowed Fernández Suárez.

—They escaped.

We will never know exactly what happened in the Chief of Police's office when the distressed Chief Inspector came in to deliver his report. In a statement before the judge seven months later, Rodríguez Moreno will say that he "was treated severely" by Fernández Suárez.

The Chief of Police's problem is easy to explain, but difficult to solve. He has arrested a dozen men before martial law was instated. He has executed them without trial. And now it turns out that seven of these men are alive.

Judging by what he does next, it is clear that he understands his situation. The first thing he does is scatter the killers and the witnesses. He sends Rodríguez Moreno and Cuello to the Mar del Plata District Police Department, and later he will send Commissioner De Paula (who saw Livraga in Moreno) to the precinct in Bernal.

On June 12, the papers publish a list—provided by the national government—of five "men executed in the region of San Martín," with the mistakes that I already noted. The report does not say who arrested them, who ordered for them to be killed and why; it does not so much as allude to the escape of the other seven. An interesting precaution.

But Fernández Suárez feels compelled to talk. There are some who ask why he was not at Headquarters when the attack began, why he left the building undefended, why he only came back when the situation was resolved. Some will suggest that the Chief of Police was hedging his bets that night and that the executions he later ordered were his alibi. He brings in the press and, according to the June 11 and 12 La Plata newspapers, explains to them:

"It was only by fortunate coincidence that I happened to be outside the Department during the uprising. During the emergency, I had traveled to the town of Moreno, where the accidental explosion of a bomb led us to discover a house belonging to the engineer Sarrabayrouse, who was affiliated with the Peronist party. We confiscated thirty-one high-powered time bombs from his arsenal. I was in the middle of this operation on Saturday when I was informed that a secret meeting that included General Tanco had taken place in a house in Vicente López.

"The operation led to the arrest of fourteen individuals, but the aforementioned member of the military was not apprehended. *At 11:00 p.m., when I was in that house*, I found out about the revolt at the Mechanics School and in Santa Rosa."

Not a word about the final destination of these individuals. Who would connect the dots between a group of "men executed in the region of San Martín" and an apartment in Vicente López?

And yet, Fernández Suárez has already given himself away. Because the crucial thing that he says here before anyone has even accused him of anything is that he arrested these individuals at 11:00 p.m. *An hour and a half before martial law was instated.*

It looks like Fernández Suárez will be able to sleep soundly. For nearly four months, no one asks him for any explanations.

But when the bomb explodes, it's not two thousand kilometers away, it's not across a border that has already been opened and closed for three survivors.

It's in the Chief of Police's very office.

At the start of October 1956, Naval Information Services inform him, confidentially, that one of his own men has denounced him.

Fernández Suárez does not need to walk ten paces to find the culprit. It is Jorge Doglia, Esq., head of the Police Judicial Division.

—The only case during my tenure —F. S. will later say, deeply dejected— of a man from the street becoming a chief inspector.

This is true. For the police, Doglia is a "man from the street," just like Fernández Suárez, who appointed him. A man genuinely committed to civil rights and liberties (thirty-one years of age, a *Radical Intransigente* at the time), Doglia the lawyer has taken that fleeting slogan from '55 seriously: "The Rule of Law." But right after he assumes his post, he learns that the prisoners giving him their statements complain of torture and bear traces of their punishment. He brings the problem to Fernández Suárez, who first pretends to be shocked and later mocks him openly.

The he goes to the second-in-command, Captain Ambroggio, and shows him photos of the prisoners who, by the look of it, have been whipped with wires. The second-in-command looks at the photos with a critical eye.

—That's not wire —he explains.— That's rubber.

Now Doglia knows what to expect. The problem is systemic, so the only thing he can do is document it. In August or September he meets Livraga. Then he goes to Naval Information Services and all his cards are revealed.

There is a heated exchange between Doglia and the Chief of Police. Fernández Suárez openly threatens him. On the tenth of October, Doglia presents his indictment again, this time before the Governance Ministry of the Province.

Doglia's indictment has two parts to it: the first refers to the system of torture; the second, to the illegal execution of Livraga. On this point, Doglia cannot know more than what Livraga himself tells him, which is that they wanted to execute him and a bunch of other people, the majority of whom he did not know by name, and that he and Giunta escaped.

Fernández Suárez strikes back by accusing Doglia of "having gone to an organization outside the department to report acts committed in the heart of the police department." He fabricates a shameful allegation with the support of the Governance Ministry and the Attorney General, Dr. Alconada Aramburú. On January 18, 1957, Doglia's name will appear in the papers, flanked on one side by the name of a policeman who was a drunk, and on the other by the name of a policeman who had committed acts of torture. All three of them were removed from their offices "for ethical reasons."

But Doglia spoke to Eduardo Schaposnik, the socialist representative for the Advisory Board, and at the beginning of December, in a secret session, the charges are made again, this time from Schaposnik's lips.

On December 14, it is Livraga himself who appears in court to sue "whoever was responsible" for attempted homicide and damages.

Fernández Suárez starts seeing ghosts. On December 18, in a fit of courage, he appears in front of the Advisory Board to rebut Schaposnik.

33. FERNÁNDEZ SUÁREZ CONFESSES

—*There are charges here* —exclaimed Lieutenant Colonel Fernández Suárez— *but no proof!*

It was eleven o'clock on the morning of December 18, 1956. The Governance Minister and the six members of the Province Advisory Board had come together in a secret session; they were listening to the Chief of Police's response to Schaposnik's accusations:

—A number of circumstances are being referred to here —proceeded Fernández Suárez with passion in his voice,— but there's no talk of who is creating them, when they took place, what evidence might exist . . . *There needs to be proof, because if there isn't, the Chief of Police should be singled out as well!*

What happens next is very strange. Up until this moment, there is actually no proof of the secret execution. There is only Livraga's formal accusation against "whoever was responsible" and Fernández Suárez's statements, which have been buried in the June 1956 newspapers, and which no one has thought to look for. But now it is the Chief of Police himself who, compelled by a dark, self-incriminating fate, confirms and expands upon those statements.

So it is he who provides the necessary proof.

At this time I would like to ask the reader to disbelieve all the claims I have made, to distrust the sound of the words, the possible language games that any journalist turns to when he wants to prove something, and to believe only the parts of my story that match what Fernández Suárez has said.

Begin by doubting the very existence of those men whom, according to my account, the Chief of Police in Florida arrested on the night of June 9, 1956. Now listen to Fernández Suárez before the Advisory Board on December 18, 1956, as per the stenographic transcription:

> WITH RESPECT TO MISTER LIVRAGA, I WANT TO MAKE KNOWN THAT ON THE NIGHT OF JUNE 9 I RECEIVED THE ORDER TO RAID A HOUSE IN PERSON . . . ON THAT PROPERTY I FOUND FOURTEEN PEOPLE . . . AMONG THEM WAS THIS MAN.

So those people existed, and among them was Livraga. But I have claimed that he arrested those men *before* martial law was put into effect. And to determine the time at which it was instated, I have not limited myself to consulting the newspapers of June 10,

1956, which unanimously report that it was announced at 12:30 a.m. of that day. I have gone beyond that by locating the State Radio registry book of announcers and photocopying it to prove, to the minute, that martial law was made public at 12:32 a.m. on June 10.

And when I maintain that the Chief of Police arrested those men an hour and a half prior, and technically a day early, that is to say at 11:00 p.m. on June 9, the reader should not take my word for it, but rather that of the Chief of Police before the Advisory Board:

AT 11:00 P.M. I RAIDED THE PROPERTY IN PERSON . . .

And when I say that those men did not participate in the rebellion of June 9, 1956, the reader should doubt me more than ever. But believe Fernández Suárez when he states:

. . . THESE PEOPLE . . . WERE ABOUT TO PARTICIPATE IN THESE ACTS . . .

Were about to. That is to say, had not participated.

I have said, moreover, that those men did not put up any resistance. And Fernández Suárez says:

. . . THEY DID NOT HAVE TIME TO RESIST . . .

Whether it was because they did not have the time or because they did not think to do it, what we know is that they did not resist.

I don't want to be accused of Jesuitically extracting the segment of Fernández Suárez's report that refers to Livraga's case and of making him say something he didn't say. I am going to reproduce it here unabridged because what it constitutes—rather than a defense—is the very proof that he was demanding.

With respect to this Mister Livraga, I would like to make

known that on the night of June 9 I received the order to raid a house in person where General Tanco was meeting with the leaders of the group that were going to attack the Mechanics School. At 11:00 p.m. I raided that property in person. I was half an hour late; if I had done it a bit earlier, I would have arrested General Tanco. I found fourteen people on that property who did not have time to resist— they were armed with Colt pistols—because we came in through the doors and the windows. Among them was that man. When I found out about what was happening in La Plata, I went to Headquarters and placed these men in the commissioner's custody. At dawn, the Executive Power ordered the execution of these people who were about to participate in these acts or who had adopted some kind of revolutionary attitude.

The reader will observe that, in addition to the points of convergence between the two versions, the first discrepancies begin to emerge. From a legal perspective, these discrepancies are unimportant. Yet it is worth noting that the Chief of Police of the Province has not yet found, nor will he find, witnesses who saw ex-General Tanco inside that house. He also has not shown, nor will he be able to show, that those men were armed with Colt pistols. Because here, indeed—to recall his apt phrase—there are charges, but no proof.

This man —Fernández Suárez went on— fled the police. Subsequently, the father sent a telegram to the President of the Republic saying that his son had been admitted to a hospital, seriously injured by the police. If the police had wanted to kill him, they would not have left him wounded, seeing how there was already an order out for his execution. Thus, he escaped. Afterward, during that confusing night, his actions and whereabouts remain unknown. He can say that the police injured him, but it's strange that, given the existence of an order for execution, they didn't execute him.

Fernández Suárez's version of the particular case of Livraga is simply childish. He tries to make them believe that Livraga wasn't a part of the execution. But rising up in opposition to the solitary word of Fernández Suárez is not only the overwhelming circumstantial evidence—which includes Livraga's scars, the receipt issued in his name by the same San Martín District Police Department that is included in this legal file, and the statements of the doctors and nurses who aided him at the San Martín polyclinic on the morning of June 10—but also the testimony of the other survivors.

Most importantly, what remains DEFINITIVELY PROVEN based on Fernández Suárez's own confession is:

1. That on June 9, 1956, he arrested a group of men in person, one of whom was Livraga.
2. That the arrest of these men occurred at 11:00 p.m. on June 9, namely an hour and a half before martial law was instated.
3. That these men had not participated in the rebellion.
4. That these men did not put up any kind of resistance to the arrest.
5. That these men were executed at dawn, "by order of the Executive Power," according to Fernández Suárez.

34. THE LIVRAGA FILE

The events that I recount in this book were systematically denied or distorted by the government of the Liberating Revolution.

The first official version of the story appears in the form of a telegram addressed to Livraga's father on June 12, 1956, from the head of the Presidential Military House, Captain Manrique. It states that Juan Carlos was "wounded during a shooting."

We have already seen what that shooting was like.

Fernández Suárez falsely claimed that Livraga had not even been wounded, let alone executed.

In the indictment that was fabricated against Doglia, Esq., the Governance Ministry of the Province claimed that Livraga fled "moments before his execution" and added with true candor that "it was unclear whether shots of any kind had been fired at him."

The same indictment then admits that Livraga "exhibited injuries," but considers them to be "evidence of his active participation in the revolutionary movement."

It was a charming way of flipping the evidence on its head: Livraga's injuries proved not that he had been executed, but that he was a revolutionary . . .

There were other sophisms, denials, and communiqués. I tore them apart one by one in my articles. Examining them at this point is unnecessary.

The evidence I collected over the course of many months of investigation allowed me to accuse Fernández Suárez of murder, which I did to the point of monotony without his ever deigning to sue me.

Still, there was something missing from this evidence: the document based on Livraga's formal accusation that was prepared by Judge Belisario Hueyo in La Plata.

I knew the basic contents of this document, but I only held a photocopy of it in my hands when the first edition of this book had already been published (1957).

I was then able to compare the two investigations, the judge's and mine. The two are practically identical and round each other out. In some ways, mine was more detailed: it included signed statements from the survivors. Judge Hueyo could not take statements from Troxler, Benavídez, and Gavino because they were in Bolivia. I had records of interviews with Horacio di Chiano, Torres, "Marcelo," and dozens of minor witnesses who did not go through an official intake of any kind. And I had a photostatic copy of the State Radio registry book of announcers, which established the time at which martial law was instated.

In other ways, the Livraga file goes beyond what I could have imagined. In addition to being the official account of the case, it contains confessions from the executioners themselves.

It is therefore this file that, as of the second edition of this book (1964), I call upon as evidence.

My personal experience with judges, as a journalist, has not been encouraging. I could name a dozen whom I know to be factious, inept, or simply corrupt. I choose instead to offer, as a model of determination, speed, and efficiency, the actions of Judge Hueyo throughout this case.

The way he carried out his investigation was truly exemplary. He does the justice system of this country an honor.

The Livraga file begins on December 14, 1956, with the report he gave to Judge Viglione who, for reasons of jurisdictional competence, remits it to Judge Hueyo five days later.

It is a detailed account of his arrest, transfer to the San Martín District Police Department, failed execution, brief stay at the San Martín polyclinic, imprisonment in Moreno, and recovery in Olmos. It includes a piece of physical evidence: a small square of paper dated June 10, 1956 at the San Martín District Police Department, with signatures from three officers confirming that "a White Star watch, a key ring, ten pesos and a handkerchief" were confiscated from Livraga that night.

There are three mistakes in the report that would make the judge's investigation (and my own) more difficult. It says there were five men arrested in the back apartment of the house in Florida when there were at least eight. It says there were ten of them taken out in the assault car to be executed when there were at least twelve.

It claims there were two survivors (he and Giunta) when in reality there were seven. Of all of them, he only knew Vicente Rodríguez, who was dead. And as for the executioners, he only knows that they were policemen from the Province.

The places and events, on the other hand, are described with photographic precision.

On December 24, Judge Hueyo issues the first orders: to ask the head of the Presidential Military House, by way of an subpoena, to identify "which reports were used to draft the telegram" where it is stated that Livraga was injured during a shooting; to send an official letter to the Chief of Police requesting that he report whether Livraga was detained in mid-June at the San Martín District Police Department and at Moreno, then at Olmos, and to identify "the judge who was in charge of his case"; to solicit the same reports from the head of the San Martín District Police Department, the commissioner in Moreno, and the director of the penitentiary in Olmos; and finally, to ask the San Martín polyclinic if Livraga received treatment there (page 26).

The head of the Presidential Military House, Captain Manrique, was a busy man: he never responded. Fernández Suárez will only respond one month later, when the complicity of the central government has already been ascertained.

The San Martín District Police Department, on the other hand, replies immediately: "On the requested date I report no record exists detention Juan Carlos Livraga." The telegram (p. 27) is signed by O. de Bellis, who has replaced Rodríguez Moreno as chief of the department.

The new commissioner of Moreno, in turn, responds with a cryptic dispatch: "Regarding report 3702 made by Juan Carlos Livraga I inform you Your Honor these premises no record books exist marking detention of aforementioned." Signed F. Ferrairone.

The judge's reply:

As the police commissioner of Moreno has failed to report on whether prisoner Juan Carlos Livraga stayed or did not stay in that precinct, I am issuing a new letter to ask as a matter of urgency that you report specifically on whether the aforementioned Juan Carlos Livraga was detained on the premises in the middle of last June, if affirmative, then dates of intake and release and the name of the judge who was in charge of his case.

The Moreno precinct insists on its ignorance: "Regarding detention Juan Carlos Livraga I inform Your Honor these premises no record books exist his detention. Ferrairone."

Was the allegedly executed man's story then false? Doubt begins to dissipate on page 29 when Doctor Marcelo Méndez Casariego, from the San Martín polyclinic, responds with a note:

In reference to your telegram dated the 24th of this month requesting records of Mr. Juan Carlos Livraga, this administration communicates to Your Honor that the aforementioned man was brought to the emergency room on June 10 of this year, at 7:45 a.m., under the custody of the San Martín District Police Department of the Province of Buenos Aires, who took him away at 9:00 p.m. on the same day.

But De Bellis and Ferrairone weren't lying either. The arrest of Livraga and the others did not appear in the San Martín and Moreno books for the simple reason that the formality of recording their intake was not carried out. Without a record, an arrest becomes a simple abduction. So the entire operation bore the indelible stamp of secrecy.

On behalf of Aramburu and in response to one of the desperate letters that Livraga's father sent when he didn't know the whereabouts of his son, the general secretary of the presidency, Colonel Víctor Arribau, had informed him by telegram on June 29, 1956 that: "The investigation is being taken up with urgency." Now Judge Hueyo, on page 32, orders that a subpoena be issued to Colonel Arribau to report on "the result of the investigation that he refers to in the telegram that appears on page 8 and, if possible, to remit a summary so that the Court may see it."

The reply, of course, never came. But in the meantime, the press campaign that I had just set in motion produced its first results. Livraga's accusation had landed in my hands on December 20. I submitted it to Leónidas Barletta, who published it in *Propósitos* on the twenty-third. The governing authority of the Province, newly appointed by the Liberating Revolution, and the Chief of Police considered themselves obligated to issue an explosive press release that was published in the papers on the twenty-seventh and the twenty-eighth. Judge Hueyo would not let the opportunity pass him by. On page 33 he stipulates: "In response to the declaration made by the Chief of Police, as it appears in the December 28 edition of the newspaper *El Plata*, wherein he claims that the man himself (Juan Carlos Livraga) was arrested in San Martín for his participation in the subversive acts of June 9 and that it was proven that he was part of the group of people who were receiving orders from ex-General Tanco, and who were subjected to martial law regulations; the Chief of Police is requested to make known which judge oversaw the investigation in question."

Fernández Suárez did not reply. There had been no other judge than him.

On page 35, for the first time, the police of the Province respond to a request made by the court. The Documents Division releases Livraga's file, which states that he was arrested on June 9, 1956, *one day before martial law was instated.*

Meanwhile, Colonel Aniceto Casco, the general manager of penal institutions, provides new confirmation of Livraga's story by reporting that "he entered Unit 1 (the penitentiary in Olmos) on July 3, 1956."

On January 8, 1957, Commissioner Ovidio R. de Bellis appears before the court. As successor to Rodríguez Moreno for the San Martín District Police Department, he states that he knows nothing about what happened because he was not there on that date, and reasserts that Livraga's arrest is not listed in the Department's books.

The judge shows him the receipt. De Bellis claims that the form "is not the one usually used as a receipt for prisoners' personal items" and that "he cannot explain who the undersigned autographs belong to." When questioned about the executions, he replies: "the person who was chief of the District Police Department at the time, Mister Rodríguez Moreno, will be in a better position to report to the court on the matter."

Upon leaving the judge's office, de Bellis comes across someone who is in the best possible position to confirm or deny Livraga's formal accusation. It is Miguel Ángel Giunta, the second survivor, who finally decides to talk.

Giunta's story is even more precise than Livraga's. He explains both the circumstances that led him to Horacio di Chiano's apartment, as well as the raid, which he says took place at 11:15 p.m. or 11:30 p.m. on June 9. Without naming him, he describes Fernández Suárez: "a large man, that is to say strong, with a mustache and a good amount of hair, who was wearing sand-colored pants and a short, olive green, military jacket; this person was carrying a .45 caliber pistol in his hand and, having told everyone to put their hands up, placed the barrel of the gun on the declarant's throat, saying to him again: 'Put your hands up, don't be smart with me.'" First there are blows to his stomach and to his hip, then there's the transfer to the Department, where the officer who interrogates him is "under thirty years old, chubby, curly-haired, with a handlebar mustache." The one overseeing the interrogations is the second-in-command, last name Cuello, "a person of short stature who walks with a stoop and with his hands behind his back." Giunta also identifies Rodrí- guez Moreno, and among the prisoners he naturally remembers Mr. Horacio, Vicente Rodríguez, Livraga, and "a person with the last name Brión or Drión." He recounts the story of the trip all the way to the garbage dump, getting off the truck in the night, the preparations for execution:

> . . . they walked like that for twenty or thirty meters and then the guards stayed back and ordered them to keep on in the same direction . . . that was when everyone knew for sure that they would be killed . . . once the truck's headlights were shining on them . . . they realized what was happening and everyone panicked, some getting on their knees and begging for mercy not to be killed . . .

He gives an account of his getaway amidst the bullets, of the way he saved himself, and of how they arrested him again. Then he describes in detail the places he had been: the precinct in Munro, the District Police Department and San Martín's First Precinct, the cell where they locked him up, even the dog that they were training in the prison block.

On page 42, Navy Lieutenant Jorge R. Dillon who, until very recently had run the policemen's health and welfare program, shows up voluntarily to make a statement. Here is his account:

> That at daybreak on June 10, at approximately 0045 hours, the declarant was in his home, which is located opposite the police department; that upon hearing the shooting which sparked the assault on said department, the declarant, armed, entered the Department and, from there, aided in its defense . . .; that thus he was present during the assault he has made reference to and partici-

pated in its suppression; that when the movement had already been stifled with respect to the attack on Headquarters, some time after four o'clock in the morning, the Chief of Police arrived together with the Vucetich Academy cadets and other personnel; that those who had been defending the building came down the stairs where they were met with those who had recently arrived; that they shared impressions and accounts of the events that had transpired . . . and that in that instance the declarant heard Chief of Police Lieutenant Colonel Desiderio Fernández Suárez say, addressing either Mr. Gesteira or another officer, the declarant does not recall which, the following words verbatim: "Send the order to the San Martín District Police Department to execute the group of individuals that I arrested immediately"; the order was sent via radio.

Lieutenant Dillon then adds:

Hours later, at the main office of Headquarters, the declarant heard someone say that the order had been carried out, but that it had been done inadequately because a group of prisoners had been taken out to an open field where some had managed to escape, and the police had felt obligated to shoot at them as they ran away, having failed to make them stand in line in front of the firing squad, as is protocol; according to the same source, that's how it had all turned into a "bloodbath" and, upon gaining knowledge of said event, the Chief of Police expressed indignation regarding the incompetence displayed and, a few days later, the then-chief of the department, Rodríguez Moreno, was suspended.

Pursuant to this statement, the judge considered it an opportune moment to communicate to Fernández Suárez "the reason why the present case is being tried in this court, asking at the same time for you to please make known by way of a written report as much information as you deem appropriate."

Fernández Suárez, who had proffered thirty thousand words in his defense before the Advisory Board, now cannot muster one sentence in response.

The judge: "As no response has been received from the Chief of Police, let the official letter sent on p. 26 be reissued."

Silence.

On page 51, the aforementioned new commissioner of Moreno, Francisco Ferrairone, appears before the court on January 11, 1957. He confirms that Livraga's arrest does not appear in his precinct's books, but that "given the requests that were sent and resent from the Court, as well as similar requests for a response that came in from Police Headquarters, he asked among the department's staff to find out whether the books were a faithful reflection of the truth, and was able to ascertain that this was not the case. He was told that one Juan Carlos Livraga had indeed been detained in that station, or at least had stayed there, and neither his intake nor his release had been recorded in the books . . ."

The police front begins to crumble. "The witness received this unofficial information," Commissioner Ferrairone cautiously clarifies, "after submitting his answers in response to the request for information issued by the Court; had it been any other way he would have reported the information not in the way that he did, but otherwise."

—Who was in Moreno in the month of June? —asks Judge Hueyo.

—Commissioner Gregorio de Paula —Ferrairone says.

On page 53, Principal Officer Boris Vucetich of the Moreno precinct gives a statement. The judge asks him if he saw Livraga there:

—Yes —the officer says.— He had two gunshot wounds, one with an entry wound beneath his jaw and an exit wound in his cheek, and the other in his arm.

The story that Livraga told Vucetich is the same one he will tell months later: "[T]hat he was at his friend's house listening to the Lausse match when they were caught off-guard by the police, dressed in civilian clothes, and taken to the San Martín District Police Department, that after being interrogated, he and other arrested individuals were loaded onto a vehicle and relocated to a place he cannot identify, that they made them get off there, ordered them to walk, he felt a few shots, threw himself to the ground, and then lost consciousness . . ."

Regarding other details, Vucetich seems to differ from Livraga. He says that the police medic Doctor Carlos Chiesa tended to him daily. It is a rare doctor, you have to admit, who lets a man with a serious gunshot wound recover in a prison cell.

Next in line to give his statement is Deputy Inspector Antonio Barbieri of the Moreno precinct. His testimony is a repeat of the last. The basic idea is that Livraga was very well attended in Moreno, that he was given a special diet and so many blankets to cover himself with that he couldn't move. The surviving executed man kept insisting that they had him in the cell half-naked and that his bandage was falling off in pieces . . .

Commissioner Gregorio de Paula, on page 55 and following, admits that Livraga was held prisoner in Moreno, that he arrived wounded, and that his intake was not recorded in the books.

—Is that normal? —asks the judge.

The commissioner acknowledges that it is not normal, but that in "this exceptional case," he understood that his intake had already been recorded at the San Martín District Police Department.

Was Livraga well cared for? Splendidly, says the commissioner. They even gave him "food that didn't need to be chewed."

Did Livraga experience any cold? No, says the commissioner, "in his memory he sees him wrapped in something warm, but he cannot say exactly what kind of garment it was."

—Did you take his statement?

—No.

—Did you tell him the charges?

—No.

—Did anyone come to visit him?

—No.

January 17. A sullen and dejected man comes to give his statement. He is forty-eight years old, a chief inspector by the name of Rodolfo Rodríguez Moreno. His testimony practically brings the case to a close. Here it is:

Asked by Your Honor whether he was head of the San Martín District Police Department last June, he responds: that indeed, he was appointed to that position in February of 1956 and held it until approximately June 15 of that same year. Asked by Your Honor whether, under his command as Head of the District Police Department, an operation took place in which police officers arrested Juan Carlos Livraga, Miguel Ángel Giunta, and other individuals, the declarant responds: that he himself did not carry out that operation but remembers a radio communication that came in from Police Headquarters calling for a group of twenty men to be gathered at the Florida precinct and put under the command of the Buenos Aires Province Police Chief himself. The commissioner of the Florida police station, last name Pena, had received word that this group would be under the command of the aforementioned Police Chief and other military officers, among them a captain with the last name San Emeterio and a major. Asked by Your Honor whether the individuals arrested during this operation were held in the San Martín District Police Department, the declarant responds: that indeed at 2400 hours or perhaps a bit later, on June 9, approximately twelve people were transferred on a bus to the San Martín District Police Department, and that then two or three more arrived who had been arrested on the street where the operation took place. Asked by Your Honor whether he remembers the names of those individuals, he responds that he cannot say exactly because he did not make a mental note of them, and to another question he responds: that indeed among them were Livraga, Giunta, and a person with a foreign last name who later on was staying at an embassy—the declarant thinks the last name sounded something like Carnevali. Asked by Your Honor whether the intake of these prisoners was recorded in the department's books, the declarant responds that the police officers on duty may have done it, that the prisoners actually found themselves in a special situation because, according to the Florida precinct, they were all being held incommunicado, by order of the Chief of Police. Asked whether they were questioned by the declarant, he states that he did not do so, that he does not believe a formal statement was taken from them, but that he ordered the second-in-command of the department, Commissioner-Inspector Benedicto Cuello, to question them about the events because, according to information that the declarant had been provided, said individuals had allegedly been arrested for taking part in a meeting connected to the subversive acts that transpired that night. Asked by Your Honor if the declarant received an order to execute all of the prisoners, the declarant states: that of his own accord, he ordered the release of the three people who were brought in later, having been arrested in the street, as there were no grounds for their arrest. He recalled that one was a local driver whom the Boulogne precinct knows well, another was a fifty-six-year-old Italian night watchman who worked in a factory near the site of the operation, and the third he cannot recall. As for the rest, he did indeed receive the strict order by radio, dispatched by the Chief of Police himself, to proceed immediately with the execution of all the individuals who had been arrested; this order as stated was sent directly by radio transmission from the Chief of Police himself to the declarant himself. Asked by Your Honor if he also received instructions as to where the execution was to take place, he responds: that he did not receive exact orders to that effect, only to look for an appropriate open field to do it. Asked by Your Honor what time he received the order, he states that it was approximately 4:30 in the morning. Asked by Your Honor if the declarant was personally leading the operation with which he had been charged, he states: that indeed the police officers in charge of the execution were under his direct and immediate command. Asked by Your Honor how it was carried out, he states: that the prisoners were loaded onto an assault car, each one matched with a guard, and that following behind them in a van were the declarant, the second-in-command, and an officer whose last name he thinks is Cáceres. That they moved to a wasteland that was twenty blocks from Route 8, on the road that links said route to the town of Boulogne, and stopped the vehicles there. The declarant got off to look for an appropriate place, which he had trouble doing due to the lack of light, and noticing a cluster of eucalyptus trees there, he decided that the place would be efficacious for the desired action, and at that point told four or five officers to form a firing squad. With the police force thus diminished and the individuals in question suspecting the reason they had been taken to the site, all of them started to run except for the five who stayed in the vehicle. Asked by Your Honor whether Livraga and Giunta were among these five, the declarant states that it is not possible because, had they been, they would have been thoroughly executed and the declarant is certain that only five corpses were left on site. He goes on to say that after the escape he has already mentioned, he made the five individuals in question get out and submitted them in pairs to execution*, leaving their bodies on site. Subsequently, the declarant requested instructions regarding what destination to assign these bodies, was told to deliver them to the nearest Polyclinic, and since the closest one was in San Martín, the five bodies of the individuals in question were sent to that location. The declarant had been given the final deadline of six o'clock that morning to execute the order, and approximately at that hour the declarant communicated to headquarters by radio that the order for execution had been carried out, without specifying whether all of them had been executed, or only five, as was the case. The declarant adds that the task with which he had been charged was horribly unpleasant, and went far beyond the stipulated duties of the police, but since the declarant understands that in an emergency the police stops taking its orders from headquarters and takes its orders directly from the Army, he was entirely certain that, were he to disobey such an order, the declarant himself would be the one executed. Asked by Your Honor at what time he reported to headquarters the incomplete way in which the order had been carried out, the declarant says that at approximately six o'clock in the morning, when he communicated that the order had been carried out, he does not know who

---

*   On this point, Rodríguez Moreno's version differs from the one that I provide in the text, which is based on the testimony of six of the seven survivors.

received his communication because he was informed that the chief had already left. Subsequently he was instructed to send the list of executed men and in response he sent the names of the five individuals who had been killed; as a result, he was called to headquarters to explain and the declarant faithfully recounted how the events had occurred and assumed personal responsibility for the escape of the other seven prisoners, as he did not think it fitting to delegate that responsibility to the officers who were serving as guards for the prisoners. He was therefore treated severely by the Chief of Police, who took this opportunity to call for his immediate replacement, which resulted in his being suspended from work for more than twenty days. The version that appears in Livraga's formal accusation and Giunta's statement is promptly explained in general terms to the declarant, who states that what he has declared in this hearing is the absolute truth, that it is not possible for Livraga to have been wounded in this instance because the gun used on him was a Mauser and its bullet would have completely destroyed Livraga's jaw;* moreover, he repeats again, there were five individuals who stayed and did not escape, and the declarant can categorically affirm that there were five bodies sent to the San Martín polyclinic. Asked by Your Honor whether the executed men received a coup de grâce, the declarant states that out of a sense of humanity and according to protocol, he gave the order for it to be done; it was carried out using

---

* R. Moreno is mistaken. The bullet did in fact destroy Livraga's jaw, but more than that, Julio Troxler saw him walking wounded, eight blocks away from the garbage dump, at the José León Suárez rail crossing. He saw a police officer pick him up there. Di Chiano and Benavídez saw him get off at the site of the execution. Troxler even remembers exactly where he was sitting in the assault car and also saw him get off. It's not plausible that Livraga, having saved himself, would have run off somewhere to shoot himself, as R. Moreno seems to suggest, and as F. Suárez has alleged.

a .45 caliber pistol, which is currently the only weapon that the police have in their possession. Asked by Your Honor at what time the removal of the bodies took place, the declarant responds that, on his way back from the execution—he believes this was at approximately six o'clock in the morning—he contacted headquarters by radio and relayed that the order had been carried out. He requested instructions regarding the destination of the bodies and an individual from the headquarters office informed him that the chief's order was to take them to the nearest polyclinic so the declarant gave the order right away to return to the site with the assault car, load up the bodies, and deliver them to the San Martín polyclinic, which was the closest. Asked by Your Honor whether after the previously mentioned episode, he had given the order for Juan Carlos Livraga to be arrested again, he responds: that indeed this is what happened, that he was told that the man in question was at the San Martín polyclinic and, when he went to this establishment in search of him, was informed that the man was allowed to travel in his condition. The declarant ordered for him to be held at the Moreno precinct because the District Police Department does not hold prisoners in custody and there was no room available at the other San Martín precincts. Asked by Your Honor how he explains the absence of any record of the two arrests in the San Martín District Police Department books, the declarant states: that he has no explanation to give because normally every prisoner's intake is properly recorded in the books. Asked by Your Honor if he received an express order in this case not to follow regulations in this respect, the declarant states: that at no point was he given the order or instructions not to record the intake of the individuals in question as prisoners. Asked by Your Honor whether he was at all involved in the second arrest that Giunta claims he was subjected to and in transferring him to the San Martín District Police Department the following Monday, the declarant states: that he does not remember Giunta being arrested for a second time at the District Police Department, but this does not mean he would rule out the possibility. The declarant is then shown a photocopy* that appears on page 1 and asked to state whether it is authentic. He replies that, since the Department does not usually keep prisoners in custody, it lacks the forms that are generally given to detained individuals as a receipt for their personal items, and it is possible that he is being shown a photocopy of the form that is used for these purposes. As for the undersigning signatures, he does not recognize them, but believes that the one at the bottom belongs to an officer with the last name Albarello. With no further questions to ask, the hearing is considered concluded. Having read the present document and verified its contents, the declarant signed in consent after Your Honor and before me, in witness thereof.

Signed Hueyo, Rodríguez Moreno, secretary Paladino, page 58 and following in criminal case number 3702 tried before the Eighth Criminal Court of First Instance in the city of La Plata.

This, then, is the document that the Liberating Revolution needs to answer to, and never will.

It proves everything that I claimed in my articles for *Mayoría* and in the first edition of this book: that a group of men were arrested before martial law was instated; that they were not given due process; that their identities were not verified; that they were not told what their crime was; and that they were massacred in an open field.

---

* The receipt they gave to Livraga.

Judge Hueyo dives right into this gaping hole in the State's disavowal. The ink of Rodríguez Moreno's signature is still fresh when the court gives its orders:

> 1) To summon the second-in-command at the Mar del Plata District Police Department, Commissioner Benedicto Cuello, to offer a statement on Monday the 21st at 10:00 a.m.; 2) To summon the medic of the Moreno Police Precinct, Doctor Chiesa, to offer a statement that same Monday at 9:30 a.m.; 3) To establish the court on Tuesday the 22nd in the San Martín District Police Department to collect statements from the department staff; 4) To appear at the polyclinic of said city immediately to collect statements from the doctors, nurses, and other personnel, and to proceed to examine the institution's books; 5) To authorize non-working days and non-working hours in order to continue with this investigation from the 22nd of the month onwards.

The judge's urgency was justified. Fernández Suárez, feeling cornered because of Rodríguez Moreno's confession and the rumor (which took La Plata by storm) that his preemptive incarceration was imminent, went looking for help at the highest echelons of the Liberating Revolution. On the morning of Monday, January 21, 1957, accompanied by Colonel Bonnecarrere—the Province authority appointed by the Liberating Revolution—he requested a hearing with General Aramburu and was received in the presence of General Quaranta. Once there, he asked for and received assistance from the President of the Nation.

That same night, Bonnecarrere called an emergency meeting, which Fernández Suárez attended. A special airplane was chartered to bring the president of the Supreme Court of the Province, Judge Amílcar Mercader, from the town of Ayacucho, which is where he was at that time. Discussed at length during this meeting were: the José León Suárez executions, the danger that the judge's obvious determination to establish the truth posed to the Liberating Revolution, and the means that the Executive Power had at its disposal to avoid it.

The following information about these desperate maneuvers leaked to the papers:

> Upon returning from our city, after interviewing the provisional president of the Nation in the early hours of the morning, State authority Colonel Bonnecarrere . . . is said to have met with his ministers and the Chief of Police around 8:30 p.m. in the Government House . . .
>
> This coincided with a visit from the head of the Supreme Court of the Province, Judge Amílcar A. Mercader.
>
> In both instances there was allegedly discussion of . . . issues connected to the workings of the Police Department of the Province of Buenos Aires, regarding recent events that are public knowledge, were discussed. (*El Argentino* from La Plata, January 22, 1957.)

The Buenos Aires periodical *La Razón* also alluded to the proceedings in a text box with the heading "A Meeting," reporting a discussion of "the events that took place last year in the region of San Martín." These euphemisms were the extent of the freedom of the press that the country so enjoyed: the public was never informed about the existence of the Livraga file.

It's possible that the way things are going influences the tone of Commissioner Cuello, the ex-second-in-command of the San Martín District Police Department, when he gives his statement on Monday the twenty-first. His gives a defiant, at times furious testimony. It begins with a lie that, albeit easily disproven, shows that Fernández Suárez and his henchmen now understand what the core of the issue is: Cuello says that "at approximately 2300 hours on June 9, he was informed that the establishment of martial law had been broadcast over the radio."

This is false. State Radio played music by Bach at 10:31 p.m.; Ravel at 10:59 p.m.; Stravinsky at 11:30 p.m., and ended its programming at 12:00 a.m. with a marching song as usual. At 12:11 a.m. on June 10 it resumed its broadcast unexpectedly on all State Radio stations at once, aired light music for twenty-one minutes, and at precisely 12:32 a.m. began to read the text of the martial law.

Cuello goes on:

that at approximately 0030 hours on the 10th, or rather closer to midnight, a group of individuals was driven to the District Police Department. It was said that they were being held incommunicado and under the command of the Chief of Police, who had allegedly carried out the procedure of apprehending them . . . Asked by Your Honor if the intake of these prisoners was recorded in the department's books, he states: that it was not done because they were being held incommunicado and under the Chief of Police's command, so it was understood that they were stopping there briefly and would then be driven to headquarters. Asked by Your Honor if the regulation is not that prisoners are to be registered as soon as they arrive at the station, he responds: that the San Martín District Police Department does not have stations designated for holding prisoners, and when a few do come through, they stay only temporarily . . . Asked by Your Honor if the prisoners were questioned, the witness states: that he cannot quite recall if they were questioned, that they might have been asked a question or two because the reason for their arrest was unknown, but he does not remember if this was recorded in writing . . . Asked by Your Honor if he can provide the names of those who were arrested, he remembers Rodríguez and thinks he remembers a last name like Brión. Actually he thinks the last name was Lizazo, and he also remembers distinctly that Giunta was there; as for Juan Carlos Livraga, he does not remember him . . . Asked by Your Honor what happened next, he states: that at approximately five o'clock in the morning his chief, Rodríguez Moreno, stated that he had received, via direct communication over the police radio between himself and the Chief of Police, an order to execute the group that the Chief of Police had arrested in Florida, that in compliance with said order he made all the prisoners get into an assault car, each prisoner with his respective guard. Asked by Your Honor whether it was covered with the appropriate curtains, the witness states: that he is almost certain that it was; that said vehicle set out followed by the Department van, which was being directed by the chief of the District Department, who was accompanied by the declarant and perhaps another officer or another person, he does not recall; that they arrived at an open field, the precise location of which the declarant cannot affirm. He can only say that it was in the jurisdiction of San Martín, that the assault car came to a stop there and was lit up by the headlights of the van. They then proceeded with the execution of the prisoners and, upon completion, or rather upon establishing how many individuals had been executed, they realized that there were only five instead of the twelve or thirteen who had been driven there, and at that moment they realized that some of the prisoners had escaped.

—When was that? —asked the judge.
Cuello doesn't know. He participated only "as a witness and as

moral support [sic] for the chief, who had taken command of the execution."

It seems obvious that, when giving oneself to a moral task of this caliber, you cannot get too hung up on the details. But the escape, Cuello explains, "happened before the execution."

THE JUDGE. —How many were left dead?

CUELLO. —Five.

THE JUDGE. —Is it possible that, of those who faced the firing squad, some were left unharmed?

CUELLO. —I don't believe so.

THE JUDGE. —How were these five executed?

CUELLO. —I don't recall, I think it was done in two groups.

At this point, the commissioner takes a polemical turn that the judge records on the back of page 62:

"At this moment the witness says he considers it necessary to explain that he does not see the reason for the investigation that is being conducted regarding these executions, that they had been ordered in compliance with martial law, that he seems to recall that it was instated on the night of the ninth between 10:30 p.m. and 11:00 p.m., and is almost certain that all the prisoners knew it had been put into effect, because he even seems to recall that the District Police Department acquired knowledge of these circumstances based on statements made by the prisoners themselves."

It's funny what this commissioner "seems to recall" considering how forgetful he is about other things (including the testimony he gave half an hour prior). First he says that "at approximately 2300 hours on June 9, he was informed that the instatement of martial law had been broadcast over the radio." Then he said that the prisoners arrived "at approximately 0030 hours on the tenth, or rather closer to midnight." And now he is saying that it's these same prisoners who gave the news to the District Police Department, and therefore to him. But if they arrived at midnight, how could they have told him the news at eleven?

Asked by the judge what they did with the bodies, Cuello says "that he does not know if it was immediately or by way of a subsequent order that they were driven to the morgue at the San Martín polyclinic."

Judge Hueyo shows him Livraga's receipt and asks him if he recognizes it. Cuello admits it is "possible that this form was filled out at the District Police Department."

Does he recognize the signatures?

He does not recognize them.

Does he know that Livraga was subsequently arrested at the Department?

He does not.

Does he know that Livraga was in Moreno?

He has no idea.

Does he know if the executed men received a coup de grâce?

He can't say for sure.

Does he know if the men who were executed were told what their crime was?

He doesn't know.

His testimony is a web of inaccuracies and evasions. As opposed to Rodríguez Moreno, this officer believes that the dead are completely dead and that there is no reason to go around asking so many questions.

On Tuesday, January 22, the judge goes to Florida in search of the "third man," Horacio di Chiano. He doesn't find him. He is in hiding and will only appear twenty days later when Enriqueta Muñiz and I manage to speak with him. Judge Hueyo questions Di Chiano's wife, who confirms Giunta's testimony and provides a new description of Fernández Suárez, "a large person who was wearing a military jacket with sand-colored gabardine pants, a person with dark hair and a mustache."

The judge asks what's become of her husband. She responds that "the declarant has not seen her husband since the night in question either; she suspects that he is still alive, but he has not been home since."

On page 69 and following, two guards from the Florida precinct state that they participated in the raid. Their testimonies add nothing to the case.

From Florida, the judge headed to the San Martín District Police Department, where he intended to establish the court. Waiting for him there was an urgent radio message from Police Headquarters, informing him that the judge's presence was needed in the capital of the Province. Once he arrives in La Plata, the judge sits down to talk with the president of the Supreme Court of the Province.

What was said during that meeting was never reported, but the game being played was plain to see. Advised by the best in the business, Bonnecarrere and Fernández Suárez figured out the magic formula for saving themselves: to get a military court to claim jurisdiction over the case.

On that same day, January 22, Fernández Suárez deigns to respond to the judge's requests for the first time. His response appears on page 71 and is stamped "Confidential." It reads as follows:

> In response to His Honor's official requests dated the 24th and 31st of December, 1956, and the 10th and 11th of the current month of January, related to Case Number 3702 entitled "Livraga, Juan Carlos – report," I have the pleasure of addressing the judge and informing him of the following:
>
> 1) Juan Carlos Livraga was condemned to death by the June 9, 1956 Decree 10.364 of the National Executive Power, the punishment to be carried out at the site of the events, in the district of San Martín, in accordance with martial law; it was not possible to complete the sentence regarding the person in question due

to his having escaped moments before the execution.

2) The corresponding records of this decree can be found in the Decree Office Archives of the President of the Nation.

3) Due to the escape of the condemned, the execution could not be carried out at the time, and it was even less possible to complete it subsequently, after arresting him, as martial law had been lifted.

4) As a result, since there had been a definitive ruling on the case, it was then also impossible to have any other authority intervene, given that he had already been tried for these charges.

5) Instead, by Decree Number 11.219, he was put under the command of the National Executive Power and held in custody at the Olmos jail.

Furthermore, I would like to inform Your Honor that martial law was instated by Decree-Law 10.362, of June 9, 1956, and put into effect by Decree 10.363, also on June 9, 1956.

This latter decree establishes the following, in short:

1) While martial law is in effect, the stipulations of Law 13.234 regarding the governance of the Nation during times of war will be applied.

2) Every active officer of the armed forces carrying out his military duties will be able to call for a summary trial and have the power to apply a death sentence by execution to any disturber of the peace.

3) Any person carrying weapons, disobeying po-

> lice orders, or exhibiting suspicious behavior
> of any kind is considered a disturber of the
> peace.

Since the case seems to originate with an alleged execution
under abnormal circumstances, I think it fitting to note, as
far as legality is concerned, that in every instance the application of these decrees requires only an oral order (Art.
138 of the Military Justice Code).

In any event, given the press scandal that, with rather unclear motives, has been unleashed regarding this issue, it is
appropriate to stress that the accountability of the authorities or of those in charge of applying a military decree can
only be decided effectively by military courts and not by
civil magistrates (Art. 136 of the Military Code of Justice).
Remaining very sincerely yours, Your Honor.

D. A. Fernández Suárez

Lieutenant Colonel Chief of Police.

So everything was legal. Livraga had been executed in compliance with a decree. There is just one tiny detail: *the decree does not
exist.* Or rather, it exists, but it does not affect him at all, because
it is a list of military personnel condemned to death, and it *does not
include Livraga.*

Fernández Suárez's argument is one more blatant lie to add to all
the previous ones.

As for the "press scandal": it was an exaggeration to give such
a label to the articles I had printed out on a little sheet of paper
that was hardly even circulated—articles which constituted the only
reference to the matter that could be found in the press at the time.

Judge Hueyo understood that the issue of jurisdictional competence had already been established by F. Suárez's note, but he did
not pass up the opportunity to tear apart the latest fabrication of this
cornered military man. On page 74, he orders the following:

With the purpose of resolving the issue of jurisdictional competence that has been established, to send an official letter to the judge currently presiding over the criminal court of the Capital asking him to demand from wherever necessary, and as a matter of urgency, authenticated copies of decree numbers 10.362, 10.363 and 10.364, as well as the date and exact time that they were in effect.

The June 14, 1956, Official Bulletin with the three decrees appears as page 82 of the file. 10.362 and 10.363, which establish and stipulate regulations for martial law, are dated June 9, without any mention of the time, and support Fernández Suárez's version of the events. But 10.364, dated June 10, says that considering "their involvement in the military uprising that occurred one day prior . . . the following individuals are sentenced to death by execution: (RET) Colonel Alcibíades Eduardo Cortínez, (RET) Colonel Ricardo Salomón Ibazeta . . ." and goes on to list five more men from the military. Of course neither Livraga's name, nor those of the other executed men, appear among them.

As a result, the court rules on January 28:

To add issue number 18.171 of the Official Bulletin, published June 14, to the investigation and, based on this document, to conclude that the National Executive Power ordering the execution of Juan Carlos Livraga does not fit the facts, as the Chief of Police asserts in his note dated the 22nd; to inform the aforementioned civil servant of said circumstance, and to request, in the event that such a decree does exist, that he report its exact number . . .

. . . To resend the official letters cited on page 74 and to let it be known that the original text of the decrees is not of interest but rather, as a supremely urgent matter, the date and exact time of their enactment and announcement.

From Judge Hueyo to Fernández Suárez, page 83:

> I have the pleasure of writing to you, Dear Sir, regarding
> the report offered by Juan Carlos Livraga. I am hereby
> making it known to you that your note dated the 22nd
> of this month states "that Juan Carlos Livraga was con-
> demned to the death penalty by the National Executive
> Power's decree number 10.364 dated June 9, 1956," and
> informing the undersigned that in the aforementioned de-
> cree-law, published in Official Bulletin Number 18.171 on
> the 14th of last June, the name of the declarant, Livraga,
> does not appear; I have addressed this letter to you, Dear
> Sir, to inform you of the erroneous information, and re-
> quest that, in the event that such a decree does exist, you
> report its exact number.

Fernández Suárez does not respond. But on January 30 he sends
a copy of the note that he has just presented to the Minister of the
Army, General Ossorio Arana, with the purpose, he says, of having
"the military justice system hear the case that is being tried, which
falls exclusively under its jurisdiction." The note to Ossorio Arana
reviews the background for the case (without mentioning decree
number 10.364) and requests:

> a) that the military justice system hear the case that is being
> tried; b) that the relevant issue of the judge's withdrawal
> for lack of jurisdictional competence (Art. 150, paragraph
> 1 of the Military Justice Code) therefore be brought for-
> ward.

That same day, the military judge, Colonel Abraham González,
took up the case as follows:

I have the pleasure of writing to Your Honor regarding the higher-order investigation that I am conducting concerning alleged infractions of the application of martial law as it was ordered by higher decree numbers 10.362 and 10.363. I request that you kindly report to this military court of justice number 27 . . . on whether a case is being tried before your court . . . that was initiated based on a report or complaint lodged by Mister Juan Carlos Livraga, which is tied to the same event that the undersigned is investigating. If affirmative, since the event in question falls within military jurisdiction either by *ratione materiae* or likewise by *ratione personae* (based on the assumption that it deals with whether military personnel acted in compliance with what Article 2 of the aforementioned higher decree number 10.363 stipulates), and considering that such a case calls for the strict application of Article 108, paragraph 1, of the Military Justice Code . . . I hereby leave Your Honor with the motion to contest jurisdiction, which is delineated in articles 150 (paragraph 1) and 151 of the aforementioned legal code.

Consequently, I ask that Your Honor desist from continuing to hear the referenced case and submit the matter at hand to this military court of justice, or, should the motion that has been made not be accepted, that the decisions be left to the National Supreme Court such that the matter in question be resolved conclusively.

On February 1, 1957, the La Plata judge resolves to retain jurisdiction, claiming the following: that *ratione personae*, it is premature to make a motion for recusal because, as it stands, the case does not directly charge any one person and the event to date does not involve "military personnel on active duty"; and that *ratione materiae*, there are similarly insufficient reasons to relinquish the case. He adds that, when the same matter was brought forth by the Chief of Police, he expressed his resolve to retain jurisdiction,

> even though said person bringing forth the issue was not involved in the case and, to that end, on January 23, he ordered the release of an official letter to the judge currently presiding over the criminal court of the capital to demand, from wherever necessary, an original copy of decree 10.362 and 10.363, as well as the date and exact time they were enacted. Said official letter was resent on the 28th, and was met no reply.

Judge Hueyo has understood from the beginning that the crux of his investigation is this: the hour at which the law was announced. He did not have enough time to obtain the evidence that I would obtain months later, once the State Radio registry book of announcers had been photocopied and published. But the following analysis seems irrefutable to me:

> The goal of the requested information —he says— was to determine whether the detention of the declarant, which occurred between 2315 and 2330 on June 9, took place after or before the instatement of martial law.
>
> In the former case, the investigation and penalty pertain to whether an infraction occurred, either regarding the application of said martial law or regarding pertinent regulations of the military code of justice. In this case, the matter does not fall under the jurisdiction of civil authorities and, with the necessary information, the undersigned would have stated as much.
>
> But in the latter case, that is, that the detention of these individuals took place prior to the instatement of martial law: even if the execution was ordered after the law had

come into effect, the law would not have applied to said individuals as no criminal law can have retroactive effect and, in that case, those in question, whatever their connection to the subversive movement may have been, were not given the opportunity to desist and lay down their weapons because they had already been seized.

Given this hypothesis, the detention in question, the subsequent execution of several of these individuals, the attempt to execute others and the repeated detention of the declarant that ultimately placed him under the jurisdiction of the National Executive Power, are events that are not within the scope of military law or its interpretation, but rather, should they be duly proven, are classified as crimes under the penal code, which the undersigned is qualified to apply. For the above reasons, it is resolved to inform the solicitor that the undersigned retains jurisdiction.

35. BLIND JUSTICE

The case went to the National Supreme Court, which, on April 24, 1957, passed one of the most shameful rulings in our judicial history, signed by all the members—Judges Alfredo Orgaz, Manuel J. Argañarás, Enrique V. Galli, Carlos Herrera, Benjamín Villegas Basavilbaso—following a prior report from the Attorney General of the Nation, Sebastián Soler.

Once the case was transferred to a so-called military justice system that was equally complicit and partisan, this ruling is what left the crime of the José León Suárez massacre forever unpunished.

Half a page was enough for Judge Soler to give his ruling on the events that I have recounted in this book. Here is his opinion:

According to the statements of the declarant, the event being investigated in the proceedings was carried out by the staff of the Police Department of the Province of Buenos Aires.

However, beginning on page 24, it appears that during the happenings of June 9, 1956, police forces acted "in accordance with military commands and authority."

Consequently, considering what is mandated by Article 108, paragraphs 2 and 3, and by Article 109, paragraph 6, of the Military Code of Justice, it is my opinion that the competence of the military justice court *sub judice* should be declared and I underscore, moreover, that this decision is supported by Article 136 of the same legal text in its stipulation that "the accountability of military authorities regarding the decrees that they pass, or of those entrusted with their application, should they overstep their authority, can only be established by military courts."

Note that the ruling does not even mention the basic discrepancy raised by Judge Hueyo. It tiptoes around all the significant elements of the issue. It is founded on the childish equivocation that the police were reporting to the Army during "the events of June 9, 1956," which is *false* because throughout the entirety of June 9, given that no decree was enacted that day to change the situation, the police were legally subordinated not to the Army, but rather to the Governance Ministry of the Province. Moreover, though, besides being false, *this is all irrelevant* because Livraga's formal accusation, which is what is being considered, refers to a crime committed on June 10, which is like saying a day later, a year later, a century later. Or is it that a famous jurist came to believe he was an angel, or a Wells character, who could play with time like this? In half a page, Judge Soler does away with everything he has taught in decades of lectures and texts.

The Court's ruling states:

Findings of fact and conclusions of law:

WHEREAS the actions that prompted this case are imputed to functionaries and employees of the Province of Buenos Aires Police, who acted during the emergency in accordance with commands and authority that were military in nature, per what is reported on page 24 by request of this Court, and what emerges as well from the proceedings is that the aforementioned events were motivated by the revolutionary movement stifled on that occasion, namely, under exceptional circumstances during which the keeping of internal order was specifically assigned to the military, according to doctrine established as of the end-date of the "Todesco, Hernando" case; and

WHEREAS in such conditions and considering what is ordered by Article 136 of the Military Code of Justice and what has been decreed by the Attorney General, it is appropriate to declare the jurisdictional competence of the presiding military judge in this case;

THEREFORE and given the report of the Attorney General, be it declared fitting for the proceedings to be heard by the presiding military judge, to whom the trial will be transferred.

In the first edition of this book I said—without its occurring to anyone to sue me for contempt—that the attorney general's report and the ruling of the Court were an evil corruption of the rule of law. I want to sum up, in the most straightforward way possible, the reasons behind this "report" that made me believe I was authorized to make such a statement.

An individual, Livraga, is arrested on a day when the ordinary rule of law is in effect. He is not formally accused of anything during the arrest, but this in itself does not yet constitute a crime. They do rough him up a bit; let's say we forget that part.

The person who arrests him is a civil servant, the Chief of Police of the Province. It is true that this civil servant is, *additionally*, a lieutenant colonel; but, for the purposes of this case, it is as though he isn't; he does not arrest him in his capacity as a lieutenant colonel, but as a civil servant under the authority of the Governance Ministry of the Province.

While detained, Livraga of course does not commit any crimes. That day—like every day—ends at twelve o'clock at night. *The following day* (it does not matter that hardly thirty-two minutes have gone by, it is already the following day, June 10), a law is instated—martial law. This law is put into effect on June 10. Livraga, imprisoned since the previous day, cannot violate it. It is as though this law does not exist for Livraga, and Livraga does not exist for it; they are spheres that do not make contact; whatever is done to him and whatever punishment is inflicted upon him in the name of this law will be a crime. Livraga exists in the penal realm that precedes this law; he cannot be judged or punished except according to the criminal code that was in effect at the time of his arrest, which entitles him to guarantees, the right to defense, an impartial judge, due process.

Now a man enters the picture. He is the same man as before, the civil servant, the Chief of Police who has undergone a *Doctor Jekyll and Mr. Hyde* kind of transformation and appears in the form of a military authority; his rank of lieutenant colonel—which earlier was insignificant—now serves him well. This man cannot be unaware that he, a civilian, has arrested Livraga, a civilian, and that their interactions are entirely frozen on this plane; that he has *arrested* Livraga at a time governed by civil law, and can only deal with him on this plane; and that any transgression he commits regarding this clear rule will have to be judged on that same, unabandonable plane—that is to say, will have to be judged by a civil judge. Because this time of civil relations between authorities and mere citizens does not expire when a revolution hits; at most, civil rule under-lies military rule: one can be superimposed on the other, but they cannot merge. This civil servant cannot act as a military authority toward someone he has *arrested* in his role as a civil servant. But he does. He orders for him to be killed. But it is clear that when he acts, when he sends Livraga to be killed, he continues acting like a civil servant, even though he believes the opposite to be the case, because that is the only way he has of relating to this detainee. If he commits a criminal offense within this relationship, he absolutely must be judged as a civil servant. What he orders is not an execu-tion; it is a murder.

To get a clearer picture of things, let's suppose that during this revolution-inspired interval of metamorphosis, this civil-servant-cum-military-authority takes advantage of the situation to commit some kind of crime, to rob a bank or murder a creditor. Would he then be judged by the military justice system? It seems clear to me that he wouldn't. His dual nature as a civil servant and military authority does not prevent him from committing a crime according to the penal code and correspondingly being tried under this very code.

Now let's suppose the opposite. Let's suppose that the mere instatement of martial law gives the chief of police the unchecked authority over all *persons previously detained* in precincts, etc., that Fernández Suárez exercised over Livraga. This man, then, can murder all of the prisoners in his custody, and later—if the issue is raised—be "judged" by a military court, that is, by his colleagues and comrades-in-arms involved in the same splinter groups and possibly guilty of similar exploits.

Isn't that how it happened? Did Lieutenant Colonel Abraham González, the military judge, penalize Lieutenant Colonel Fernán-dez Suárez or even disclose any of the results of this "trial"?

I want somebody to tell me what the difference is between this conception of justice and the one the Nazi gas chambers created.

Let's return now to Livraga. When this man, already arrested, gets on a bus at 11:30 p.m. on June 9, he is, despite everything, protected by Article 18 of the Constitution, which says that "No inhabitant of the Nation can be punished without a trial governed by the law that was in effect prior to the act that gave rise to the proceedings . . . or deprived of the judges appointed by law before the act for which he is tried."

What does Livraga do to lose these rights? Nothing. And yet, he loses them, and this is one more of the phases of legal monstrosity validated by the Court's ruling and by the military "trial"—two stones along the same path because in 1957 you did not need to be a genius to know that Lieutenant Colonel González was not going find Lieutenant Colonel Fernández Suárez guilty.

This, then, is the irremovable stain that soils a government, a justice system, and an army equally:

That the men arrested in Florida were punished, condemned to death without trial; that they were deprived of the judges appointed by law before the act that gave rise to the case, and under law instated subsequent to the act in question; and that there was in fact no act and no justification for any of it.

No amount of finagling will manage to erase the horrific evidence showing that the government of the Liberating Revolution retroactively applied a martial law that was instated on June 10 to men who were arrested on June 9.

And that is not execution. It is murder.

36. EPILOGUE

One of my concerns upon finding out about this massacre and telling its story while the executioners were still in power was to keep it separate, to the extent possible, from the other executions, whose victims were primarily military personnel. Here was an incident that the Liberating Revolution could not even respond to with sophistries.

This approach forced me to make a specific allegation instead of a historical argument. It meant presenting the Liberating Revolution and its heirs to date with the borderline case of an unjustified atrocity, and asking them a question: Did they acknowledge the atrocity as their own, or did they explicitly disapprove of it? The only way to show that they had not authorized it was to punish those responsible and offer moral and material compensation for the victims. Three editions of this book, about forty published articles, a bill presented to Congress, and countless smaller initiatives have all served to pose the question to five successive governments over the course of twelve years. The response has always been silence. The ruling class that these governments represent supports this act of murder, accepts it as a part of itself, and does not punish anyone for it simply because it does not want to punish itself.

The executions of military personnel in the barracks were, of course, just as barbaric, illegal, and arbitrary as the civilian executions in the garbage dump.

The six men who, following Colonel Yrigoyen's orders, attempted to establish Valle's command in Avellaneda, put up no resistance when they were caught. They are executed in the Lanús District Police Department at dawn on June 10.

Colonel Cogorno, the leader of the uprising in La Plata, is executed during the first minutes of June 11 in the Seventh Regiment barracks. The civilian Alberto Abadíe, wounded in the skirmish, is first *treated.* Then, at nightfall on the twelfth, he is ready for the firing squad, which he has to face in the Bosque de La Plata park.

On June 10 at noon, Colonels Cortínez and Ibazeta, along with five junior officers, are tried at Campo de Mayo. The court, presided over by General Lorio, decides that the case does not warrant the death penalty. The Executive Power completely disregards *res judicata* and passes Decree 10.364, which condemns six of the seven accused men to death. The order is carried out at 3:40 a.m. on June 11 near an embankment.

At the same time, the four NCOs who had momentarily taken control of the Army Mechanics School are executed there, and the three NCOs of the Palermo Second Regiment who were also allegedly "involved" are executed in the National Penitentiary. Sometime afterward, I spoke to the widow of one of these men—the military band sergeant Luciano Isaías Rojas. She told me that on the night of the uprising, her husband had been sleeping beside her at their home.

On June 12, General Valle turns himself in to put a stop to the killings. They execute him that same night.

That makes for twenty-seven executions in less than seventy-two hours at six locations.

They all fall under Article 18 of the National Constitution, active in that moment, which says: "The death penalty for political reasons is hereafter abolished."

In certain cases, martial law is applied retroactively. In others, *res judicata* is invoked over and over again in an abusive cycle. In yet others, the fact that the accused abandoned their weapons at the first opportunity is not taken into account. In short, it is a massive, arbitrary, illegal murder whose greatest culprits are the men who signed the decrees designed to validate it: Generals Aramburu and Ossorio Arana, Admirals Rojas and Hartung, and Brigadier General Krause.

37. ARAMBURU AND THE HISTORICAL TRIAL

On May 29, 1970, a Montonero commando kidnapped Lieutenant General Aramburu from his home. Two days later, they condemned him to death and listed the charges that the Peronists had against him. The first two included "the killing of twenty-seven Argentines without trial or just cause" on June 9, 1956.

The commando bore the name of the executed General Valle. Aramburu was executed on June 1 at seven o'clock in the morning and his body turned up forty-five days later in the south of the Province of Buenos Aires.

The incident shook the country in a number of different ways. The people did not cry over the death of Aramburu. The Army, the institutions, and the oligarchy raised an angry outcry. Among the hundreds of protests and statements that were made, there is one worth recalling. It classifies the event as a "monstrous and cowardly crime for which there is no precedent in the history of the Republic." One of the signatories is General Bonnecarrere, Governor of the Province at the time of Operation Massacre. Another is General Leguizamón Martínez, who had executed Colonel Cogorno in the La Plata barracks. A third is Colonel Fernández Suárez himself. They did not seem like the best people to be talking about precedents.

The execution of Aramburu provoked the fall of General Onganía one week later, whose dictatorship had already been damaged on a different May 29 (of the previous year) by the saga of the popular uprising known as Cordobazo;[16] it also momentarily set back the plans of Liberal groups who saw in the executed general a second chance for the failed Argentine Revolution.[17]

The dramatic nature of this death accelerated a process that usually takes years to accomplish: the creation of a national hero. In a matter of months, Liberal doctors, the press, and Aramburu's political heirs canonized him in an unending stream of praise and elegy. Champion of democracy, soldier of liberty, beloved son of the fatherland, a military man cast in the classic mold of the San Martín tradition, an honest and unassuming ruler whose temperament did not allow him to overstep his authority, these are some of the incantations that hide the true portrait of Aramburu from history. Two years later he had his mausoleum, decorated with Virtues.

Not all of Aramburu's supporters were so foolish as to buy the image of him that was crafted in that language. Those who were smart enough to understand why the people hated him maintained that "the Aramburu of 1970 was not the Aramburu of 1956" and that the Aramburu of 1970, put in the same circumstances, would not have ordered executions, persecutions, or proscriptions. You could say the same for Lavalle, Dorrego's murderer, that he only committed the terrible acts he committed because he was under the influence of devious advisers: all you had to do was switch Salvador del Carril's name for Américo Ghioldi's.[18] Both of them would have regretted what they had done and, at the very last moment, come together in a puzzling union with their land and their people. From this perspective, one can see how Aramburu would come to warrant, in addition to the anti-Peronist memorial he received, an expiatory cantata written by some future Sábato.[19]

In a less partial trial, this kind of transformation would not matter, even if it had truly happened. Here was an executor of a class policy whose foundation—exploitation—is in itself inhuman and whose acts of cruelty derive from this foundation like branches from a tree trunk: Aramburu's perplexing turns, when he was already far removed from power, just barely illuminate the discrepancy between the abstract ideals and the concrete acts of the members of that class. The evil that he perpetrated was in his acts, and whatever goodness he had in his thoughts was a belated tremor of the bourgeois consciousness. Aramburu was obliged to execute and ban in the same way that his successors to this day have been forced to torture and murder: for the simple fact that they represent a usurping minority that can only stay in power through deceit and violence.

The June massacre exemplifies but does not represent the height of this regime's perversity. Aramburu's government imprisoned thousands of workers, stifled each and every strike, and did away with union organizing. Torture became the norm and spread throughout the entire country. The decree that prohibited mention of Perón's name or the secret operation that snatched his wife's body, mutilated it, and took it out of the country, were expressions of a hatred that even inanimate objects could not escape—sheets and silverware from the Foundation were burned and melted because they bore the imprint of this name that was thought to be demonic.[20] An entire health and welfare program was destroyed, public swimming pools that called to mind "the cursed deed" were drained, and liberal humanism reached medieval lows: rarely has such hatred been seen here, rarely have two social classes clashed so strikingly.[21]

But if this kind of violence reveals the true nature of Argentine society, fatally split, it is actually a different, less sensational and more pernicious violence that insinuates itself into the country with Aramburu. His government gives shape to a second *década infame*: enter the Alsogarays, the Kriegers, and the Verriers, who neatly rejoin the bonds of dependency that were broken during Perón's government.[22] The Argentine Republic, one of the countries with the lowest foreign investment (5 percent of total investments), which had barely been sending remittances abroad of one dollar per inhabitant annually, begins to administer loans that only benefit the lender, to be duped into investing in technology scams, to build foreign capital with the national savings and to accumulate the debt that today saps 25 percent of our registered exports. One decree alone, number 13.125, divests the country of two billion dollars in nationalized bank deposits and places them under the control of the international bank that can now control national credit, throttle small businesses, and prepare for the massive influx of big monopolies.

Fifteen years later, we are able to see the outcome of these policies: a dependent and stagnant country, a sunken working class, rebellion bubbling everywhere. This rebellion finally reaches Aramburu, confronts him with his deeds, and paralyzes the hand that was signing the loans, the decrees, the executions.

APPENDICES

The garbage dump in José León Suárez where the killings took place.

PROLOGUE TO THE BOOK EDITION
*(from the first edition, July 1957)**

Operation Massacre was published in the journal *Mayoría* between May 27 and July 29 of 1957: nine articles in total.

I had already covered the events that I recount there in a half-dozen articles that were published by the newspaper *Revolución Nacional* between January 15 and the end of March 1957.

Now the book is being published by Ediciones Sigla.

The names I mention here might suggest that I have an exclusive preference for tough, nationalist presses. That is not the case. I wrote this book for it to be published, for it to *act*, not so that it could join the vast number of reveries dreamed up by ideologues. I investigated and recounted these awful events to bring them to light in the fullest way possible, to provoke fear, to have them never happen again. I consider whoever helps me publish and circulate the story to be an ally; I will not ask what your politics are.

That is how I respond to cowards and to those who are weak of spirit when they ask me why I—someone who considers himself a man of the Left—am collaborating journalistically with men and publications of the Right. I reply: because they dare to take the risk, and right now there is no hierarchy that I recognize or accept as being more noble than that of civil courage. Or would they prefer that I kept quiet about these things on account of ridiculous parti-

---

* *Necessary clarification*: In the editions of *Operation Massacre* that appeared during Walsh's life, there is some confusion regarding this prologue (which the author signs "La Plata, July 1957"), the "Introduction" (p. 157) (signed "La Plata, March 1957"), and the "Obligatory Appendix" (p. 165), also dated March of that year. The first book version, published by Sigla, finished printing on November 30, 1957, and included these texts (without further clarifications), which were written beforehand during different months. *[Ediciones de la Flor Editor's Note.]*

san prejudices? While the ideologues dream, more practical people torture and kill. That is concrete, that is urgent, that is of the here and now.

If necessary, I can renounce or put off all political philosophies whose truths are, in the end, of a speculative nature. I cannot, I will not, and I should not renounce one basic feeling: indignation in the face of abuse, cowardice, and murder.

I have also learned that partisan differences are perhaps the most superficial rifts that come between men. It's other ones that matter: the insurmountable, irreducible differences in character. Among people who think like I do about the majority of abstract issues, I have discovered an alarming pragmatism when it comes to concrete situations that require almost instinctive reactions, the kinds of reactions that make being human worthwhile.

The torturer who becomes an executioner at the slightest provocation is a present-day problem, a clear target that the civil conscience ought to obliterate. We have ignored the fact that there has been a beast lurking among us. Even in Nazi Germany, years of misery, fear, and bombings were necessary to bring it to light. In the Argentine Republic, six hours of rebellion were enough to make its repulsive silhouette emerge. Here it is, with the name it happens to carry today, for all to see. And to act accordingly.

The rest, at this exact moment, does not interest me.

INTRODUCTION
(to the first edition, March 1957)

News of the massacre in José León Suárez first came to my ears by pure chance, on December 18, 1956. The news was not quite accurate, which was only fitting for the place where I heard it—a café. It suggested that a man who was allegedly executed during the Peronist uprising of June 9 and 10 of that year had survived and was not in jail.

The story sounded like a movie to me, primed for all sorts of exercises in disbelief. (It had the same effect on many people, which was unfortunate. An official of the armed forces, for example, whom I told about the events before publishing anything, described them in all sincerity as "a serialized novel.")

But this kind of disbelief can be thinly disguised wisdom. The absolute nonbeliever can be as naïve as he who believes everything; at bottom, the two fall under the same psychological category.

I asked for more information. And the following day I met the first key player of the drama: Jorge Doglia, Esq. The interview with him left a strong impression on me. It may be that Doglia, a thirty-two-year-old lawyer, had his nerves shredded from waging a battle without respite for a number of months against the police "methods" he had witnessed as head of the Judicial Division of the Police Department for the Province. But he sounded utterly sincere to me. He told me about horrific cases of torture using the *picana* and burning cigarettes, of rubber and wire whips, of common criminals—usually "drifters" and pickpockets with no families to come looking for them—beaten to death in various precincts throughout the Province. And all of this under the regime of a "liberating revolution" that many Argentines received with hope because they believed it would put an end to abuses of police authority.

Doglia had fought valiantly against all of this, but now he was starting to feel defeated. Two months earlier, he had reported the illegal executions and the torture to a branch of Intelligence Services. But a bureaucrat there who could easily have spent the rest of his days looking up rules in basic textbooks for how to handle an informant—an ethical principle that we assume is basic knowledge for every branch of this kind—could think of nothing better than to expose him. Instead of protecting him, they put his life in danger, and he has received unequivocal death threats ever since.

Doglia presented a similar report to the Ministry of the Government of the Province that generated a stack of abstruse documents. Within this file—the prose worthy of Gracián in his weakest moments—a certain undersecretary comes to the conclusion that there is something there, but he isn't sure what it is.[23] At this juncture, the file keeps expanding, accumulating pages, dust, and rhetorical phrases. But, in short, nothing. In short, sloth and ineptitude when it is obvious how important it is for the matter to be resolved quickly and completely. This is what some of today's public servants have to offer.

Doglia did not put too much faith in journalism. He assumed the official newspapers were not going to take on such a prickly issue, and on the other hand he didn't want the voices of the opposition to exploit it for political reasons. He didn't expect very much from the same justice system that had just been presented with the surviving executed man as a plaintiff. From the very start, Doglia predicted: 1) that the case would be claimed by a Military Court and 2) that this motion would be approved. (The first happened promptly at the start of February 1957. The second remained to be seen. Everything depended on what the ruling of the National Supreme Court would be on the jurisdictional conflict. By the time this book was being published, Doglia's second prediction had also come true.)

As for the surviving executed man, I acquired the first piece of concrete evidence that night: his name was Juan Carlos Livraga. On the morning of December 20, I had in my hands a copy of the report that Livraga had filed. Later on, I was able to verify that his account of events was essentially accurate, though it contained a few significant omissions and inaccuracies when it came to details. But it was still too cinematic. Seemed as though it'd been pulled straight out of a movie.

And yet, the report was already a *fact*. What he alleged there could have been entirely false or not, but it was a fact: a man who said he had been executed in an unusual and illegal fashion was appearing before the reviewing judge to charge "whoever was responsible" with attempted homicide and assault.

There was something else. The document made mention of a second survivor, a certain Giunta, which opened up the immediate possibility of checking the facts that had already been reported. We were already quite far away from that first rumor overheard in a café thirty-six hours earlier.

That same afternoon the copy of the report landed in the hands of Mr. Leónidas Barletta, who ran *Propósitos*. Barletta spoke little and promised nothing. He only asked whether the circulation of this text might not disrupt the ongoing legal investigation. He received a reply stating that the most pressing concern was to use the right kind of publicity to protect the plaintiff's life, Doglia's life, and the lives of other witnesses who were thought to be in danger. Three days later, on the night of December 23, the report was out in the streets, brought there by *Propósitos*.

In the meantime, on the twenty-first, I had my first encounter with Livraga in his lawyer von Kotsch's study. I talked to him for a long while, gathering information that I would later use for the story that came out in *Revolución Nacional*.

What I first noticed about Livraga, naturally, were the two bullet wound scars on his face (entry and exit wounds). This was also a *fact*. The circumstances under which he received these injuries could be discussed, but the fact that he had received them could not. Nonetheless, there was an official version that went so far as to claim, absurdly, that "no shots of any kind had been fired on him."

What also came to mind immediately was the fundamental question of Livraga's innocence or guilt vis-à-vis the June 9 uprising. If he had been guilty, even in his intentions, was it normal, psychologically speaking, for him to appear before the judges and demand compensation? Wouldn't it have made much more sense for him to keep quiet, to thank God for making it out alive and gaining back his freedom? I believe a man has to feel *innocent* in order to present such a report against a Power as great as the Police Department of the Province. Of course, one could argue that everything is possible in abnormal psychology. But if there is something remarkable about Livraga, it is how normal he is and how reserved, how able he is to reason and observe.

Moreover, as I have already said, he was set free. This was also a *fact*. How could they let someone who was directly involved in the June incidents, a "revolutionary," an executed man, be free? The only explanation was the innocence hypothesis. We were already getting further and further away from the "serialized novel," which would from now on be perpetuated solely in official versions of the story.

I won't say here how the skein came untangled; how, starting with the first thread, we were able to stitch together a nearly definitive overview of what happened; how, starting from just one character in the drama, we were able to find almost all the rest. I would rather share the results we have obtained.

Over the course of the four months that this search has already lasted, I have spoken with the three survivors of the tragedy who are still at large in the country. I was the first journalist to reach all of them. I found and interviewed the third one even before anyone in the justice system did. I have figured out the names of three more survivors who are now in Bolivia, and the name of a seventh who is locked up in Olmos. I have stated and proven that a man who was recorded as dead in the official list of those executed (Reinaldo Benavídez), whose death certificate even exists, is perfectly safe and unharmed. Inversely, I was sorry to ascertain that another man (Mario Brión), who did not appear on that list and whom I harbored the hope of finding alive at one point, was killed by the firing squad.

I have spoken to witnesses who were there at every one of the stages that ended in the massacre. Some of the physical evidence in my possession has not yet reached its rightful recipient. I have obtained stenographic transcriptions of the Province Advisory Board's secret sessions in which the issue was discussed. I have spoken to the families of the victims and I have cultivated direct or indirect relationships with conspirators, political refugees and fugitives, alleged informers, and anonymous heroes. I can also say with confidence that I have always taken the greatest precautions to protect my informants, insofar as my obligation as a journalist has allowed. Throughout this entire process, I have benefited from the invaluable help of the person to whom this book is dedicated.

Of course, I am not trying to suggest that I was the first to arrive everywhere. I know that a legal investigation was carried out, and although I was not entirely privy to its conclusions, I have every reason to believe that it was very serous, efficient, and expeditious, up until the jurisdictional conflict got in the way. I hope that when the results of the case are made public—if they ever are—they can fill the unavoidable gaps in my story.

Some of the material gathered here appeared in the weekly publication *Revolución Nacional*, which was run by Dr. Cerruti Costa. I hope Dr. Cerruti will not think me ungrateful if I say that my having brought this material to him does not imply a preference or sympathy for his particular brand of politics. As a journalist, I am not that interested in politics. For me, it was a decision I was forced to make, which is not to say that I regret it. My first story about Juan Carlos Livraga had already been rejected by the various weeklies I had approached when Dr. Cerruti found the courage to publish it and use it as a launch pad for the series of stories and coverage about the executions that followed.

The suspicions that I anticipate raising oblige me to state that I am not a Peronist, have never been one, and do not have the intention of becoming one. If I were a Peronist, I would say so. I don't think that saying it would jeopardize my comfort or peace of mind more than this publication already does.

I am also no longer a supporter of the revolution that, like so many others, I believed was going to Liberate us.

I know perfectly well, however, that under Peronism I would not have been able to publish a book like this or the news articles that preceded it, or to even attempt to investigate police killings that were also taking place at the time. That's the little we have gained.

Most of us journalists and writers have come to consider Peronism our enemy in the last decade. And with very good reason. But there is something we should have realized: you cannot conquer the enemy without first understanding it.

In recent months, I've had to arrange first contact with these terrible beings—Peronists—who stir up newspaper headlines. And I have come to the conclusion (so banal that I am shocked more people don't share it) that, as mistaken as they may be, they are human beings and ought to be treated as such. Mainly, they should not be given reasons to keep following the wrong path. Executions, persecutions, and torture are reasons powerful enough to turn the wrong path into the right one at a certain point.

Most of all, I fear the moment when, humiliated and offended, they begin to be right. Right in a dogmatic way—in addition to being right in the sentimental or humane way that is already working in their favor and is, ultimately, where their dogmatism comes from in the first place. This moment is imminent; it will be unavoidable if this misguided politics of revenge, directed more at the working class than at anyone else, continues. Until now, every act of repression against Peronism has only worked to strengthen the case for it. That is not just regrettable: it is idiotic.

I will say again that this book does not have a political agenda, and its intention is certainly not to stir up completely futile hatreds. It is one among many other books that has a social agenda: to do away—in the short- or long-term—with murderers who have gone unpunished, with torturers, with *picana* "technicians" who remain in their posts despite changes in the government, with this posse of armed criminals dressed in uniform.

If people ask me why I have decided to speak now after keeping quiet as a journalist when others reported on government crimes under Peronism—though I never wrote a single signed or unsigned word in praise of Peronism, I was also never confronted with this level of atrocity—I will say with complete honesty: I have learned my lesson. But now my teachers are the ones keeping quiet. I have witnessed the willful silence of all the "serious press" in the face of this heinous massacre for many months, and I have felt ashamed.

People will also say that the José León Suárez execution was an isolated affair of rather minor importance. I believe the opposite. It was the perfect culmination of an entire system. It was one case among many; the clearest, not the most barbaric. I have learned things that are difficult to keep quiet about, but that would be unbearable to say right now. An excess of truth can madden and annihilate the moral conscience of a people. One day the complete, tragic story of the June killings will be written. That's when the shock will travel beyond our national borders.

Meanwhile, the Chief of Police who gave the order for this particular massacre is still in office.

This means that the battle against what he represents is ongoing. And I have the strong conviction that the final outcome of this battle will have an influence on the nature of our repressive systems in years to come; it will decide whether we live like civilized individuals or like Hottentots.

I know the Chief of the Police Department of the Province of Buenos Aires has expressed great curiosity—which I presume remains unsatisfied—about the author of the articles allegedly attacking him. The truth, I must say, is that I had no intention of attacking him personally; I was attacking him only to the extent that he constitutes one of the two faces of Civilization and Barbarism as articulated by a great Argentine one century ago.[24] It is precisely this face that needs to disappear, whose disappearance we all need to fight for.

When this book is published with my name on it, the Chief of Police will have no more doubts. I am not revealing my identity like this out of some foolish sense of bravado or defiance. I know perfectly well that in this country a chief of police is powerful, while a journalist—an obscure one to boot—is hardly anything. But I happen to believe, with complete earnestness and conviction, in the right of every citizen to share any truth that he comes to know, however dangerous that truth may be. And I believe in this book, in the impact it can have.

I hope I am not criticized for believing in a book—even if it does happen to be written by me—when there are so many more people believing in machine guns.

OBLIGATORY APPENDIX
(to the first edition, March 1957)

LYING AS A PROFESSION

The article that I published in *Mayoría* on July 15, 1957, served as a provisional epilogue to my book. The "provisional" part was not an accident. There were many things I still wanted to say. I preferred to leave them for another time because, first of all, I didn't want to abuse the space that the magazine had given me; secondly, I didn't want people to think I gained any pleasure from reporting on the moral wretchedness that prevails over some parts of this country; and thirdly, I hoped that the people whose duty it is to react against this kind of misery would be the ones to do so. This kind of hope, which I held onto for so long, is proof that I am one of the most naïve men ever to set foot on this soil.

Because the reaction came from somewhere else. The Chief of Police of the Province of Buenos Aires, Lieutenant Colonel Fernández Suárez, decided at last to acknowledge receipt of the charges that I made against him. He did so in the most skillful yet clumsy way possible. I will explain the clumsiness later.

First note the skill. The Chief of Police of the Province learns of the decidedly real existence of a band of terrorists. In fulfillment of his duties, he arrests them. He selects a certain "Marcelo" from among them (one of the secondary witnesses I mention in *Operation Massacre*). Then he chooses a judge, Judge Viglione, who is known as a man of integrity, and grants him the immediate authority to establish whether the prisoners are being treated correctly. And I am completely certain that this, this particular act, was one of the most measured, exemplary, even kind procedures that have ever

165

been carried out in the struggle against terrorism. Judge Viglione agrees to hold a press conference—which is not objectionable in any way—where he offers some details regarding the terrorist plot. But that's when the ace in the hole is revealed, the key to everything, the bait to hook the gullible. Under the auspices of the esteemed judge, anointed by the presence of the esteemed judge, Lieutenant Colonel Fernández Suárez intervenes and addresses my colleagues, journalists from the big newspapers who believe they have come to hear a story about terrorism. But in fact they have come, without knowing it, so that Fernández Suárez can publicly "lift" the charges that I have brought against him and that are really weighing down on him. And my colleagues, journalists from the big newspapers, they write it all down. They diligently write down what Fernández Suárez has dictated without any one of them thinking to ask any questions or raise any doubts. Let's take a look at what they write.

From *La Razón*:

> The Chief of Police, in turn, gave more background re-
> garding the conspiracy plot in question, noting specifically
> that among the main characters involved was Marcelo
> Rizzoni, the same person who managed to escape on June
> 9 of last year, just before the raid in Florida that saw the
> arrest of men who were involved in the rebellion that same
> night. He added that Rizzoni is the person who, under the
> pseudonym M, went to opposition newspapers with the
> information about the executions, which was then used
> as the basis for a campaign against Lieutenant Colonel
> Fernández Suárez that included fabricated details about
> the incident.

From *La Nación*:

> The Chief of Police, Lieutenant Colonel Fernández

Suárez, then added that this Marcelo is the one who, under the pseudonym M, provided some press publications with information, unsubstantiated of course, for a campaign against the police department on account of the executions.

From *El Plata*, of La Plata:

This individual Rizzoni is the one who was providing the newspaper *Revolución Nacional* with information for its vitriolic campaign against the Chief of Police.

From *El Argentino*, of La Plata:

Afterward, the Chief of Police stated that a terrorist—who has been detained and whose name, as it turns out, is Marcelo Rizzoni—was the one responsible for assembling the bombs, and was responsible for supplying false information regarding the executions to the newspaper *Revolución Nacional*, which is publishing several articles entitled "Operation Massacre," wherein the Chief of Police is put at fault. All of the information offered by the aforementioned periodical is false because it has been supplied by a person like Rizzoni, whose only goal is to confuse.

From *El Día*, of La Plata:

Lieutenant Colonel Fernández Suárez stepped in to note that one of the detainees, Marcelo Rizzoni—who played a central role in the terrorist group, signs his contributions to a newspaper where he has reported on alleged cases of torture "Mr. M," and is the leader of "Operation Massacre"—has made statements apologizing for his behavior . . .

There are times when the lies get so intricate that you need just the right method to untangle them. For lack of a better one, and even at the risk of boring you, I will use one that I have used before. The five reported versions, which I have mentioned in order of increasing stupidity, contain the following facts that are clearly false, partially false, or unproven, namely:

1. "*Marcelo Rizzoni, the same person who managed to escape on June 9 of last year, just before the raid in Florida . . .*" False. Marcelo did not "escape." He came to the house in Florida three times, and on the third time he left quietly without suspecting anything or thinking to himself that he was "escaping." The man who escaped when the raid took place was named Juan Carlos Torres.

2. "*. . . the raid in Florida that saw the arrest of men who were involved in the rebellion that same night . . .*" Partially false. Among those arrested, only one had been involved, and that was Norberto Gavino; otherwise, there were two or three suspects, and nine or ten innocents. And from the point of view of the Martial Law that was applied to them, they were all innocent, including Gavino.

3. "*Rizzoni is the person who, under the pseudonym M, went to all the opposition newspapers with the information about the executions . . .*" False. Marcelo did not go to them with *the* information, just *one piece* of information.

4. "*. . . information about the executions, which was then used as the basis for a campaign against Lieutenant Colonel Fernández Suárez . . .*" False. Not only was Marcelo's information *not* used as a basis for the "campaign"; the moment he brought it forth, the Chief of Police's position was significantly improved, as we will see later on.

5. "*. . . that included fabricated details about the incident . . .*" False. The information provided by Marcelo, like all

of the information I have used, is correct. I have verified it and can prove it before any civil or military
court.

6. "*. . . some press publications with information, unsubstantiated
of course . . .*" There is no proof that it was unsubstantiated.

7. "*This individual Rizzoni is the one who was providing the
newspaper . . . with information . . .*" Partially false, see
subheading 3.

8. "*. . . to the newspaper* Revolución Nacional, *which is
publishing . . .*" False. *Revolución Nacional* stopped being
printed a while ago, and is therefore not publishing
anything at all. Published.

9. "*. . . which is publishing several articles entitled 'Operation
Massacre' . . .*" False. *Revolución Nacional* never published
articles entitled "Operation Massacre."

10. "*Marcelo Rizzoni—who . . . signs his contributions to a newspaper . . . 'Mr. M' . . .*" False, and also stupid. Marcelo is a
witness, not a journalist. A witness whom I have called
M. and not "Mr. M." A witness who neither writes nor
signs contributions to any newspaper of any kind.

11. "*. . . a newspaper where he has reported on alleged cases of
torture . . .*" False and ridiculous to anyone who knows
what is being discussed.

12. "*He is the leader of 'Operation Massacre' . . .*" False. It's
confirmed: the person who drafted this version is men-
tally disabled. The indisputable leader of "Operation
Massacre" was Lieutenant Colonel Fernández Suárez.

Earlier I showed that Fernández Suárez lied, statistically speaking,
every other line. Now, with the help of my colleagues in the press,
he has beaten his own record.

Fernández Suárez tries to discredit everything I have published, making it seem like the information I am using as a foundation was supplied by a terrorist. But "Marcelo" is just one witness among fifty, and perhaps the least important one at that. The information, the real information, has been supplied to me by Fernández Suárez himself. He is my chief witness.

Should a civil or military court, intelligence services, or publishers of serious newspapers want to retrace my research step by step, the following are the witnesses and statements I used, by order of importance:

1. Fernández Suárez in his report before the Province Advisory Board on December 18, 1956;
2. Juan Carlos Livraga's formal accusation, restated before the judge, and his oral statements;
3. Miguel Ángel Giunta's statement;
4. Horacio di Chiano's oral testimony; (I have spoken to each of these three survivors at least half a dozen times, thoroughly rechecking every single detail)
5. a statement signed by Norberto Gavino, which I have in my possession;
6. a joint statement signed by Julio Troxler and Reinaldo Benavídez, in my possession;
7. testimony from Vicente Rodríguez's widow;
8. testimony from Mario Brión's relatives;
9. testimony from Nicolás Carranza's widow;
10. testimony from Francisco Garibotti's widow;
11. testimony from Carlos Lizaso's relatives;
12. testimony from Juan Carlos Torres;
13. testimony from Giunta's relatives;
14. testimony from Livraga's relatives;
15. testimony from Di Chiano's relatives.

Over the course of four months, I have conducted hundreds of interviews with these witnesses and with more minor ones, the vast majority of whom have not even made statements before a civil or military judge.

Now that there is no imminent danger, I should think that my fellow journalists from the big newspapers could go to the lengths I have gone to instead of taking dictation from the lieutenant colonel executioner.

SHORT HISTORY OF AN INVESTIGATION

In my account, I mention "Marcelo" three times using the initial M. I did not know him as a terrorist, but as a witness. I can't say, however, that I am surprised he became a terrorist: he was an embittered man who suffered tremendously. The ghost of Carlitos Lizaso—his blood-spattered chest, his cheek crushed by a bullet—tormented him relentlessly. His dear friend Mr. Pedro Lizaso had made him responsible for watching over the boy. He had brought him back dead.

In order to illustrate how untrue it is that "Marcelo" supplied the "*information used as the basis*" for my articles, and in an effort to stave off any more fanciful manipulations, I will have to refer briefly to the phases of my investigation. I first heard news of the massacre on December 18, 1956. On the nineteenth, I met Judge Doglia. On the twentieth, I met von Kotsch, Esq., and obtained a copy of Livraga's formal accusation. That afternoon, I sent it to the publisher of *Propósitos*. On the twenty-first, I met Livraga. On the twenty-third, the accusation was published in *Propósitos*.

The accusation and Livraga's oral statement were relatively precise, but they contained two basic errors that significantly hindered my later investigations. The first was the claim that, in the back apartment, where Livraga's friend Rodríguez had taken him, there were only three more people. The second was the assumption that there were only ten prisoners in the assault car.

On December 26, I finished writing my story on Livraga which, after a long pilgrimage, was going to be published in *Revolución Nacional* on January 15. It of course included those two errors. But it also included a noteworthy guess, a hunch even, based on a few words that Livraga heard in a semiconscious state: the theory of a third survivor. I never could have imagined how right it turned out to be. The piece also included another guess of mine that did not make it to the public: the nearly outright mention of the Chief of Police as the one responsible for everything. The editors at the newspaper thought it was too "bold" so they scrapped it.

On December 27, while looking through newspapers from the time of the uprising, I discovered Vicente Rodríguez's name at the top of a list of "those executed in the San Martín Region." But there were unbelievable errors here as well that would prove to be real stumbling blocks. There was a "Crizaso" on the list who I later realized was Lizaso. Reinaldo Benavídez was listed as dead though he was really alive. And Mario Brión's name was missing.

So, at the time, using Livraga's formal accusation and this list, you could glean the following, somewhat erroneous overview: there were two survivors (Livraga and Giunta), five known dead (Rodríguez, Carranza, Garibotti, "Crizaso," and Benavídez); and three unknown dead.

On December 28, it occurred to me to review *all* of the newspapers from the time of the uprising. Since it was All Fool's Day, it shouldn't have surprised me to come upon the Chief of Police's statements where he told the story of the raid, saying he had arrested *fourteen* people. Thus began the endless and slightly Kafkaesque process in which I was either missing a body or a survivor, or had one too many . . .

For rather unimportant reasons, I then reached an impasse that lasted twenty days.

On January 19, I located the site of the execution and took photographs. The twentieth was an extraordinary day. I went to Florida, met Giunta, managed to break down his dogged resistance, and got him to tell me his version of what had happened. That same afternoon, I interviewed Rodríguez's widow. I used that opportunity to talk to the neighbors. There were three extremely important pieces of information that came to the fore from all of these conversations: 1) the existence of a "third man," a new survivor, just as I had thought; 2) the first mention of Mario Brión; 3) the first mention of the mysterious tenant in the back apartment, "a tall man who escaped," according to what the neighborhood kids told me. I learned more in that one afternoon than I had in an entire month of false starts.

On January 29, 1957, *Revolución Nacional* published my story on Rodríguez's widow where, for the first time, I singled out Fernández Suárez as the perpetrator of the arrests and the one responsible for the executions.

On February 7, I had in my hands transcriptions of both Province Advisory Board sessions in which the torture and executions were discussed. One of them included the now notorious confession from Fernández Suárez.

On February 10, I returned to Florida for what I knew from the start would be one of the more difficult tasks: locating the "third man." I already knew his name. I had his address. I had been told, though, that I wasn't going to find him. He was hiding somewhere as a fugitive. He would not let himself be seen by anyone. His life was still dominated by panic.

As usual, the kids from the neighborhood were my best informants. A little girl with bright eyes mysteriously approached us.

—The man you're looking for *is* in his house —she whispered.— They're going to tell you he isn't, but he *is*.

—And you know why we've come? —I asked her.

—Yes. I know everything —she replied, with the utmost dignity.

(There were dozens of scenes like this.)

I won't recount the feats of eloquence I had to display to get face to face, finally, with Mr. Horacio di Chiano. But there he was, the third survivor, alive and kicking.

With that, I thought the matter of survivors had come to an end. It was already a miracle that the three of them had saved themselves. But on the following day, February 11, I got one of the biggest shocks of my life. The letter I held in my hands was real, palpable. And in it, like a bomb, was this paragraph: "When the innocent victims stepped out of the assault car, Livraga, Giunta, and the ex-NCO Gavino managed to escape. The latter was able to get himself to the Bolivian Embassy and was granted asylum in that country."

So the number of survivors had gone up to four. I began to ask myself whether anyone had actually died. I went back to "my witnesses" and kept putting the sentence "The tall man who escaped . . ." out there as though at random, until I got the immediate, mechanical response I was looking for:

—Torres.

—At the embassy . . . ?

—The Bolivian one.

By the time my informant had raised his hand to cover his mouth, it was already too late. Aside from the children, no one said anything voluntarily. But people have reflexes. On February 19, I saw Torres at the Bolivian Embassy. On the twenty-first, I came back to see him again. You could say that the investigation came to a close that day. Torres' account was shocking. Not only was Gavino's existence confirmed; it turned out that Benavídez, the one from the official list of those executed, was not dead: he was in exile in Bolivia. And with him was a sixth survivor, whose name I heard uttered for the first time: Julio Troxler. And there may have also been a seventh who, according to some, was locked up in Olmos. Torres could not remember the last name. He only knew it was something common, something like Rodríguez . . . I looked at a list of the prisoners in Olmos. When I saw Torres again, I hit him pointblank with a name:

—Díaz?

His face lit up.

—Díaz! How'd you do it?

—Rogelio Díaz?

—Exactly.

The list was complete. Rogelio Díaz was the seventh survivor.

That same nineteenth of February, the third and most important of my articles—"The Truth about the Executed Men"—appeared in *Revolución Nacional* and included all the facts I had gathered before going to see Torres. In it, I already made mention of Mario Brión, claimed that there were three living survivors, and speculated that there might be two more—I was certainly getting ahead of myself with all this, given the information I had in my possession when I wrote it. On the twenty-first, I managed to locate Mario Brión's relatives. In the meantime, I had already found addresses for Carranza's and Garibotti's widows.

It was then and only then, with the case completely clear and resolved, that "Marcelo" came into the picture.

REGARDING "MARCELO"

At first, "Marcelo" was simply a voice on the telephone. A tense, nervous voice that would call the main office at the *Revolución Nacional* bureau and ask to speak to the author who wrote the articles on the José León Suárez executions. We set up an interview for February 22, 1957. "Marcelo" was devastated when he found out that he was taking a risk unnecessarily, since Torres had already provided me with all the information he brought me. The funny thing is, even if I had never met either of these two men, I still would have found out about the other survivors. Because on the twenty-third or the twenty-fourth of February, I received a third letter with a list of all the survivors from the informant who signed his name "Atilas." "Atilas" arrived forty-eight hours late, but I still want to take the opportunity—if he happens to be reading this—to thank him for his valuable help.

There is not one important piece of information in the text of *Operation Massacre* that hasn't been matched and double-checked with the testimony of three or four people, sometimes more. With respect to the basic facts, I have ruthlessly thrown out any information that was not corroborated, as sensational as it might have been. It's possible that some minor mistakes in detail have slipped, but the account is fundamentally accurate and I can prove it before any civil or military court.

Returning now to "Marcelo": his and Torres's matching testimony was damaging to Livraga and benefited Fernández Suárez, which demonstrates conclusively that it was true. Based on Livraga's formal accusation, I had assumed in my first articles for *Revolución Nacional* that Fernández Suárez arrested only five people at the house in Florida, and indiscriminately rounded up the rest in the surrounding area. Torres and "Marcelo" explained to me that this was not the case, that *all* the executed men had been arrested inside the house. From this perspective, the raid at least had a certain logic to it and Fernández Suárez's behavior before the mass murder seemed easier to explain. I was completely honest about this and made it clear the first chance I got. Torres went further still: he admitted that he and Gavino were involved in the uprising, even though they did not get to act. These people were completely frank with me and told me who had been involved: Torres and Gavino. The ones who had simply known about it were Carranza and Lizaso. And those who knew absolutely nothing were Brión, Giunta, Di Chiano, Livraga, and Garibotti. For lack of concrete facts, I was still in the dark about the state of mind of men like Rodríguez and Díaz. All of this is stated very clearly in my account. As for Troxler and Benavídez, it doesn't really matter if they were involved or whether they knew anything: they were taken to be executed for the sole crime of ringing a doorbell.

"Marcelo" was a short man with olive skin, dark glasses, and a bitter, disdainful expression on his face. He was thirty-seven years old but looked older. His most valuable contributions to my book were the moving, faltering words he used to speak about Carlitos Lizaso. He remembered him with almost as much intensity as a father would his son: in his way of being, in his little anecdotes, in his youthful happiness. Over the course of the months I have spent digging around in this case, I have met women who weep every rotten day as a matter of habit; I have met small children with an unmistakably distant look in their eyes ("Do you miss your father very much?" "Oh, yes, you have no idea . . ."); and I have met brothers whose clenched fists on the table are a natural extension of the murderous look in their eyes. But I have seen few things like the dull, terrible, cutting pain of this man when he remembers that boy. He would try, uselessly, to recreate him with a gesture, to bring his smile back to life with an awkward grimace, "to bring him back and ungag him"; he, a ruined and unwell man.

I am sorry that "Marcelo" decided to follow the fruitless road of terror to banish this ghost. But my question is: Have the high judges and rulers who are protecting his friend's murderer given him any other way? I know that there is nothing more difficult than justifying a bomb-thrower, and I do not even plan to try. All I can say is that, at heart, that's not who "Marcelo" was. At heart, he was a man who suffered terribly, constantly, sleeplessly. Every time he would think back on leaving the house in Florida ten minutes before the raid, he would say again: "If I had just stayed . . . If I had just . . ." A sense of male pride stopped him from saying that he, too, wished he were dead.

Now "Marcelo" is in jail, and I am happy for his sake that they caught him before his bombs could take innocent lives. But I will not be the one to call this wreck of a man an irresponsible and cowardly criminal. I leave that work to my colleagues, the serious journalists, lovers of easy truths.

Terrorism in the abstract is no doubt criminal, irresponsible, and cowardly. But if I have to choose between a desperate man like "Marcelo," eaten away by his own ghost and his thirst for vengeance, and a cold, capricious, cognizant, methodical torturer and executioner, don't ask me whom I would pick.

THE PRESS CONFERENCE THAT JUDGE VIGLIONE NEVER GAVE

On July 11, 1957, Judge Viglione called the press together at the Police Headquarters of the Province to report on a terrorist organization that had recently been discovered in Boulogne, and whose leader was allegedly "Marcelo." I think it's good that a judge intervened in the proceedings and monitored the treatment of the prisoners, because that's the main duty of a judge in the Province of Buenos Aires. I think it's great, also, that he quickly supplied the public with information because "in a democracy, dialogue is interesting," as Fernández Suárez once put it. What seems wrong to me is that he took advantage of the situation to discredit, in a childish maneuver, the unclearable charges of multiple homicide that I have made against the Chief of Police. If not for this, I would have nothing to say and I would not be publishing this article. But malice is a double-edged sword, and here we have the second edge. This is my response to the clumsiness that I mentioned earlier.

I won't say it was Banquo's ghost exactly that hovered over Judge Viglione's press conference, but rather a specter of the other failed press conference from the end of this past January in which a different judge, Judge Hueyo, was going to announce the trial of Fernández Suárez. For this reason—and because I might have wanted to ask some modest and respectful questions of the Chief of Police in attendance (as I have gathered that a press conference is basically like a question-and-answer contest)—I was sorry not to be invited. One of these days, God willing.

What I am even more sorry about is the fact that the judge

missed a nearly unique opportunity to educate and be a model for the people, which itself is another one of his duties. The judge could have explained that terrorism is not a product of spontaneous generation. He could have explained that the behavior of a terrorist down in the streets who sets a bomb is a response to the *picana* terrorism being inflicted on high by the State. He could have explained that the bomb that kills an innocent person is not so different from the firing squad rounds that kill another innocent person. And that, if any kind of subtle distinction should be made, it is in favor of the terrorist in the streets who at least does not act with complete impunity, does not believe he is defending democracy, liberty, and justice, and does not organize press conferences.

No one was in a better position than the judge to give the entire country this excellent lesson in sanity, common sense, and integrity. Because in the Province of Buenos Aires, there is no one—except the torturers themselves—who knows how police torture works better than Judge Viglione.

To demonstrate, I will limit myself to sharing just one part of the report that the Socialist representative, Eduardo Schaposnik, presented on December 27, 1956, before the Province Advisory Board. I hope *La Nación* says it is "unsubstantiated." I hope *La Razón* says it is "fabricated." I hope *El Día* from La Plata speaks of "alleged" torture. I hope all of this is used as material for Judge Viglione's next press conference. This is what Dr. Schaposnik said:

> Together with representative Bronzini, I have been to the offices of two judges in order to gather impressions that would allow us to verify whether our information (*about the torture*) was true or not. What we have learned, especially from the words of Judge Viglione—whom I value as a man for his civic activism, and whom I respect even more for the adjudication skills he has demonstrated during this brief but brilliant term, carried out with such zeal

and enthusiasm—is conclusive. And what we have verified has discouraged our faith in a number of men. It indicates a rise in the number of torture cases beginning at the start of this year and reaching its height during the uprising of June 9 and 10 . . .

This is then followed by a few paragraphs that I have already cited in the main text of *Operation Massacre*. Dr. Schaposnik then continues:

I have encountered numerous torture cases in the criminal courts that leave no shred of doubt: in one of them, the perpetrators were sentenced in the first hearing to four years in prison by Judge Viglione, and the case is currently on appeal in the appropriate chamber. Another case, which is still in its first hearing in the same court, is worth highlighting to see whether the charges—overwhelming and painful for any man with two cents' worth of sensitivity to bear—are not damaging to the reputation of the institution.

I will now summarize some of the proceedings of the criminal case based on torture claims that is currently being tried in Judge Viglione's court.

Court minutes, page one: dated April 9, 1956, Judge Viglione, having been informed that illegal punishment has been carried out against the prisoners repeatedly, in the Lanús Bureau of Investigation, resolves to establish the Court in that police division.

Back of page one: Having established the court in the aforementioned police station, Judge Viglione examines the cells together with the Court clerks and is informed by prisoners Héctor Silva, Agustín Daniel Silva and Julio Jorge Silva, Agapito Rearte, Rómulo Fernández, Héctor A. Milito, Mariano Enrique Gareca, Carlos Neme, Miguel Artemio Longhi, Alfredo Richler, Alfonso Dande, Ernesto Arturo Suárez, Domingo Cuervo and Domingo Prieto, that they had injuries from torture inflicted upon them in that same police station, and which call for the attendance of the police medic, Dr. Ricardo Alberto Díaz, who is offering his report separately. The prisoners then identify their torturers: Rearte gives the name of Officer Farina; Milito was given the *picana* by Officers Zapiola and Fernández; Cuervo reports that he was beaten by Officer Gatti and others whom he would recognize; Prieto says that Officer Fumagalli and others beat him and gave him the *picana*; Richler saw his fellow prisoners being taken to the cell completely naked and in poor condition due to the torture they had endured. The minutes are signed by all of the aforementioned prisoners, the judge, and the clerks.

The police medic's report reads:

That prisoners Héctor, Agustín Daniel, and Julio Jorge Silva have the following injuries: linear abrasions on the lateral right and left side walls of the upper abdomen. Multiple punctated ecchymoses in most of the abdomen, seven days old, produced by a hard instrument; the rest produced from mild pressure throughout the area by a small instrument with a small blunt surface, which has been applied violently enough to produce these small superficial hemorrhages.

Agapito Néstor Rearte: two scars approximately half a centimeter in diameter in the dorsal region of the penis; given their size, they look like burns and are not less than seven days nor more than fifteen days old.

Rómulo Fernández: bruises approximately eight days old in the right lower eyelid, caused by a blunt object, possibly a punch.

Milito: ecchymosis in the inguinoscrotal region, caused by a blunt object.

Carlos Neme: punctate scars on the penis and scrotum, the same type as those of Rearte.

Domingo Prieto: contusion on his right knee and a superficial wound on his right arm; these injuries are in the process of fully healing and are three or four days old.

Then Dr. Schaposnik said:

I am not going to continue reading the records of the trial that convincingly demonstrate how poorly the prisoners were treated by the Lanús Bureau of Investigation. Commissioner Mucci, who led the investigation in Lanús, is still in office . . . What I posit here are examples. My presentation would be endless if I had set myself the task of extracting all of the necessary notes from the dossiers . . .

Does this not warrant another press conference? If we admit that a public reaction must be incited against terrorism in the streets (and I don't disagree), can't we also see how urgent it is that we support a great transformation in public opinion, one in favor of eliminating the high-up terrorists, the State torturers and the executioners, for all time?

I have begun to convince myself that always seeing both sides of the coin is a kind of misfortune, some sort of psychological defect that respectable people steer clear of; it's that two-cent coin of sensitivity that Dr. Schaposnik was asking for.

PROVISIONAL EPILOGUE
(to the first edition, July 1957)

For various reasons, happenstance included, I was quite close to the three revolutions—two that were quashed in very different ways, and a victorious one in the middle—that rattled the country in 1955 and 1956.

I can say again, without remorse, that I supported the September 1955 uprising. Not only for pressing, family reasons—which I had—but because I knew with certainty that a system that mocked civil liberties, that denied the right to freedom of expression, and that promoted obedience on the one hand and excess on the other, had just been overthrown. My memory is not short: what I thought then, right or wrong, I continue to think today.

Toward the end of 1955, I wrote an article for the papers as a tribute to the three men of the naval air force who had died in an expedition to the South, fighting with simple and obvious heroism. For reasons that are better left unmentioned, the Navy authorities disavowed this article, first verbally and then in writing. Their understanding was that the fallen ones, their own dead, could do without such a tribute—a tribute that even their enemies might not have denied them—and my understanding was that I could do without the Navy's opinion. Because then as well as now I believe that the press has to be free, or it's a farce; there is no middle ground. And naturally, the article ran with my name on it, despite the explicit disavowal that I still have in my hands.

I am not just making idle mention of this incident; it was perhaps the first one in a long series of events that allowed the revolution to devour its heroes and forsake its dead, and with that, to lose its Liberating characteristic, among many other things. Because in the article I purposefully pointed out that, along with Captian Estivariz and Lieutenant Irigoin, a Peronist NCO had died. A man who could have dodged his service as many higher-ranking men had done, but instead had put his esprit de corps, his loyalty to the uniform, and his devotion to his superior first and foremost; at a very far second were his heartfelt and, in his case, respectable political opinions. The charred and unrecognizable remains of the three men—two revolutionaries and one Peronist inside the same plane that was blown to pieces, who died fighting the same battle, and who were consumed by the same fire of heroism—undoubtedly meant something. It was a sign, a warning, a massive symbol, a pact sealed with blood. What meaning does it carry now, almost two years later, when the short-sighted, the cowardly, and the dim-witted have done nothing but violate this pact? I can only think to say one thing: blessed are those three who lie dead, united, and untouched in their glorious eternity.

The June 9 revolution hit even closer to home. For purely geographic reasons, it literally came into my home. To reach my house in the early morning, I had to cross a war zone at the corner of Fifty-Fourth and Fourth in La Plata. In the thirty paces it took to cross the live fire zone of the Second Division Command, I learned what irrepressible physical fear was.

But I don't just remember this minor incident for love of the picturesque, either. On that same corner, behind a car that was being used as a barricade and amidst the crackling of gunshots, I was the final recipient of a "Haaalt!" that rang out endlessly, coming from invisible snipers all around me. I had been stopped by a short, rather fat man with a mustache, a leather jacket, and a submachine gun tucked into his belt. He asked me where I was going. My voice faltering, I told him about my family that was fifty meters away, in the area where the most intense shooting of the entire day was taking place. He didn't ask me for my ID, which I didn't have on me.

He didn't ask my opinion about what was happening. He simply said, shrugging his shoulders:

—Go ahead, if you dare.

He was the leader of the rebel Peronist group. A man who now sells balloons in a plaza in Montevideo. I thought then and I think now—take good note of this—that the man was in the wrong. Because he could not have known that, at that very moment, he was being proven right. He could not have known that, at that very moment, an individual who would not dare to stick his nose in that battle-field was coldly ordering the execution of twelve poor bastards. He could not have known that, behind the wall and the little green door of the Command, another man—Juan Carlos Longoni—was risking his life for the exact opposite idea, was going to risk and lose his job for helping those poor bastards. Neither he, nor I, nor Longoni knew any of that.

But that same Seargeant Ferrari of the rebel group let me pass; he must have regretted it. Because two hours later my house became a shelter for the forty loyal soldiers who, having overcome their fear, were shooting at him. Those men of the City Bell Communications Second Batallion will not remember my face, which they could barely see in the darkness, or my name, which they didn't check. But I am certain that not one of them—not even Lieutenant Cruset, or Decruset, who was in charge—will ever forget the tall wooden door on Fifty-Fourth street that was the only one to open for them when they were caught in rebel fire that threatened to destroy them and that, on the sidewalk across the street, had already left a trail of dead marines.

One of them had just died, ten meters away, on the other side of the street. I heard the cry of terror and loneliness that he let out when he was dying and the patrol fell back for a moment, taken by surprise: "Don't leave me here alone! You sons of b——, don't leave me here alone!" Later on, his fellow soldiers took control of the machine-gun emplacement (located in a construction site) that had killed him. But Bernardino Rodríguez perished at age twenty-one believing that his brothers-in-arms, his friends, had abandoned him in death. That pained me at the time, and continues to pain me now, like so many other useless things.

That is the moment when I understood what a revolution was, its squalid face that nothing can make up for. And I hated that revolution with all my might. As a reflex, I also hated all the previous ones, however just they may have been. I came to a deeper understanding of it in the tense hours that followed, seeing undisguised fear all around me in the almost childlike faces of the soldiers who didn't know if they were "loyalists" or "rebels," but knew that they had to shoot at other soldiers identical to themselves, who also didn't know if they were loyalists or rebels.

If there is one thing that I have tried to evoke in these pages it is the horror of revolutions, whose first victims are always innocent people like the executed men at José León Suárez or that dying soldier just a few meters from where I was. These poor people do not die screaming "Long live the nation" like they do in novels. They die vomiting from fear, like Nicolás Carranza, or cursing others for abandoning them, like Bernardino Rodríguez.

Only an idiot could not want peace.

But peace at any price is not acceptable.

And there will always be new seeds of revolution taking root, new surges of senseless revenge (that might later come to mean the complete opposite) on the rise as long as we keep men like the current Chief of Police of the Province of Buenos Aires, Lieutenant Colonel Desiderio Fernández Suárez, at the helm of repressive State institutions.

EPILOGUE
(to the second edition, 1964)

I want now to state what I have accomplished with this book, but also, mainly, what I have not accomplished. I want to note the ways in which it was a triumph, and the ways in which it was a defeat; what I have won and what I have lost.

It was a triumph to be able to clarify some facts that were at first confusing, disturbing, even implausible, with little help aside from that of a young woman and a few harrassed men, namely the victims. It was a triumph to overcome the fear that came at me with a kind of intensity, primarily in the beginning, and to get them to overcome theirs too, even though they had experienced fear in a way that I will never be able to match. It was a triumph to get a man like "Marcelo," who didn't even know us, to bring us his information, risking the ambush and the *picana* that tore him up later; to get even little Cassandra from Florida to know that she could entrust us with a man's life. It has been a triumph to find myself face to face years later with Troxler's childish grin, and to know that he saved everyone who survived, but not to say a word about that night.

As for the rest, I lost. I wanted the government—Aramburu's, Frondizi's, Guido's, any government really—to acknowledge, be it in the words of the most absent-minded and innocent of its public servants, that an atrocity had been committed on the night of June 10, 1956, in the name of the Argentine Republic.

I wanted one of the multiple governments of this country to acknowledge that its justice system was wrong to kill those men, that they were killed for no good reason, out of stupidity and blindness. I know it doesn't matter to the dead. But there was a question of decency at hand, I don't know how else to say it.

I wanted those who escaped—Livraga disfigured from bullet wounds; Giunta nearly insane; Di Chiano hiding in a basement; others in exile—to have some kind of authority, some institution, any respectable part of this civilized country, admit to them in words at least—here, where words are so easy, where they cost nothing—that there was a mistake, that there was a fatal lapse in consideration, let alone a murder.

I wanted Carranza's six children, Garibotti's six children, Rodríguez's three children, and Brión's only child, together with all of these men's wives, to be given some rights on account of the bloody corpses that the justice system of this country, and not any other, sent to their graves; on account of all the bodies that were once people loved by their families. To be given something, a testimony, a word, a monthly stipend, not as large as what they would give a general or a judge of the Court, because who could ask for so much. But something.

I failed at this. Aramburu promoted Fernández Suárez; he did not clear the names of the victims. Frondizi had a copy of this book in his hands with a dedication in it: he promoted Aramburu. After that is when I think I lost interest. In 1957 I boasted: "This case is in process, and will continue to be for as long as is necessary, months or even years." I would like to retract that flawed statement. This case is no longer in process, it is barely a piece of history; this case is dead.

I failed at other things as well. I wanted Fernández Suárez to be tried, removed from office, and punished. When it became clear that none of this was going to happen, I wanted to punish him myself, in my own way, with my own weapons: I chased him perhaps as savagely as he chased, tortured, and killed; I whipped him week after week. To the extent that I resembled him in this effort, I again request a retraction. What do I care about Fernández Suárez at this point.

There is yet another failure. When I wrote this story, I was thirty years old. I had been a journalist for ten years. Suddenly I felt I understood that everything I had done before had nothing to do with a certain notion of journalism that had been taking shape in my mind, and this—investigating at all costs, gathering testimony of what is most hidden and most painful—this *did* have something do with it and fit into that notion. I was fortified by this thought, so I investigated and wrote about another secret story right away, the Satanowsky case.[25] It made more noise, but the outcome was the same: the dead, still dead; the murderers, proven guilty, but set free.

So I asked myself if it was worth it, if what I was chasing was not a fantasy, if the society we live in really needs to hear about these things. I still don't have an answer. In any event, you can understand how I may have lost some faith—faith in justice, in compensation, in democracy, in all those words, and finally, in what was once, but is no longer, my trade.

I am rereading the story that you all have read. There are entire sentences that bother me, I get annoyed thinking about how much better it would be if I wrote it now.

Would I write it now?

PORTRAIT OF THE DOMINANT OLIGARCHY
(end of the epilogue to the third edition, 1969)

The following generalizations should not be dismissed as stemming from impatience.

Today, in light of the murders, we can begin to perfect a portrait of the dominant oligarchy, moving in orderly fashion from the smallest to the greatest detail. As opposed to others who staged uprisings before and afterward, the military personnel who were executed in June 1956 were killed for trying to speak in the name of the people: more specifically, in the name of Peronism and the working class. The torture and murders that preceded and followed the 1956 massacre are typical, inevitable incidents, not anecdotal ones about class warfare in Argentina. The Manchego case; the Vallese case; the murder of Méndez, Mussi, and Retamar; the death of Pampillón; the murder of Hilda Guerrero; the daily *picana* sessions in police precincts throughout the country; the brutal repression of labor and student protests; random raids in slums: these are all links in the same chain.[26]

It was useless in 1957 to seek justice for the victims of "Operation Massacre," just as it was useless in 1958 to seek punishment against General Cuaranta for the murder of Satanowsky, just as it is useless in 1968 to call for the prosecution of those who murdered Blajaquis and Zalazar and are being protected by the government.[27] Within the system, there is no justice.

Other writers keep refining the picture of this oligarchy that dominates Argentines and is dominated by foreign interests. When considering taking up a fight against this elite class, it is important to remember that they are temperamentally inclined toward murder. This tendency should be kept in mind, not with the thought of doing as they do, but rather the contrary: so as not to be moved by the sacred ideas, the sacred principles, and more generally, the beautiful souls of the executioners.

OPERATION IN THE MOVIES

In 1971, Jorge Cedrón decided to make a film out of *Operation Massacre*. He shot the film in secret due to the restrictions that Lanusse's dictatorship had placed on most political activities, as well as some artistic ones.[28] About thirty professional actors, most of them first-rate, accepted the risk of shooting the film.

They finished shooting in August of 1972. With the help of the Peronist Youth movement, union and student groups, and run-of-the-mill Peronism, it was screened hundreds of times in the neighborhoods and slums of the metropolitan area of Buenos Aires and throughout the country without ever falling into the hands of the police. It was estimated that more than one hundred thousand had seen it before May 25, 1973. Ever since that day, there has been a hold on a permit from the Film Institute to show it legally.

Julio Troxler plays himself nicely in the movie. After a conversation with him and Cedrón about the book, we came to the conclusion that the film should not limit itself to the events described in the text. Troxler's active militancy for nearly twenty years gave him the authority to encapsulate the collective experience of Peronism during the difficult years of resistance, proscription, and armed struggle.

So the movie includes a text that does not appear in the original book. I have included it in this edition because I understand that it makes the book whole and gives it its ultimate meaning.

FINAL SEQUENCE

José León Suárez. Dawn.	VOICE OF TROXLER (*offstage*). –I came back from Bolivia, they put me in jail, I was acquainted with the electric *picana* for the first time. I've gone back to that place many times in my mind. I wanted to find the answer to that question of what it meant to be a Peronist.
Bodies in the garbage dump.	What did this hatred mean, why were they killing us off like that. It took us a long time to understand it, to realize that Peronism was something more everlasting than a government that can be abolished, than a political party that can be outlawed.
Crowds in motion.	Peronism was a class, the working class that cannot be destroyed, the backbone of a liberation movement that cannot be crushed. Their hatred of us was the hatred exploiters have of those they are exploiting.
Bodies in Plaza de Mayo.	
The people's martyrs: Jáuregui.	Many more people would fall victim to that hatred when fighting in popular protests, through torture, through being kidnapped and murdered by the police and the army, or in combat.
Baldú. Maestre. Abal Medina.	

A young man holding a flag leads a protest.

But the people never stopped raising the flag of liberation, the working class never stopped rebelling against injustice. Peronism tried every way possible of regaining power, from logrolling to a military coup. The outcome was always the same:

An occupied factory.

Frondizi.

Exploitation

Villa Miseria.
Signs: Esso, Fiat, etc.
A fallen protestor.

Submission
Suppression.
That's how we began to learn.

Politicians.

We came to expect only deceit from the politicians,

A documentary about the Cordobazo uprising starts rolling.

the only true revolution is one sparked by the people and led by the workers.

Soldiers.

Military personnel can join it as individuals, but cannot control it as an institution.

Military trucks.

Graffiti on a wall: "FAP, FAR, Montoneros."[29]

Because this institution belongs to the enemy, and only another army, rising up from the people, can fight against this enemy.

Cut back to the Cordobazo documentary.

Blood was spilled to learn these truths,

The people push against the cavalry.

but for the first time, they made the tyrants step back and, for the first time, they unsettled the enemy,

Córdoba covered in smoke, Lanusse.
Fighting in the streets: Rosario.
Fighting in the streets: Mendoza.
Commissioner Sandoval, dead.
Newspaper headline: "General Sánchez is killed."
Aramburu.

Aramburu's funeral.
The execution of Lizaso.
Graffiti: "*Descamisados.*
The Carlos Lizaso Squad."[30]

Troxler grabs rifles from two guards in José León Suárez.

The documentary: moving crowds.

Vandor.
Alonso.
Crowds.
Crowds advancing.
Crowds advancing.
Crowds advancing.

which started seeking out impossible pacts between the oppressors and the oppressed. The tide was beginning to turn: now the bullets were hitting the torturers and the leaders of the oppression, too.

Those who had signed off on death sentences were now suffering a death sentence. The names of our dead took on new life in our combatants.

The things that we had improvised in our despair, others learned to organize rigorously and to develop in order to meet the needs of the working class—a class which, in silence and anonymity, continues to organize itself without traitors
or bureaucrats,
the long war of the people
the long road
the long march
to the Socialist Homeland.

OPEN LETTER FROM A WRITER
TO THE MILITARY JUNTA[*]

1. Censorship of the press, the persecution of intellectuals, the raid on my home in Tigre, the murder of dear friends, and the loss of a daughter who died fighting you, are some of the events that compel me to express myself in this clandestine way after having shared my opinion freely as a writer and journalist for nearly thirty years.[32]

The first anniversary of this Military Junta has brought about a year-end review of government operations in the form of official documents and speeches: what you call good decisions are mistakes, what you acknowledge as mistakes are crimes, and what you have left out entirely are disasters.

On March 24, 1976, you overthrew a government that you yourselves were a part of, that you helped bring into disrepute as the executors of its repressive policies, and that was coming to an end, given the elections that had been set for just nine months later. From this perspective, what you destroyed was not the temporary mandate of Isabel Martínez, but rather the possibility for a democratic process through which the people might remedy the problems that you have perpetuated and aggravated.[33]

Illegitimate since birth, your government could have legitimized itself by reviving the political program that 80 percent of Argentines voted for in the 1973 elections, and that continues to be an objective

---

[*] Walsh sent this letter, dated March 24, 1977, by post to the editorial departments of local newspapers and to foreign press correspondents. On March 25, 1977, Walsh was kidnapped by a "Work Group" and has been missing ever since.[31]

The letter was not published by any local media, but it gradually came to be distributed abroad. Ever since the letter was reissued in 1984, De la Flor has included it as an Appendix in all reprints of *Operation Massacre*. *[Edición de la Flor Editor's Note.]*

expression of the people's will—the only thing that could possibly be denoted by the "national being" that you invoke so often. You have gone instead in the completely opposite direction by return- ing to the ideas and interests of defeated minority groups, the ones who hold back workforce development, exploit the people, and divide the Nation. This kind of politics can only prevail temporar- ily by banning political parties, taking control of unions, silencing the press, and introducing Argentine society to the most profound terror it has ever known.

2. Fifteen thousand missing, ten thousand prisoners, four thou- sand dead, tens of thousands in exile: these are the raw numbers of this terror.

Since the ordinary jails were filled to the brim, you created virtual concentration camps in the main garrisons of the country which judges, lawyers, journalists, and international observers, are all for- bidden to enter. The military secrecy of what goes on inside, which you cite as a requirement for the purposes of investigation, means that the majority of the arrests turn into kidnappings that in turn allow for torture without limits and execution without trial.*

More than seven thousand habeas corpus petitions have been denied in the past year. In thousands of other cases of missing peo- ple, the petition has not even been presented either because people know ahead of time how useless it is, or because they can't find a lawyer who will dare to present it, since the fifty or sixty who did have been kidnapped one by one.

This is how you have done away with any time limit on torture. Since the prisoner does not exist, there is no way to present him before the judge within ten days, as stipulated by the law that was respected

---

* In January 1977, the Junta began publishing incomplete lists of new prisoners and of those "released," the majority of whom were not actually released; they have been charged and are no longer under the Junta's jurisdiction, but remain in jail. The names of thousands of prisoners are still a military secret and the conditions that allow for their torture and subsequent execution remain un- changed.

even at the heights of repression during previous dictatorships.

The lack of any time limits has been accompanied by a lack of any limits when it comes to your methods: you have regressed to periods when victims' joints and internal organs were operated on directly, only now you use surgical and pharmacological aids that the old executioners did not have at their disposal. The rack, the drill, skinning alive, and the saw of the medieval Inquisition reappear in testimonies alongside the *picana* and waterboarding, the blowtorch of today.*

By succumbing repeatedly to the argument that the end of killing guerrillas justifies all your means, you have arrived at a form of absolute, metaphysical torture that is unbounded by time: the original goal of obtaining information has been lost in the disturbed minds of those inflicting the torture. Instead, they have ceded to the impulse to pommel human substance to the point of breaking it and making it lose its dignity, which the executioner has lost, and which you yourselves have lost.

3. The refusal of this Junta to publish the names of the prisoners is, moreover, a cover for the systematic execution of hostages in vacant lots in the early morning, all under the pretext of fabricated combat and imaginary escape attempts.

Extremists who hand out pamphlets in the countryside, graffiti the sidewalks, or pile ten at a time into vehicles that then burst into flames: these are the stereotypes of a screenplay that was written not to be believed, but to buffer against the international reaction to the current executions. Within the country, meanwhile, the screenplay only underscores how intensely the military lashes back in the same places where there has just been guerrilla activity.

---

* The Peronist leader Jorge Lizaso was skinned alive; a former member of Congress, Mario Amaya, was beaten to death, and the former member of Congress Muñiz Barreto had his neck broken in one blow. One survivor's testimony: "*Picana* on my arms, hands, thighs, near my mouth every time I cried or prayed . . . Every twenty minutes they would open the door and you could hear the saw machine they said they'd use to make cold cuts out of me."

Seventy people executed after the Federal Security Agency bombing, fifty-five in response to the blasting of the La Plata Police Department, thirty for the attack on the Ministry of Defense, forty in the New Year's Massacre following the death of Colonel Castellanos, and nineteen after the explosion that destroyed the Ciudadela precinct, amount to only a portion of the twelve hundred executions in three hundred alleged battles where the opposition came out with zero wounded and zero forces killed in action.

Many of the hostages are union representatives, intellectuals, relatives of guerrillas, unarmed opponents, or people who just look suspicious: they are recipients of a collective guilt that has no place in a civilized justice system and are incapable of influencing the politics that dictate the events they are being punished for. They are killed to balance the number of casualties according to the foreign "body-count" doctrine that the SS used in occupied countries and the invaders used in Vietnam.

Guerrillas who were wounded or captured in real combat are being killed just to make sure they are dead. This additional piece of evidence was taken from the military's own press releases which stated that, over the course of one year, there were six hundred guerrilla deaths and only ten or fifteen wounded—a ratio unheard of in even the bloodiest of conflicts. This suggestion is confirmed by a sampling from a secret news source which showed that, between December 18, 1976, and February 3, 1977, over the course of forty live battles, the armed forces suffered twenty-three deaths and forty wounded, and the guerrillas suffered sixty-three deaths.[*]

More than one hundred prisoners awaiting their sentence have also been slain in their attempts to escape. Here, too, the official story has been written not to be believable, but rather to show the guerrillas and the political parties that even those who have been acknowledged as prisoners are held on strategic reserve: the Corps Commanders use them in retaliation depending on how the battles

---

[*]   *Cadena Informativa*, message No. 4, February 1977.

are going, if a lesson can be learned, if the mood strikes them.

That is how General Benjamín Menéndez, Commander of the Third Army Corps, earned his laurels before March 24: first with the murder of Marcos Osatinsky, who had been arrested in Córdoba, and then with the death of Hugo Vaca Narvaja and another fifty prisoners through various, merciless applications of the escape law; the official story of these deaths was told without any sense of shame.*

The murder of Dardo Cabo, arrested in April 1975 and executed on January 6, 1977, with seven other prisoners under the jurisdiction of the First Army Corps led by General Suárez Mason, shows that these incidents do not constitute the indulgences of a few eccentric centurions, but rather are the very same policies that you plan among your general staff, that you discuss in your cabinet meetings, that you enforce as commanders-in-chief of the three branches of government, and that you approve as members of the Ruling Junta.

4. Between fifteen hundred and three thousand people have been massacred in secret since you banned the right to report on the discovery of bodies; in some cases, the news still managed to leak, either because it involved other countries, or because of the magnitude of your genocide, or because of the shock provoked among your own troops.**

---

* A precise version of events appears in this letter from the prisoners at the Remand Center to the Bishop of Córdoba, Monsignor Primatesta: "On May 17, five fellow prisoners are taken out under the pretext of a trip to the infirmary and then executed: Miguel Ángel Mosse, José Svaguza, Diana Fidelman, Luis Verón, Ricardo Yung, and Eduardo Hernández. The Third Army Corps reported that they died in an attempted escape. On May 29, José Puchet and Carlos Sgadurra are taken out. The latter had been punished for not being able to stand on his feet, as he had suffered a number of broken bones. Later they are also reported as having been executed in an attempted escape."

** During the first fifteen days of military government, sixty-three bodies turned up, according to the papers. This makes for an annual projection of fifteen hundred. The assumption that the number could double is based both on the fact that since January 1976, the data in the press's hands has been incomplete, and also on the fact that there has been a general increase in repression since the coup. What follows is a plausible overall estimate of the number of deaths caused by the Junta. Dead in combat: six hundred. Executed: thirteen hundred. Executed in secret: two thousand. Miscellaneous: one hundred. Total: four

Twenty-five mutilated bodies washed up on Uruguayan shores between March and October 1976. This was a small portion perhaps of the heaping number of those tortured to death at the Naval Mechanics Academy and dropped into the La Plata River by navy ships, among them a fifteen-year-old boy, Floreal Avellaneda, his hands and feet bound, "with bruising in the anal region and visible fractures," according to the autopsy.

In August 1976, a local man went diving in the San Roque Lake, Córdoba, and discovered a genuine swamp of a cemetery. He went to the precinct, where they would not file his report, and he wrote to the papers, where they would not publish it.[*]

Thirty-four bodies turned up in Buenos Aires between the third and the ninth of April 1976, eight in San Telmo on July 4, ten in the Luján river on October 9; this, plus the massacres on August 20 that left a heap of thirty people dead fifteen kilometers from Campo de Mayo and seventeen dead in Lomas de Zamora, are all part of the same pattern.

These reports put an end to the make-believe story spun about right-wing gangs, alleged heirs to López Rega's *Triple A*, who would be able to get past the largest garrison in the country with military trucks, carpet the La Plata River with bodies, or throw prisoners to the sea from the First Aerial Brigade[**] without General Videla, Admiral Massera, or Brigadier General Agosti knowing about it.[35] Today, the *Triple A* has become the 3 Branches, and the Junta that you are running is not the balancing point between "two kinds of violence," nor is it the impartial referee between "two terrorisms"; rather, it is the very source of the terror that has lost its way and can do nothing more than babble on in its discourse of death.[***]

---

thousand.

[*]   Letter from Isaías Zanotti, circulated by ANCLA, the Clandestine News Agency.[34]

[**]   A "program" run by Admiral Mariani, Head of the First Aerial Brigade of Palomar, between July and December of 1976. They used *Fokker F-27* planes.

[***] Foreign Minister Vice Admiral Guzzetti admitted in an article published by *La Opinión* on October 3, 1976, that "the terrorism of the right is not terrorism as such" but rather "an antibody."

The same historical continuity ties the murder of General Carlos Prats, under the previous government, to the kidnapping and death of General Juan José Torres, Zelmar Michelini, Héctor Gutiérrez Ruiz, and dozens of political refugees whose death killed off any chances of democratic regimes in Chile, Bolivia, and Uruguay.*

That the Federal Police's Department of Foreign Affairs—which is led by officials who received grant money from the CIA via USAID (like Commissioners Juan Gattei and Antonio Gettor) and are themselves under the authority of Mr. Gardener Hathaway, Station Chief of the CIA in Argentina—was undeniably involved in those crimes is the seed for future revelations like the ones that today shock the international community. The revelations will keep coming, even after a light is shined on the role that both this agency and high-ranking officers of the Army, led by General Menéndez, played in the creation of the Libertadores de América Society—the same Society that replaced the *Triple A* until their general mission was taken on by this Junta in the name of the 3 Branches.[36]

This tally of destruction even includes the balancing of personal accounts—like the murder of Captain Horacio Gándara, who had been investigating the dealings of high-ranking Naval Chiefs for the past decade, or of the *Prensa Libre* journalist, Horacio Novillo, stabbed and burned to death after that paper reported on ties between Minister Martínez de Hoz and international monopolies.[37]

In light of these incidents, the definition of the war, as phrased by one of its leaders, takes on its ultimate significance: "The battle we are waging knows neither moral nor natural limits; it takes place beyond good and evil."***

---

* General Prats, President Allende's last Defense Minister, killed by a bomb in September 1974. The former Uruguayan members of parliament Michelini and Gutiérrez Ruiz were found riddled with bullets on May 2, 1976. The body of General Torres, former president of Bolivia, turned up on June 2, 1976, after General Harguindeguy, Isabel Martínez's Minister of Interior and former Chief of Police, accused him of "faking" his kidnapping.

** Lieutenant Colonel Hugo Ildebrando Pascarelli, according to *La Razón* on June 12, 1976. Chief of the First Artillery Group of Ciudadela, Pascarelli is the one

5. These events, which have shaken the conscience of the civilized world, are nonetheless not the ones that have brought the greatest suffering upon the Argentine people, nor are they the worst human rights violations that you have committed. The political economy of the government is the place to look not only for the explanation of your crimes, but also for an even greater atrocity that is leading millions of human beings into certain misery.

Over the course of one year, you have decreased the real wages of workers by 40 percent, reduced their contribution to the national income by 30 percent, and raised the number of hours per day a worker needs to put in to cover his cost of living* from six to eighteen, thereby reviving forms of forced labor that cannot even be found in the last remnants of colonialism.

By freezing salaries with the butts of your rifles while prices rise at bayonet point, abolishing every form of collective protest, forbidding internal commissions and assemblies, extending workdays, raising unemployment to a record level of 9 percent** and being sure to increase it with three hundred thousand new layoffs, you have brought labor relations back to the beginning of the Industrial Era. And when the workers have wanted to protest, you have called them subversives and kidnapped entire delegations of union representatives who sometimes turned up dead, and other times did not turn up at all.***

The results of these policies have been devastating. During this first year of government, consumption of food has decreased by 40 percent, consumption of clothing by more than 50 percent, and

---

allegedly responsible for thirty-three executions that took place between January 5 and February 3 of 1977.

* Swiss Banks Union data from June 1976. The situation grew even worse afterward.

** *Clarín* newspaper.

*** Among the national leaders who were kidnapped are Mario Aguirre of ATE, Jorge Di Pasqual ve of Farmacia, Oscar Smith of Luz y Fuerza. The number of union leaders from metal and naval industries who have been kidnapped and murdered has been particularly high.

the consumption of medicine is practically at zero among the lower class. There are already regions in Greater Buenos Aires where the infant mortality rate is above 30 percent, a figure which places us on par with Rhodesia, Dahomey, or the Guayanas. The incidence of diseases like Summer Diarrhea, parasitosis, and even rabies has climbed to meet world records and has even surpassed them. As if these were desirable and sought-after goals, you have reduced the public health budget to less than a third of military spending, shutting down even the free hospitals while hundreds of doctors, medical professionals, and technicians join the exodus provoked by terror, low wages, or "rationalization."

You only have to walk around Greater Buenos Aires for a few hours before quickly realizing that these policies are turning it into a slum with ten million inhabitants. Cities in semi-darkness; entire neighborhoods with no running water because the monopolies rob them of their groundwater tables; thousands of blocks turned into one big pothole because you only pave military neighborhoods and decorate the Plaza de Mayo; the biggest river in the world is contaminated in all of its beaches because Minister Martínez de Hoz's associates are sloughing their industrial waste into it, and the only government measure you have taken is to ban people from bathing.

You have not been much wiser it comes to the abstract goals of the economy, which you tend to call "the country." A decrease in the gross national product of around 3 percent, a foreign debt reaching $600 dollars per inhabitant, an annual inflation rate of 400 percent, a 9 percent increase in the money supply within a single week in December, a low of 13 percent in foreign investment—these are also world records, strange fruit born of cold calculation and severe incompetence.

While all the constructive and protective functions of the state atrophy and dissolve into pure anemia, only one is clearly thriving. One billion eight hundred million dollars—the equivalent of half of Argentina's exports—have been budgeted for Security and Defense in 1977. That there are four thousand new officer positions in the Federal Police and twelve thousand in the Province of Buenos Aires offering salaries that are double that of an industrial worker and triple that of a school principal—while military wages have secretly increased by 120 percent since February—proves that there is no salary freezing or unemployment in the kingdom of torture and death. This is the only Argentine business where the product is growing and where the price per slain guerrilla is rising faster than the dollar.

6. The economic policies of this Junta—which follow the formula of the International Monetary Fund that has been applied indiscriminately to Zaire and Chile, to Uruguay and Indonesia—recognize only the following as beneficiaries: the old ranchers' oligarchy; the new speculating oligarchy; and a select group of international monopolies headed by ITT, Esso, the automobile industry, US Steel, and Siemens, which Minister Martínez de Hoz and his entire cabinet have personal ties to.[38]

A 722 percent increase in the prices of animal products in 1976 illustrates the scale of a return to oligarchy, launched by Martínez de Hoz, that is consistent with the creed of the Sociedad Rural as stated by its president, Celedonio Pereda: "It is very surprising that certain small but active groups keep insisting that food should be affordable."*

The spectacle of a Stock Exchange where, within one week, some have enjoyed 100- and 200 percent gains without working; where there are companies that doubled their capital overnight without producing any more than before; where the crazy wheel of speculation spins in dollars, letters, adjustable values and simple usury calculates interest on an hourly basis—it all seems rather strange, considering that this government came in to put a stop to the "feast of the corrupt." By privatizing banks, you are placing the savings and credit of the country in the hands of foreign banks; by indemnifying ITT and Siemens, you are rewarding companies that swindled

---

*   *Prensa Libre*, December 16, 1976.

the State; by reinstalling fueling stations, you are raising Shell's and Esso's returns; by lowering customs tariffs, you are creating jobs in Hong Kong or Singapore and unemployment in Argentina. Faced with all these facts, you have to ask yourself: Who are the unpatriotic people being referred to in the official press releases? Where are the mercenaries who are working for foreign interests? Which ideology is the one threatening the nation?

Even if the overwhelming propaganda—a distorted reflection of the evil acts being committed—were not trying to argue that this Junta wants peace, that General Videla is a defender of human rights, or that Admiral Massera loves life, it would still be worth asking the Commanders-in-Chief of the 3 Branches to meditate on the abyss they are leading the country into under the pretense of winning a war. In this war, even killing the last guerrilla would do nothing more than make it start up again in new ways, because the reasons that have been motivating the Argentine people's resistance for more than twenty years will not disappear but will instead be aggravated by the memory of the havoc that has been wreaked and by the revelation of the atrocities that have been committed.

These are the thoughts I wanted to pass on to the members of this Junta on the first anniversary of your ill-fated government, with no hope of being heard, with the certainty of being persecuted, but faithful to the commitment I made a long time ago to bear witness during difficult times.

Rodolfo Walsh. - I.D. 2845022
Buenos Aires, March 24, 1977

Next pages: Survivor Juan Carlos Livraga's formal accusation as published in the newspaper Propósitos. *The title, "Castigo a los culpables," translates as "I Call for the Punishment of the Guilty".*

pechas: Declaraciones Tomadas por Personal de Policía a Detenidos en la Cárcel de Olmos a Disposición del P. E. Nacional, Sin Fecha y luego Antidatadas: en el apartado Torturas dice la citada denuncia):

"TORTURAS"

"Han tomado estado público por su frecuencia y gravedad. Se tortura especialmente en las brigadas de investigaciones

caso el mérito de las torturas c al comisario Tarragona de la S de La Plata.

"René OTEGUI, en el mism el anterior.

"Juan PENDEL" y señora, e situación que los anteriores. To caña, inclusive la esposa, a esta quemaron con colillas de cigar bién detenidos en Olmos.

CASTIGO A L

COPIA de la demanda contra la Policía de la Provincia de Buenos Aires, por tentativa de homicidio y daño, presentada por Juan Carlos Livraga, el 14|XII|56, ante el Juzgado del Dr. Viglione secretaria González Arsac (La Plata. Fué trasladada al Juzgado del doctor Hueyo, por estar de turno a la fecha de los acontecimientos).

FORMULA DENUNCIA

Señor Juez del Crimen:

JUAN CARLOS LIVRAGA, mayor de edad, soltero, de profesión chófer, con domicilio real en la calle Florencio Varela, número 1624, de Florida Provincia de Buenos Aires, y constituyéndolo a los fines de esta presentación en el escritorio de mi abogado patrocinante, calle 47, número 792, a V. S. digo:

1. — Que vengo a denunciar a los funcionarios de Policía de la Provincia que resulten responsables por los hechos delictuosos de que fuera víctima y que paso a relatar.

2. — Fuí detenido por personal de dicha policía la noche del 9 de junio próximo pasado.

La tarde de ese día llegué a mi domicilio entre las 18.30 y 19 horas, por haberse descompuesto el auto colectivo que manejo habitualmente: conocen esta última circunstancia las autoridades de la línea número 10, Ciudad de Vicente López, con domicilio en Maure y Avenida Forest. Permanecí en mi domicilio hasta las 22 horas y 15 minutos, por hallarme ligeramente descompuesto, y a esa hora, un poco mejorado, salí en dirección al bar que frecuento, sito en Avenida San Martín y Franklin Caminaba hacia ese lugar, cuan

con una radio en recepción en la emisora que había de transmitirla Así decidido, comenzó Rodríguez un juego de cartas con sus amigos.

Escuché por mi parte el desarrollo íntegro del encuentro de box, y cuando hubo terminado, manifesté el deseo de retirarme, por hallarme todavía algo indispuesto. Saludando a Rodríguez y a los dueños de la casa y a punto de salir, irrumpieron en el domicilio policias de uniforme y civil, portando armas largas. Fuí arrojado al suelo de un empellón y retirado luego de la casa, con mis ocasionales acompañantes. Ya en la esquina fuí golpeado en el estómago con la culata de una pistola de gran calibre que portaba un hombre que vestía campera verde, siendo subidos a un colectivo de la línea 19 — el número 40—, por el que fuimos trasladados a la Unidad Regional de la Policía, sita en San Martín. Arribamos a ese sitio aproximadamente a la hora 24.

Una vez en el local policial me fué retirado el registro de conductor, un pañuelo, un reloj y la su

ta. Nada l mientos f estos caso permanecí que se nos La Plata, no ofrecía mi concer trataba de cuanto a jor.

Habíam lómetros, dónde, cu y se nos cimos y na oscuri cuando se tros apro las fuerza necía en que marc nifestó t adelante", subidos n daban poc destino. R estimo en nos indic cendiéram campo y a pacho y delante de muchos otros detenidos que salían en libertad, después de haber estado en Olmos, pegó tal bofetada que lo tiró de la silla. Pobre Petit ya había recibido "atenciones" en la sección 5a. El comisario Tarragona lo había picaneado a gusto. No otra cosa pueden atestiguar todos los funcionarios policiales que por un momento u otro han debido soportar a un funcionario que no ayuda a la revolución".

en vísperas de las fiestas.

* * *

Que a los comensales de los Comedores Populares Israelitas Argentinos, Yea Literat y Marlo Clar se les haya prohibido la entrada porque... leen "Propósitos". Damos traslado de esta arbitrariedad a las autoridades y prevenimos al señor Kreichman que está incurriendo en falta penada por la ley.

S CULPABLES

r aconteci_ omunes en te — todos — pensé a ciudad de olicía. Esto a lo que a alguno. Se situación y igara, me_

lgunos ki_ cisar hacia se detuvo der. Lo hi_ os en ple_ apado, aun a cien me_ El jefe de que perma_ ta policial uestro, ma_ no, más en fuimos carro. Que_ de nuestro trecho que etros y se que des_ en pleno z más cer_

a me_ de los ues de s cul_ os ma_ o. ide el

Y es_ pre de s y de

sonal, aprestaban su retirada, cuando sucedió lo imprevisto. Al recorrer la camioneta con sus focos el grupo de cadáveres, la potente luz, al darme de lleno en la cara, provocó un parpadeo que no pude evitar. Casi en forma simultánea sentí una voz que partía de la camioneta policial, que decía: "Dale a ese que todavía respira", y tres detonaciones: un impacto levantó tierra al incrustarse cerca de mi cara; luego un fuerte dolor en la cabeza, como el provocado por un hierro candente, y la misma sensación en un brazo. Traté de orientarme, caminé unas pocas cuadras y unos veinte metros antes de llegar a la casilla policial existente en la estación de José León Suárez, caí al suelo, prácticamente no podía dar un paso más. Una persona me levantó y con su ayuda pude llegar al destacamento.

Una vez allí, un oficial de cabello rubio, que no me preguntó cuál era el motivo de mis heridas, tal vez por la gravedad de mi estado, me trasladó al Policlínico San Martín, establecimiento que se halla sobre la ruta ocho, cerca del Liceo del mismo nombre. Practicadas las primeras curas, una enfermera llamó a mis padres y ellos, y también primos míos, se notificaron, por la constancia escrita en un libro, que si bien mis heridas son serias, mi vida no corre peligro. Tal vez, las autoridades del establecimiento, al conocer la verdad de los hechos, quisieron protegerme en previsión de futuros atentados.

Se me había practicado la primera cura, ya que el tratamiento definitivo debía durar mucho más, entre otros motivos por la pérdida de piezas dentales y el destrozo

unas horas, que según me manifestó el comisario "era contrabando, ya que él tenía estrictas órdenes que no se me maltrató de hecho y con golpes, es que no se me trataba mal, pero tampoco se me podía tratar bien. Poco y nada podía comer, con la boca casi destrozada. Y así permanecí hasta la fecha indicada, 3 de julio, sin poderme asear, sin ser curado, sin ni siquiera poder afeitarme, hasta que la venda cayó sola.

Luego fuí trasladado a Olmos e informado que me hallaba a disposición del Poder Ejecutivo Nacional. Y allí terminaron mis padecimientos. Fuí curado y atendido como un ser humano. Me restablecí y permanecí preso hasta el día 16 de agosto, en que se me concedió la libertad. Llegué a Olmos con diez kilos menos de peso, que había perdido en 25 días — lo prueban las historias clínicas — y de allí me retiré prácticamente recuperado. Faltaba solamente el arreglo de mi dentadura, que luego realizó particularmente un especialista.

Creo, y me parece evidente, que no fui sometido a juicio sumarísimo, por varios motivos. Fuí detenido antes de la vigencia de la Ley Marcial y no se me hizo conocer nada, ninguna circunstancia, que pudiera hacerme prever lo que luego se intentó contra mi persona. Tampoco he sido fusilado. Es obvio que los fusilados normalmente no relatan sus experiencias; nadie escapa vivo de una ejecución formal. Por otra parte, las autoridades no hubieran tenido por qué no reconocer o negar tal circunstancia — la de un fusilamiento en forma — en caso de que se hubiera producido. Y que intentaron ocultarlo, no hay duda. Un tele_

NOTES

1. *Keres, Nimzowitsch, Schlechter, Aramburu, Rojas.* (p. 33). Paul Keres, Aron Nimzowitsch, and Carl Schlechter were world-renowned chess masters of the late nineteenth and early twentieth centuries. **General Pedro Eugenio Aramburu** served as the de facto President of Argentina from November 1955 to April 1958 and **Admiral Isaac Francisco Rojas**, originally of the Argentine Navy, served as his de facto Vice President. Aramburu had replaced **General Eduardo Lonardi**, who had served for less than two months. Lonardi headed the Liberating Revolution movement (see Note 8), which had originally ousted the twice democratically elected **President Juan Perón** in a military coup on September 16, 1955. Perón had championed a brand of populism and anti-capitalism throughout his term as President that has been reconfigured and fractured multiple times up until the present day. While he claimed to fight in the name of the people and for social justice, his detractors considered his regime corrupt and authoritarian.

   Aramburu was determined to erase Peronism from the public consciousness, and employed executive measures to that end. In 1970, Aramburu was kidnapped and killed by the Peronist guerrilla group, the **Montoneros**. Some accounts of this history suggest that he was killed in response to the execution of General Juan José Valle in 1956 (see Note 2).

   For a more comprehensive version of events, please refer to Luis Alberto Romero's *A History of Argentina in the Twentieth Century*.

2. *Valle's failed rebellion* (p. 33). A group of Peronist officers in the military, led in part by **General Juan José Valle**, together with **General Raúl Tanco**, other military leaders, and a number of civilian groups, staged an uprising against the de facto government on June 9, 1956. The uprising was immediately and definitively quashed by Aramburu's regime. Valle and others were executed by firing squad three days later. Tanco managed to escape.

3. *Picana* (p. 38, 197, 213, 215, 225, 233). The *picana* was a torture device

used by the police and the military in Argentina during the twentieth century, especially throughout the years of dictatorship. A metal prod was electrified and applied to the victim's body, generally in highly sensitive areas. The high-voltage shocks were continually applied and the torture could be prolonged due to the fact that the current was kept at a relatively low level.

4. *Lausse match* (p. 48, 66, 68, 154). Argentine middleweight boxer Eduardo Lausse fought and beat Chilean middleweight boxer Humberto Loayza in round three of twelve on the night of June 9, 1956, at the Luna Park Stadium in the City of Buenos Aires.

5. *Radical Civil Union* [Unión Cívica Radical] (p. 55). **The Radical Civil Union** was first formed as a political party at the turn of the nineteenth century. Since then, it has undergone a series of transformations while maintaining a generally oppositionist stance until the early 1950s, when it came to power with President Arturo Frondizi. The party's political orientation has been primarily centrist and leftist, but not in any way radical, in the traditional sense of the word. Its relationship to Peronism has been antagonistic for the most part, though certain leaders over the course of the party's existence have been more prone to reconciling with Peronist supporters, most often in exchange for political support.

6. *Década infame* (p. 77, 185). *Década Infame* (The Infamous Decade) refers to the thirteen years between the military coups that ousted President Hipólito Yrigoyen in 1930 and President Ramón Castillo in 1943, respectively. The term was coined by Argentine historian and writer José Luis Torres, who characterized the period as plagued by state corruption, corporatization and privatization, popular flight from rural areas, and an ever-increasing national deficit. Walsh considers the possibility here of a second *década infame*.

7. *The Liberating Revolution* [Revolución Libertadora] (p. 82, 86, 90, 126, 144, 149, 161, 162, 180, 191). The **Liberating Revolution** began as a movement run by General Lonardi (see Note 1), who wanted to rid Argentina of Peronism's corruption and economic policies while also reconciling with the traditionally Peronist unions. Less than two months after assuming power, Lonardi was forced to resign because his policies were considered insufficiently anti-Peronist. A more staunchly anti-Peronist General Aramburu took control of the Liberating Revolution in November 1955. The regime came to an end in 1958, when elections were held and **Arturo Frondizi**, of the *Radical Civil Union* party, triumphed (see Note 5).

8. *Hartung, Krause, Ossorio Arana, Landaburu* (p. 82, 182). Teodoro Hartung, Julio César Krause, Arturo Ossorio Arana, and Laureano Landaburu were all ministers in President Aramburu's cabinet. For Aramburu and Rojas, see Note 1.

9. *P. V.* (p. 89). Abbreviation for "Perón Vuelve"—"Perón Returns."

10. *Camino de Cintura highway* (p. 96). *Camino de Cintura*, also known as Provincial Route 4, is a highway in the Province of Buenos Aires that encompasses the City of Buenos Aires.

11. *German Club* [Club Alemán] (p. 98, 108n). Chain of sports and social clubs founded in the mid-nineteenth century in response to the growing German-Argentine population.

12. *Contradanza* (p. 104). A traditional, fast-paced dance that originated in aristocratic, eighteenth-century Europe and migrated to the Southern Hemisphere in the nineteenth century, where it became a more popular art form.

13. *General Quaranta* (p. 120, 162). General Domingo Quaranta was head of the State Intelligence Service at the time.

14. *Pink House* (p. 124, 129). The Pink House (*Casa Rosada*) is the Presidential Office. The mansion is relatively centrally located in the city of Buenos Aires, and is so called because of its pink façade. In the book, Walsh also refers to the building using its alternate name, the "Government House" (*Casa de Gobierno*).

15. *Radical Intransigente, Unión Cívica Radical Intransigente* [Intransigent Radical Civil Union] (p. 130). After Perón was ousted in 1955, the *Unión Cívica Radical* (see Note 5) party split into two factions, the *UCR Intransigente* and the *UCR del Pueblo* [The People's Radical Civil Union]. The *Intransigente* party was more prepared to work together with Peronist supporters and was led by Arturo Frondizi, while the more rigidly antiPeronist faction, *UCR del Pueblo*, was led by Ricardo Balbín.

16. *Onganía; Cordobazo* (p. 183, 247). **Juan Carlos Onganía** was the de facto President of Argentina from 1966 to 1970. He enforced social and economic policies that disempowered universities and unions, and his dictatorship was heavily bruised by the **Cordobazo** of May 1969—a civil protest coordinated by student and labor activist groups in the city of Córdoba that lasted three days and resulted in a number of deaths and hundreds wounded.

17. *Liberal groups* (p. 183). Right-leaning, conservative groups who traditionally opposed Peronist policies.

18. *Lavalle, Dorrego, Salvador del Carril, Américo Ghioldi* (p. 184). Manuel Dorrego was the governor of the Province of Buenos Aires from 1827 to 1828, when his office was overtaken by General Juan Lavalle in a military coup. Lavalle executed Dorrego, only to be ousted himself not seven months later. Salvador María del Carril, the first vice president of the nation, advised Lavalle to execute Dorrego. Walsh suggests that Socialist Américo Ghioldi was similarly recruited to

advise de facto President Lonardi's regime on how best to dismantle Peronism.

19. *Expiatory cantata written by some future Sábato* (p. 184). Walsh is referring to Argentine author Ernesto Sábato's 1961 work *Sobre héroes y tumbas* (*On Heroes and Tombs*), which contains a somewhat vindicating description of General Lavalle's struggles and his death (see Note 18). Walsh considers the possibility of such a work, revisionist in nature, being written about Aramburu.

20. *Foundation* (p. 185). The Eva Perón Foundation was founded by the First Lady herself in 1948, and kept running for three years after her death as a charitable institution, until her husband was ousted in 1955.

21. *The "cursed deed"* (p. 185). Argentine Peronist elected official John William Cooke characterized Peronism as the "hecho maldito" ("cursed deed") of the middle class. The phrase is most commonly interpreted as pertaining to Peronism's complicated relationship to the middle class—specifically, to the movement's tendency to submit to its desires.

22. *Alsogarays, the Kriegers, and the Verriers* (p. 185). Ministers of the Argentine Economy under Presidents Aramburu and Frondizi. For *década infame*, see Note 6.

23. *Gracián* (p. 192). **Baltasar Gracián** was a seventeenth-century Spanish and Jesuit writer and philosopher.

24. *The two faces of Civilization and Barbarism that have been studied for the past century by a great Argentine* (p. 198). Walsh is referring here to the work of **Domingo Faustino Sarmiento**, a nineteenth-century writer and political activist whose most well-known work was *Facundo: Civilización y barbarie* (1845) (*Facundo: Civilization and Barbarism*). Written while he was in exile in Chile, *Facundo* was Sarmiento's attempt to capture the complexity of Argentina as he saw it through the literary biography of an early nineteenth-century military leader and landowner, Juan Facundo Quiroga. Sarmiento himself was opposed to everything that Quiroga represented. Within the book, Sarmiento provides a survey of the geography, history, and culture of Argentina as well as his own version of what the country ought to look like.

25. *The Satanowsky Case* (p. 223). See Note 27.

26. *Manchego, Vallese, Méndez, Mussi, and Retamar, Pampillón, Hilda Guerrero* (p. 225). These are all student or labor activists who were either killed or disappeared under the Argentine dictatorships of the 1960s and '70s.

27. *General Cuaranta, Satanowsky, Blajaquis, Zalazar* (p. 225). Marcos Satanowsky was a lawyer who was killed in his Buenos Aires office in 1957. Walsh wrote an entire book about the crime entitled *El Caso Satanowsky* (1973) (*The Satanowsky Case*) in which he incriminates Gen-

eral Juan Constantino Cuaranta of the State Intelligence Service. No one was ever brought to justice for Satanowsky's murder. **Domingo Blajaquis** and **Juan Zalazar** were killed in a shootout among members of the Metal Workers Union in Avellaneda, in the Province of Buenos Aires. Walsh recounts this event in great detail in his 1968 non-fiction investigative work, *¿Quién mató a Rosendo?* (*Who Killed Rosendo?*).

28. *Lanusse* (p. 227, 230) Alejandro Lanusse was first appointed in 1968 as one of the commanders of the Armed Forces under General Onganía's de facto presidency. He himself then served as the de facto President of Argentina from 1971 to 1973.

29. *FAP, FAR* (p. 229). The FAP (*Fuerzas Armadas Peronistas* [Peronist Armed Forces]) and the FAR (*Fuerzas Armadas Revolucionarias* [Revolutionary Armed Forces]) were left-wing Peronist guerrilla groups that were started in the late 1960s and mainly active during the early 1970s. In 1973, after much negotiation, the FAR merged with the Montonero movement. Walsh himself worked with the FAP before joining the Montoneros in 1973.

30. *Descamisados* (p. 230). The *Descamisados* (The Shirtless) were another left-wing Peronist guerrilla group active in the early 1970s that merged with the Montoneros in 1973.

31. *"Work Group"* (p. 231n). Once the dictatorship of 1976 began, Work Groups (*grupos de tarea*) were formed to carry out the extermination of any individuals considered enemies of the state. These groups, composed mainly of men with experience in the military, state security, or the police department, were notorious for kidnapping victims, torturing them, killing them, and leaving no trace of their bodies.

32. *The loss of a daughter* (p. 231). Walsh's younger daughter, María Victoria ("Vicki") Walsh, was a journalist who became involved with the Montonero movement even before her father did (see Note 1). She died on her twenty-sixth birthday, September 28, 1976, in a shootout. With her group on the rooftop of a house entirely outnumbered by over a hundred men and a tank on the ground, she chose to take her own life. Walsh writes further of Vicki's death and his feelings of loss in two letters, both published in 1976: "Carta a Vicki" ("Letter to Vicki") and "Carta a mis amigos" ("Letter to My Friends").

33. *Mandate of Isabel Martínez* (p. 236, 242n). **María Estela ("Isabel" or "Isabelita") Martínez** was Juan Perón's third and final wife. She served first as his vice president from 1973 to 1974 and, after her husband's death in 1974, as the interim President of Argentina until the military coup of March 24, 1976.

34. *ANCLA* (p. 236n). *Agencia de Noticias Clandestina* (Clandestine News Agency). Walsh founded this underground news agency in June of

1976, less than a year before his death, in response to the increasingly limited access to information regarding State terrorism and corruption in Argentina.

35. *López Rega, Triple A, General Videla, Admiral Massera, Brigadier General Agosti* (p. 236). **José López Rega** was appointed Minister of Social Welfare in 1973 under Perón; after Perón's death, López Rega became the heart of Isabel Martínez de Perón's political program. The **Triple A** (Argentine Anticommunist Alliance—*Alianza Anticomunista Argentina*) was a facet of this program: throughout the 1970s, its death squads sought out and eradicated elements of the Left or any suspected enemies of the State. General **Jorge Rafael Videla**, Admiral **Emilio Eduardo Massera**, and Brigadier General **Orlando Ramón Agosti** were responsible for the military coup that ousted Isabel Martínez de Perón in 1976. Videla then served as the de facto President of Argentina from 1976 to 1981, overseeing one of the most brutal eras in the country's history.

36. *Libertadores de América Society* (p. 237). This Argentine death squad was similar in nature to López Rega's *Triple A* and was responsible for hundreds of deaths during the 1970s.

37. *Minister Martínez de Hoz* (p. 237, 239, 240). **José Alfredo Martínez de Hoz** was Minister of the Economy during the years that Videla served as de facto president (see Note 35). He is known for leading Argentina in the direction of less state intervention in the economy and more free-market capitalism. He froze wages in an effort to decrease inflation, but in doing so brought on heavy speculation and social unrest. He maintained relationships with foreign investors abroad, and was criticized for depending too heavily on foreign investments and loans, on corporations and big money, while neglecting the effects of his ambitious economic decisions on the welfare of the middle class. One of his lasting legacies was an enormous increase in Argentine foreign debt.

38. *International Monetary Fund (IMF), old ranchers' oligarchy* (p. 240). Martínez de Hoz's 1976 policy was similar to the formula prescribed by the IMF that Walsh mentions here. The general idea was to restructure the State's economic program, cutting down on domestic spending and any State regulation, to allow for growth through the international economy. The **old ranchers' oligarchy** ("oligarquía ganadera") refers to cattle-ranching families that owned Argentine land and gained high social status starting in the nineteenth century. De Hoz himself came from such a family.

GLOSSARY

Berta Figueroa: Nicolás Carranza's widow.

Captain/Commissioner-Inspector Benedicto Cuello: Second-in-command to Rodríguez Moreno, Commissioner of the San Martín District Police Department at the time of the execution.

Carlos Lizaso: Works with his father at an auction house. On the night of the José León Suárez execution, he leaves his girlfriend a note that says "If all goes well tonight . . ." Killed on site at twenty-one years old.

Chief Inspector Rodolfo Rodríguez Moreno: Chief of the San Martín District Police Department who obeyed the order from Fernández Suárez to carry out "Operation Massacre."

Colonel Bonnecarrere: Appointed by the Liberating Revolution to the highest position of State authority in the Province of Buenos Aires.

Colonel Desiderio A. Fernández Suárez: Chief of Police of the Province of Buenos Aires, responsible for ordering the executions at José León Suárez.

Commissioner F. Ferrairone: Replaces Commissioner Gregorio de Paula as commissioner of the Moreno precinct after the José León Suárez execution.

Commissioner Gregorio de Paula: Commissioner of the Moreno precinct at the time of the José León Suárez execution.

Doctor Carlos Chiesa: Police medic at the Moreno precinct.

Eduardo Schaposnik: Socialist representative for the Advisory

Board of the Province of Buenos Aires who reports on alleged cases of torture within the justice system.

Enriqueta Muñiz: Walsh's right hand in the investigation.

Florinda Allende: Francisco Garibotti's widow.

Francisco Garibotti: Father of six and longtime railroad worker. Killed at thirty-eight years old in the José León Suárez execution.

Horacio di Chiano: Works as an electrician, lives with his wife and daughter, around fifty years old at the time of the José León Suárez execution. He survives and hides in his basement, consumed by fear.

Jorge Doglia, Esq.: Head of the Police Judicial Division at the time of Operation Massacre.

Juan Carlos Livraga: Critically injured survivor of the José León Suárez execution. He was nearly twenty-four years old and a bus driver at the time. Livraga's formal accusation was published in the newspaper *Propósitos*.

Juan Carlos Torres: Tenant of the apartment where most of the victims of the José León Suárez executions were gathered on the night of June 9, 1956.

Judge Belisario Hueyo: Judge from La Plata who, aside from Walsh himself, most avidly seeks justice in the case of "Operation Massacre."

Judge Viglione: Judge for the Province of Buenos Aires who is appointed to adjudicate Walsh's charges against Police Commissioner Fernández Suárez.

Julio Troxler: Twenty-nine-year-old Peronist and former police officer. He survives the José León Suárez execution and goes into exile in Bolivia.

"Marcelo": a.k.a. Marcelo Rizzoni, an informant for Walsh in the investigation who never forgives himself for Carlos Lizaso's death and becomes a terrorist.

Mario Brión: Working man who lives with his wife and son. Killed at thirty-three years old in the José León Suárez execution.

Máximo von Kotsch, Esq.: Lawyer who represented survivors

Giunta and Livraga.

Miguel Ángel Giunta: Critically injured survivor of the José León Suárez execution. Works at a shoe shop.

Nicolás Carranza: Father of six, Peronist, and fugitive. Killed in the José León Suárez execution.

Norberto Gavino: Fugitive from the law whose wife was taken hostage on account of his subversive activity. He is around forty years old at the time of the José León Suárez execution. He survives and goes into exile in Bolivia.

Ovidio R. de Bellis: Replaces Rodríguez Moreno as Chief of the San Martín District Police Department

Pedro Livraga: Father of Juan Carlos Livraga.

Reinaldo Benavídez: Around thirty years old at the time of the José León Suárez execution. Survives and goes into exile in Bolivia.

Rogelio Díaz: NCO who served as a sergeant, has retired from the Navy at the time of the José León Suárez execution. He survives.

Señora Pilar: Mr. Horacio's widow.

Vicente Damián Rodríguez: Dockworker and father of three. Killed at thirty-five years old in the José León Suárez execution.

AFTERWORD

For many of us, Rodolfo Walsh serves as a synthesis of what one would call the political tradition in today's Argentine literature: he was a great writer who pushed the question of the intellectual's civic responsibility to its limit. He started by writing detective stories à la Borges, and went on to write longer works based on true crimes that made him a threat in the eyes of the State. *Operation Massacre* (1957) is one of the great Latin American texts of documentary literature. In a 1970 interview, speaking about another one of his works in which he exposed a true, unpunished crime, he told me:

> A journalist asked me why I hadn't made a novel out of this subject that seemed so suitable for a novel. What he was clearly hiding was the notion that a novel on this subject is better or in a higher category than an indictment about this subject. I think that translating an indictment into the art that is the novel renders it inoffensive, namely, consecrates it as art. On the other hand, building upon a document or a testimony allows for every degree of perfection: immense artistic possibilities emerge from the process of selection and the work of investigation.

With *Operation Massacre*, Walsh puts forward and elevates the raw truth of the facts. He offers a direct accusation, a documentary story instead of a novel based on fictionalized political events. The political use of literature ought to take a step away from fiction. This is Walsh's great lesson.

He notes in his *Diario* that "[T]o be absolutely diaphanous" is the goal of his writing. Clarity is a virtue, but not because things need to be simplified in order for people to understand—that's just the rhetoric of journalism. The virtue lies in confronting a deliberate darkness, a global jargon, a certain established rhetoric that makes clarity difficult to attain. "For a rigorous man it becomes more difficult each year to say anything without raising the suspicion that he might be lying or mistaken," he wrote. Aware of this difficulty and his social circumstances, Walsh produced a unique, flexible, and inimitable style that permeates every text he wrote and that we remember him for.

Throughout his work, Walsh engages with two distinct poetics. On the one hand, fiction for Walsh is the art of ellipsis: it deals with allusion and that which is not said. Its construction is in total opposition to the simplification and the aesthetic of urgency that characterize social realism. Walsh's second poetics manifests as the documentary story, the autobiographical treatment of testimonies, pamphlets, and diatribes: the writer is a historian of the present who speaks in the name of truth and denounces misuses of power. Walsh's "Open Letter to the Military Junta" is the greatest example of this kind of political writing.

There is one exemplary story in which the two poetics clearly play out and interact. "Esa mujer" ("That Woman") is a story Walsh wrote in 1963 about someone who speaks to a former State Intelligence Services officer in an attempt to find the body of Eva Perón. The narrator is a journalist confronting and negotiating with this figure who symbolizes the world of power. He wants to unveil the secret that will lead him to Eva Perón's body, with everything that goes along with finding that woman who embodies the history of an entire people. This intellectual's investigation, this search, is the driving force of the story.

The first indicator of Walsh's poetics is that Eva Perón is never mentioned explicitly in the story. We all know that she is the one being discussed, but the most important aspect of a story should never be named. Walsh practices the art of ellipsis, which clearly calls for the reader to crack the encoded context to seek out the implicit story, what is said in the unsaid. Walsh moves his style in this direction of allusion and condensation, of saying the most with the fewest number of words.

We catch a glimpse of Walsh's other poetics in the stance of this educated man, this journalist who is confronted with an historical enigma. For Walsh, Eva Perón appears first as a secret, a problem that has to be solved, but also as a destination. "If I could find that woman I wouldn't feel alone anymore," the narrator says. Finding Evita, who represents the masses and the popular tradition of Peronism, means the intellectual must cross over to the other side. But crossing over no longer means finding a world of terror; instead, it allows for the possibility of finding friends and allies. Suddenly the intellectual does not feel that the barbaric world of the masses is adversarial and antagonistic, but that it is a place to escape to, a point of arrival. This story can be read as a very early allegory foreshadowing Walsh's decisions to join the Montoneros and convert to Peronism.

Everything in the story is condensed into the blind search for Eva Perón's missing body, but at the same time, Walsh is exploring two separate tensions. First, we have the tension between the intellectual and the masses. And second, we have the tension between the ex-Intelligence officer who knows where that woman is, on the one hand, and, on the other, we have the narrator of the story—the journalist who happens to share some of Walsh's traits in his commitment to decoding secrets and investigating manipulations of power. This is where the writer comes in: his task is to establish the truth, to act like a detective, to discover the secret that the State is hiding, to reveal the truth that is being hidden—buried, in this case, in a hidden body, a historical, symbolic body that has been stolen and disgraced.

Walsh summons both poetics again when he confronts the question that many writers of the 20th century, among them Primo Levi, Osip Mandelstam, and Paul Célan, have wrestled with: How can you narrate horror? How can you convey horror without just reporting on it? The experience of the concentration camps, of the Gulag, of genocide. Literature shows us that there are events that are nearly impossible to convey and that thus suggest a new relationship to the limits of language. The most poignant example of this in Walsh's work is the way he tells the story of his daughter's death in what is known as "Letter to Vicky," which he wrote to Maria Victoria Walsh in 1976, in the thick of the military dictatorship. This piece of writing is by no means a work of fiction, but Walsh practices ellipsis and displacement nonetheless. After recreating the exact moment when he finds out about her death over the radio and the gesture that comes with this revelation ("I heard your name mispronounced, and it took a second for it to register. I automatically started to cross myself the way I used to as a child"), he writes: "Last night I had a terrible nightmare. There was a pillar of fire, powerful, but contained within its borders, that was flaring up quite intensely." A nightmare with virtually no content, condensed into a horrific abstract image.

He then writes: "Today on the train a man said 'I suffer greatly, I'd like to go to sleep and wake up in a year.'" And Walsh concludes: "He was speaking for himself but for me as well." He puts words in the mouth of someone else who is speaking about his pain, a stranger on the train, a stranger who happens to be around. The small step he takes away from what he is trying to say is a metaphor that conveys the experience of limits: someone speaks for him and expresses the pain in a somber, direct, and very moving way. From this displacement you get everything: the pain, the compassion, a lesson in style. Through this movement, Walsh shows what cannot be told.

Walsh uses the same displacement in his "Letter to My Friends" (written several days later), when he reconstructs the circumstances of Vicky's death. He reconstructs the ambush on the house where his daughter is in the middle of the city, the siege, the resistance, the combat, the military forces that surround the house. In order to tell the story of what happened, he once again endows someone else with a voice: "I received the testimony of one of those men, a conscript." He then transcribes the story as told by this man who was there, besieging the place: "The fighting lasted more than an hour and a half. A man and a woman were shooting from up top. The woman caught our attention because every time she shot a burst and we ducked, she laughed." The laughter is there, the extreme youth, the shock, everything is condensed and narrated by someone else. The impersonality of the story and the admiration for his own enemies reinforce the heroism of the scene: those who are going to kill her are the first ones who recognize her bravery, just as the best epic tradition dictates. Just like the case of the man on the train, here too there is a displacement and the voice is given to another who condenses what he is trying to say, and therefore becomes the solder who tells the story. This displacement recalls the form of a fiction that is intending to tell the truth. Maybe that soldier never existed, just as maybe that man on the train never existed, it doesn't matter. What matters is the vision it produces, the fact that they are there to witness and can then tell the story of the experience.

We see this movement as well in the prologue to the third edition of *Operation Massacre* (1968), where he describes the first scene, the origin of how history and politics came into his life. Walsh is at a café in La Plata where he always goes to talk about literature and play chess. One night in June of 1956, they hear shooting, people are running in the streets, a group of Peronists and rebel officers attack the Second Division Command: it is the start of Valle's failed rebellion that will result in secret repression and the José León Suárez executions. And that night, Walsh leaves the café, runs along the tree-lined streets, and finally finds shelter in his house. This is when he tells the story: "I also haven't forgotten how, standing by the window blinds, I heard a recruit dying in the street who didn't say 'Long live the nation!' but instead: 'Don't leave me here alone, you sons of bitches.'"

The other conscript who is lying there terrified and about to die, in him we see the truth of the story. A displacement to the other, a fictional movement towards a scene that condenses and crystallizes a network of multiple meanings. That is how the experience is conveyed; it is far beyond simple information. Walsh had a natural ability to depict a scene using what is heard and to condense pure experience. It is a movement that occurs within the story, an ellipsis that displaces truth-telling onto the Other.

Walsh is wise enough to know, however, that the writer is not the only one using fictions to his advantage. The State also narrates, constructs fictions, and manipulates certain stories, while literature and the writer construct alternative stories that are in tension with them. The French poet Paul Valéry confronts these questions with the following logic: "A society rises from brutality to order. Barbarism is the age of the fact, so the age of order is necessarily the realm of fictions, because there is no power capable of establishing the order of the body solely through bodily force. Fictional forces are necessary." The State cannot function by pure coercion alone; it needs what Valéry calls *fictional forces*. It needs to construct consensus, to construct stories and make people believe a certain version of events.

What matters is not only the content of these State fictions, not just the material that they manipulate, but also the form that they take. To begin to understand their form, we can look to the methods and devices used to construct them. During the period of the military dictatorship, for example, one of the stories being constructed was what we might call the *surgical* story, a story that pertained to bodies. The military used a medical metaphor to explain what they were doing. They concealed everything that was happening, but simultaneously *did* say what was happening, just in the form of a story about sickness and health. They spoke of Argentina as a sick body that had a tumor, a cancer that was spreading—this was the subversive element or revolution—and the role of the military was to operate on it. As doctors, their work was aseptic, beyond good and evil, an appropriate response to the needs of science, which calls for destruction and mutilation for the sake of saving a life. Everything that was secret was actually revealed in this story, just displaced. There were, as in every story, two stories being told: there was the attempt to make people believe that Argentina was a sick society and that the military was coming in from the outside as technicians to fix the problem, and then there was the idea that a painful operation had to be performed and, as Videla used to say, it was an operation that had to be performed without anesthesia. That was the discourse, the fictional version, that the State used: it told the truth about what it was doing, but in a covert and allegorical way.

This is a very small example of a State fiction. Running in tandem with these fictions are a series of anti-State stories, stories of resistance and opposition that circulate within a society and resist the State fictions. I have often thought that these social stories—anonymous fictions, micro-stories, testimonies that are exchanged and circulated—are the greatest context that literature uses. The writer is the one who knows how to hear them, who is attuned to this social narration; he is also the one who imagines them and writes them.

As just one example of these anonymous stories, consider an anti-State fiction that circulated during the military dictatorship, around 1978 and 1979, at the time of the conflict with Chile. The war was about to become one of the political schemes that the military was looking for, just as the Malvinas later were. Attempting to construct political consensus through war was the only way that the military had of generating public support. There was a pervasive feeling of repression in the country, and the idea of going to the South in search of conflict was in the air. Multiple versions of an anonymous story began circulating in the city. It was said that somebody knew somebody who had seen a train stacked with coffins headed south at a deserted train station in the suburbs at dawn. A cargo train that someone had seen pass by slowly, like a ghost, in the silence of the night. Those empty coffins corresponded to the disappeared, to the bodies with no graves. It was also a story that foresaw the war in the Malvinas because there was no question that those coffins in that imaginary train were headed towards the Malvinas, to where soldiers were going to die and need to be buried.

This seemingly insignificant, forgotten story presents a clear, compact version of the way alternative stories are created, anonymous stories that, in their condensed and extraordinary form, have multiple meanings. Some truth has been captured briefly in the metallic sound of a train passing through the night. There is a very important difference between showing and telling in literature: this story does not tell or say anything directly, but it allows the reader to see and to understand, which is why it lives on in our memories as an unforgettable vision. The image of an unending train that passes at dawn through an empty station and the fact that someone is there to see it who can then tell the story—this is a very good telling of what it was like to live in Argentina during the dictatorship. Because it is not just that there is a train crossing in the story, but that there is a witness who tells someone what he has seen. There will always be a witness who has seen and will tell the story, someone who survives so that the story is not forgotten.

On some level, this tension between the State story and the contradictory stories of the masses that circulate, is the story that Walsh has always tried to tell. Because, in a sense, Walsh has tried both to discover the truths that the State is manipulating, and also to listen to the story of the masses, the alternative versions that circulate and contradict. *Operation Massacre* is a definitive text in this sense. On the one hand, again, the intellectual, the educated one, confronts the

State and exposes it for constructing a false version of the facts. In order to construct an opposing reality, Walsh records the antagonistic versions, looks for the truth in other versions and voices. He tries to show how this State story hides, manipulates, and falsifies, and tries to show the truth through the version provided by the witness who has seen everything and survived. If you read *Operation Massacre*, you will see how he goes from one voice to the next, from one story to the next, and this story as a whole runs parallel to the dismantling of the State story. The individuals who have lived through that brutal experience and who give the writer fragments of that reality, they are the witnesses who, in the night, have seen the horror of the story. The narrator is the one who knows how to transcribe these voices. The voice you hear has the spoken quality of the voice of the masses.

Walsh essentially listens to the Other. He knows how to hear the story that emerges from the popular voice and tries to get closer to the truth by using it. The truth is in the story and the story is partial: it modifies, transforms, alters, and sometimes deforms the facts. A web of alternative stories needs to be constructed in order to bring back what has been lost. Walsh the craftsman deftly handles this basic dual movement of hearing and transmitting the popular story while also disarming the State fiction. The conquerors write the story and the conquered tell it. Walsh dismantles the written story and contradicts it with the witness's story.

With Walsh, the nonfiction story moves towards the truth and reconstructs it from the perspective of a well-defined political stance. This reconstruction presumes a neatly defined position within the social realm and a clear conception of the relationships between truth and struggles for social justice. In this sense, Walsh's nonfiction books present a departure from the more neutral versions of the genre as it has been practiced in the United States, starting with Capote, Mailer, and what's been called "New Journalism." In Walsh's work, access to the truth is tangled up with political struggle, social inequality, power relations, and the State's strategizing. Since he is dealing with a notion of the truth that escapes the most immediate evidence, he must first dismantle the fictional forces constructed by the powers that be, and then rescue the fragments of truth, the allegories, the stories circulating among the people. Walsh is fighting for this latter, social truth that has been lost, and is recording and reconstructing it. The truth is a story that someone else tells.

—Ricardo Piglia

ABOUT THE TRANSLATOR

Daniella Gitlin is a writer, translator, and editor. She studied comparative literature at Princeton University and received her MFA in nonfiction writing from Columbia University, where she taught for two years. Her translation of Pablo Martín Ruiz's *Epifanías del Danubio* ("Epiphanies on the Danube") appeared in the January 2011 inaugural issue of *Asymptote*. She lives in New York City.